ACCOUNTING AND AUDITING FOR EMPLOYEE BENEFIT PLANS

By

GEOFFREY M. GILBERT, CPA
Ernst & Ernst

GREGORY J. LACHOWICZ, CPA
Ernst & Ernst

JAMES F. ZID, CPA
Ernst & Ernst

WG
&L

WARREN, GORHAM & LAMONT
Boston
New York

GEOFFREY M. GILBERT, CPA, is a Partner of Ernst & Ernst and is the firm's National Director of Services to Employee Benefit Plans. He is currently serving on the AICPA Auditing Standards Executive Committee and the Employee Benefit Plans and ERISA Committee.

GREGORY J. LACHOWICZ, CPA, is a Manager in the National Accounting and Auditing Department of Ernst & Ernst. He has had extensive experience in auditing insurance companies and employee benefit plans. He is a fellow of the Life Office Management Association.

JAMES F. ZID, CPA, is a Partner of Ernst & Ernst and is National Partner in Charge of the firm's specialized industries practice. He is a member of the AICPA Committee on Relations With Actuaries and served on the FASB Task Force on Accounting and Reporting by Employee Benefit Plans.

Preface

The Employee Retirement Income Security Act of 1974 (ERISA) was signed into law in September 1974. The Act was designed to achieve the following broad objectives:

(1) To increase the number of employees covered by retirement plans by establishing minimum age and service eligibility conditions for participation.

(2) To establish minimum periods during which participating employees must acquire vested interests in the benefits provided under these plans.

(3) To better protect participants' pension interests by increasing the disclosure requirements of plans and establishing minimum standards of conduct by fiduciaries and others who administer plan assets.

(4) To establish minimum requirements for funding promised benefits under such plans.

(5) To make the tax rules more equitable for self-employed persons by reducing the differences in treatment of benefits and allowable deductions that depend on the form of the employer's business organization.

(6) To encourage employees to save for their retirement needs by providing tax incentives for those not covered by plans.

Insuring that participants' interests are better protected involves, among other matters, increasing plan disclosure requirements. One of these requirements is the annual report to the Department of Labor. This report includes plan financial statements which, for plans with 100 or more participants, have to be audited by independent public accountants. This single requirement has dramatically increased the involvement of independent accountants with employee benefit plans.

Thus, accountants need to gain a better understanding of the development and operations of employee benefit plans to conduct plan audits effectively.

Therefore, the first three chapters of this book are designed to provide the auditor with a basic background in the various types of employee benefit plans, the statutory requirements of ERISA, and the regulatory requirements of the Department of Labor and the Internal Revenue Service.

Another extremely important aspect of the operation of a retirement benefit plan providing fixed or determinable future benefits is the actuarial estimate of the periodic and ultimate cost of those benefits. An effective plan audit requires an understanding of the actuary's role. Even if the auditor does not express an opinion on an actuarial report, he may, from time to time, need to use data from it in his own efforts. Therefore, we have attempted to provide an introduction to actuarial concepts and theory, as well as practical information (with examples) on the actuarial valuation process.

Although the Financial Accounting Standards Board is currently studying accounting for employee benefit plans, the current lack of codified generally accepted accounting principles for these plans adds an additional element of complexity for plan auditors. Thus, the book offers guidance on interim standards plus practical suggestions for accounting, auditing, and reporting on plan audits, including model financial statements and footnote disclosures and a comprehensive internal control questionnaire.

We would like to acknowledge the contributions of the following individuals to this book: Our associates at Ernst & Ernst—Chuck Bell, Jim Blair, Jon Haber, Don Nichols, Jim Ogorek, and Jim Walker—provided invaluable assistance in researching, preparing and reviewing its contents. Dave Kass and Jim Germain of the actuarial consulting firm of Kass, Germain and Co. provided a critical review and a number of excellent suggestions for the actuarial chapters. Finally, Ray Groves, Managing Partner of Ernst & Ernst, and Bob Neary, National Partner in Charge of Accounting and Auditing, provided the necessary support and encouragement for this project.

GEOFFREY M. GILBERT
GREGORY J. LACHOWICZ
JAMES F. ZID

Table of Contents

Part I

Background Information

Chapter 1

TYPES OF EMPLOYEE BENEFIT PLANS

Part II

Actuarial Valuations

Chapter 4

ACTUARIAL VALUATIONS AND THEORY—OVERVIEW

Chapter 6

ACTUARIAL DETERMINATIONS OF ASSET VALUES, UNFUNDED SUPPLEMENTAL VALUE, AND ANNUAL PENSION COST

Chapter 7

ACTUARIAL ASSUMPTIONS

Chapter 8

ACTUARIAL VALUATION METHODS

Chapter 9

PLAN EXPERIENCE GAINS AND LOSSES

Part III

Regulatory Requirements; Generally Accepted Accounting Principles

Chapter 10

REGULATORY REPORTING AND DISCLOSURE REQUIREMENTS

Chapter 11

CURRENT STATUS OF FASB, AICPA, AND SEC GUIDELINES FOR PLAN ACCOUNTING

Chapter 12

INTERIM ACCOUNTING GUIDELINES

Part IV

Auditing and Reporting

Chapter 13

GENERAL AUDITING CONSIDERATIONS

Chapter 14

REVIEW OF INTERNAL ACCOUNTING CONTROL

Chapter 15

CONDUCTING THE AUDIT

Chapter 16

REPORTING ON PLAN FINANCIAL STATEMENTS

Part I

BACKGROUND INFORMATION

Chapter 1

TYPES OF EMPLOYEE BENEFIT PLANS

¶ 1.01 INTRODUCTION

A fundamental understanding of the various types of employee benefit plans is of primary importance to an efficient audit of a plan. This chapter discusses the various types of employee benefit plans and the methods used for the accumulation and administration of assets for the payment of benefits to participants.

Employee benefit plans vary according to the types of benefits provided, how plan assets are administered, and the manner in which the amounts of benefits are determined. Employees participating in a benefit plan may be those of a single employer or several employers. The funds to finance a benefit plan can be provided by the employee (contributory plan—either jointly with the employer or by himself) or provided solely by the employer (noncontributory plan).

The selection of a particular plan depends upon several factors, including tax benefits, cost considerations, and the desire to provide employees with security and incentives. A plan may be a voluntary plan established unilaterally by an employer, or a negotiated plan established as a result of collective bargaining between the employer and a union. Negotiated plans may be either single-employer plans or industry-wide multiemployer plans.

The provisions of employee benefit plans are normally set forth in written documents describing the benefits, eligibility of participants, how the benefits will be financed, and the duties and responsibilities of the parties involved in the administration of benefits. Under Section

402 of the Employee Retirement Income Security Act of 1974 (ERISA), a written plan document is required. In addition, plans may have contracts with insurance companies, trust agreements with trustees, or other contracts with labor organizations or the employees themselves. Since plans vary so much, it is important to review all plan documents in order to determine the division of responsibilities among the parties involved in the administration of the plan and other significant features of the plan.

Employee benefit plans can be classified according to the type of benefit provided. Plans which provide retirement income are commonly referred to as *pension benefit plans*, while those plans which provide other benefits (e.g., health, vacation, education, or other similar benefits) are usually grouped together as *welfare benefit plans*. Section 3 of ERISA defines "employee benefit plans" as follows:

"Pension Benefit Plan

"The terms 'employee pension benefit plan' and 'pension plan' mean any plan, fund, or program which was heretofore or is hereafter established or maintained by an employer or by an employee organization or by both, to the extent that by its express terms or as a result of surrounding circumstances such plan, fund, or program—

"A. Provides retirement income to employees, or

"B. Results in a deferral of income by employees for periods extending to the termination of covered employment or beyond, regardless of the method of calculating the contributions made to the plan, the method of calculating the benefits under the plan or the method of distributing benefits from the plan.

"Welfare Benefit Plan

"The terms 'employee welfare benefit plan' and 'welfare plan' mean any plan, fund, or program which was heretofore or is hereafter established or maintained by an employer or by an employee organization, or by both to the extent that such plan, fund, or program was established or is maintained for the purpose of providing for its participants or beneficiaries, through the purchase of insurance or otherwise, (a) medical, surgical, or hospital care or benefits, or benefits in the event of sickness, accident, disability, death or unemployment, or vacation benefits, apprenticeship or other training programs, or day care centers, scholarship funds, or prepaid legal services, or (b) any benefit described in section 302(c) of the Labor Management Relations Act, 1947 (other than pensions on retirement or death, and insurance to provide such pensions)."

¶ 1.02 PENSION BENEFIT PLANS

Pension plans may be classified into two primary categories based upon the way pension benefits are determined. Plans which provide for a definitely determined benefit based upon a formula specified in the plan are classified as defined benefit plans. Plans which do not specify benefits, but rather state that the contributions allocated to each participant's account will be used to provide pension benefits, are classified as defined contribution plans. Upon retirement, pension plan benefits are generally paid out in the form of a life annuity or a period-certain annuity as of the participant's normal retirement date. Other methods of paying benefits are installment payments and lump-sum distributions. In some types of defined contribution plans, such as employee stock ownership plans, distributions may be made in the form of securities.

It should be noted that ERISA affects these two categories of pension plans in different ways. For example, both types of plan are affected by the participation, vesting, reporting and employee disclosure, and fiduciary responsibility provisions of the Act. However, in general, only defined benefit plans are affected by the minimum funding, actuarial reporting, and termination insurance provisions of the Act. This distinction is important to the auditor in determining the scope of his examination and the specific tests to be performed. The various provisions of the Act and their impact on employee benefit plans are discussed in Chapter 2.

[1] Defined Benefit Plans

Defined benefit plans provide definitely determinable benefits based on the plan's benefit accrual provision. The plan's benefit accrual provision is usually contained in the plan as a formula or schedule that specifies the rate at which employees' benefits are accumulated. For example, some plans specify that employees accumulate a fixed dollar (e.g., $20 a month) benefit to be paid at age sixty-five for each year of service. Other plans determine benefits based on both service and salary (e.g., a plan which provides for a benefit of 1½ percent of final or average annual compensation per year of service). Accordingly, defined benefit plans can be further categorized according to the method of calculating retirement benefits. There are four basic benefit formulas as described below:

(1) *Flat amount formula* provides a stated benefit unrelated to an employee's earnings, but subject to a minimum service requirement (e.g., a plan which states that the participant will receive an annual pension benefit of $1,000 if he has twenty-five years of credited service).

(2) *Flat percentage of earnings formula* provides a benefit related to the employee's earnings subject to a minimum service requirement (e.g., a plan which states that the participant will receive an annual pension benefit equal to 25 percent of his career average earnings if he has twenty-five years of credited service).

(3) *Flat amount per year of service formula* reflects an employee's service, but not earnings (e.g., a plan which states that the participant will receive an annual pension benefit of $20 times the number of years of credited service).

(4) *Percentage of earnings per year of service formula* reflects both an employee's earnings and service (e.g., a plan which states that the participant will receive an annual pension benefit of 1½ percent of the average of the highest consecutive five years' earnings times the number of years of credited service).

The fourth benefit formula relates benefits to both earnings and years of service and is the most common method used to compute pension benefits in plans for salaried personnel. The flat amount or flat amount per year of service formula is often found in negotiated plans. The flat amount and flat percentage of earnings formulas typically require that an employee complete a minimum number of years of service by his normal retirement date and that the benefit will be proportionately reduced if his service was less than the required number of years. Defined benefit formulas based upon earnings can vary according to whether they are based upon career average earnings, final earnings, or average earnings for a given period of time.

Contributions to a defined benefit plan are based on actuarial valuations designed to estimate the amounts necessary to fund the estimated benefits to be paid to participants at retirement. The actuarial valuation process is discussed in detail in Chapters 4 through 9.

[2] Defined Contribution Plans

Defined contribution plans, also referred to as individual account plans, provide for an account for each participant and for benefits based solely upon the amount contributed to the participant's account. In addition, any income, expenses, gains and losses, and any forfeitures of accounts of other participants may be allocated to such participant's account.

Under a defined contribution plan, the rate of contribution is either fixed, usually determined as a percentage of eligible employees' earnings or as a percentage of profits, or the contribution may be determined on a discretionary basis by the board of directors. The *employer's* contribution, together with the *employee's* contribution under a contributory plan, and the employee's share in the investment experience of the plan, provides eventual retirement income or other benefits. The amount accumulated by retirement in the employee's account will depend upon such factors as his contributions and the investment experience of the plan. Upon retirement, this amount will be paid to the employee in a lump sum or used to purchase a retirement annuity. Since the cost of a retirement annuity will vary according to such factors as age, sex, and normal retirement date, it is not possible to predict with any certainty the amount of retirement income a participant will receive under a defined contribution plan.

In general, there are five basic types of defined contribution plans:

(1) *Profit-sharing plan.* An employer's contributions are based upon a predetermined formula or determined at the discretion of the board of directors of the employer. Contributions are generally allocated to participants in proportion to their compensation.

(2) *Money-purchase plan.* An employer's contributions are based upon a percentage of compensation for specific individuals. The benefits for each participant are derived from the amounts contributed to his account.

(3) *Target benefit plan.* The employer's contributrion to each participant's account is established at a level, based upon an

actuarial valuation, sufficient to provide a "target" benefit to each participant upon retirement. The plan does not guarantee that the target benefit will be paid; its only obligation is to pay whatever can be provided by the amount in the participant's account, depending on actual investment results achieved by the plan.

(4) *Stock bonus or employee stock ownership plan* (ESOP). This type of plan provides benefits similar to those of a profit-sharing plan; however, contributions are not necessarily dependent upon profits and the benefits are usually distributed in a lump sum in stock or, in some cases, cash.

(5) *Thrift or savings plan.* This type of plan allows the partricipants to contribute within given ranges (usually a percentage of pay). The employer's contribution is then related to the amount or rate of participant's contributions.

[3] Integration of Pension Plan Benefits With Social Security Benefits

The pension benefits paid under both defined benefit and defined contribution plans can be integrated with Social Security retirement benefits. In practice, many defined benefit plans are integrated, while only some defined contribution plans are integrated. The purpose of integration is to eliminate the double cost to the employer for providing retirement benefits which duplicate or overlap with Social Security benefits. Since the employer is paying FICA taxes on all participants up to the FICA wage base limitation (referred to as the "break point"), the pension plan can be designed to exclude from the plan's retirement benefit the Social Security retirement benefit provided through employer contributions. Integration is therefore designed to provide a total retirement benefit (Social Security and the pension plan) which is a *uniform percentage of compensation* for all participants.

The Internal Revenue Service has developed a complex set of rules and regulations concerning the integration of a plan with Social Security. These requirements are discussed at ¶ 3.04[6].

[4] Joint and Survivor Annuity

ERISA requires that if a plan provides for the payment of benefits in the form of an annuity, the plan must provide for the payment of annuity benefits in a form having the effect of a qualified joint and survivor annuity unless the participant elects otherwise. Under this form of payment, the participant's spouse is entitled to receive a continuing annuity in the event of death of the participant in an amount not less than one-half of the amount paid to the participant during the joint lives of him and his spouse. However, ERISA does not require the employer to pay the cost of the additional benefit but permits the employer to reduce the pension benefit to its actuarial equivalent as discussed at ¶ 7.13.

[5] Cost of Living and Variable Annuity Provisions

Certain plans incorporate formulas that are designed to protect against the effects of inflation on a retired participant's pension benefit. Such plans provide adjustments to the amount of the benefit based upon recognized cost-of-living indexes or provide a benefit that varies to reflect changes in the value of a specific portfolio of common stock and similar investments. Plans that contain provisions for election of a benefit which varies according to the performance of common stocks are referred to as "variable annuity" plans. Defined benefit plans that contain this feature convert, at time of retirement, the dollar benefit to be received by the participant into shares or units of a fund. Payments to the retiree will vary according to changes in the investment experience of the fund.

[6] Supplemental Benefits

Pension plans may contain provisions for the payment of benefits in the event of termination, death, disability, or early retirement. The specific types of benefits provided, eligibility for such benefits, and the amounts to be paid are set forth in the plan agreement. These supplemental benefits can be paid directly out of the assets of the pension plan or can be provided through insurance policies.

¶ 1.03   WELFARE BENEFIT PLANS

The more common types of employee welfare benefit plans are as follows:

(1) *Health plans* (i.e., plans which provide for hospital expenses, diagnostic X-ray and laboratory fees, surgical and medical fees, medicine and drugs, major medical insurance, life insurance, accidental death and dismemberment benefits, and/or

dental care, visual care, psychiatric care, and preventive medical examinations);

(2) *Disability plans* (i.e., plans which provide for benefits during periods of inability to work because of physical incapacity from illness or injury);

(3) *Vacation and holiday plans* (i.e., plans which provide for cash benefits to cover time-off for vacation purposes);

(4) *Supplemental unemployment benefit plans*; and

(5) *Apprenticeship, educational, and similar plans.*

Most single-employer welfare plans are either insured plans or unfunded plans. The insured plans typically include medical insurance, such as Blue Cross-Blue Shield and/or group major medical and group term life insurance. The unfunded benefit plans that are typical for most single employers are vacation and sick-leave plans. The establishment of a separate trust to accumulate contributions and pay benefits is normally limited to multiemployer plans, distinctive characteristics of which are discussed later in this chapter. Occasionally, larger employers may provide medical and life benefits on a self-insured basis and may establish a trust to accumulate annual contributions.

Generally, ERISA requires that all assets of employee benefit plans be held in trust. Exemptions from this requirement exist for fully insured plans, and proposed regulations would exempt welfare plans where benefits are paid directly from the general assets of the employer (unfunded plans). A plan is considered funded, however, if plan participants make contributions through withholding or otherwise and if there is a separate bank account or other segregation of assets.

Because of general familiarity with the wide variety of group insurance programs providing welfare benefits and the small number of trusteed welfare benefit plans, the following material on administration of employee benefit plans and funding instruments relates primarily to pension benefit plans.

¶ 1.04 ADMINSTRATION OF EMPLOYEE BENEFIT PLANS

Under ERISA, employee benefits plans subject to the fiduciary responsibility rules, and not exempted by law or regulation, must be established and maintained in writing. The plan document must provide for one or more named fiduciaries (designated individually or determinable under procedures specified in the plan). A named fiduciary may be an individual or organization so designated or a person holding a specified office, or the plan document may provide, for example, for the named fiduciary to be designated by the board of directors.

The named fiduciary(ies) have the responsibility to control and manage the operation and administration of the plan. The plan may allocate responsibility among various fiduciaries and provide for delegation of duties to third parties who are not named fiduciaries.

The administration of a plan can take various forms. In the case of single-employer pension plans, the day-to-day administrative duties are usually performed by the employer. The plan may have an administrative committee consisting of three or more officers or other responsible employees, or an individual appointed as administrator. The committee or individual will have overall responsibility for the operation of the pension fund in accordance with the plan, trust agreement, and other applicable documents and regulations. Outside parties such as bank trust departments, insurance companies, and independent contractual administrators might be retained by the employer to handle some or all of the day-to-day administration of the plan.

Under ERISA, the administrator is a person designated by the plan or, if no administrator is designated, the plan sponsor. The officially designated administrator has certain responsibilities under ERISA, such as filing the annual report, regardless of who handles day-to-day administration of the plan.

A funding agency is an organization or individual that provides facilities for the accumulation or administration of assets to be used for the payment of plan benefits. Funding agencies include life insurance companies, corporate trustees (bank or trust company), and individuals acting as trustees. Plans funded with an insurance company are commonly referred to as "insured plans," while the other plans are called "trusteed plans." Many plans accumulate assets with both insurance companies and trustees and are called "combination plans."

[1] Trusteed Plans

The principal responsibility of the trustee is to hold title to and possession of specific assets. The trustee is responsible for the safekeeping and management of assets to the extent this responsibility is not delegated to others. Typically, trustees will also make benefit payments based upon instructions from the plan's retirement or administrative committee, and maintain investment and transaction records.

A trust agreement sets forth the duties and responsibilities of the trustee. The typical trust agreement contains provisions among others, regarding the irrevocability and nondiversion of trust assets; the investment powers of the trustee; the payment of legal, trustee, and other fees relative to the plan; periodic reports to the employer to be prepared by the trustee; the records and accounts to be maintained by the trustee; the payment of benefits under the plan; and the rights and duties of a trustee in case of amendments or termination of the plan.

The trust fund arrangement provides the greatest degree of flexibility in the administration and funding of pension benefits. Trusteed plans can be designed to provide a wide range of benefits paid to participants and offer flexibility in investment methods. In addition, there are no required minimum deposits or limitations on the selection of investments as required by insured plans, except as specifically set forth in the trust agreement or as a result of ERISA's fiduciary responsibility provisions.

A combination of investment methods may be used by a trusteed plan. The investment powers of a trustee are usually set forth in the trust agreement. The types of investments utilized by a trusteed plan can vary according to the desire for diversification of investments in an attempt to minimize risk, the desire for high-yield investments, liquidity requirements, and the type of benefits provided by the plan. Bank trust departments are frequently used as the trustee.

[a] Services of Bank Trust Departments

Bank trust departments can provide a variety of services to employee benefit plans. These services include:

(1) Investment management;
(2) Investment safekeeping;
(3) Receipt and delivery of securities;
(4) Receipt of sale proceeds;
(5) Disbursement of purchase costs;
(6) Receipt of investment income;
(7) Disbursement of individual benefits;
(8) Disbursement of plan expenses;
(9) Accounting for and reporting of plan transactions and assets.

The extent to which these services are provided to an employee benefit plan depends upon the plan's arrangement with the trust department. Some of the more common arrangements are described below:

(1) *Full trustee*. Under this type of arrangement the trust department will perform all of the functions previously listed. In some cases, the plan may retain the right to approve investment decisions before the transactions are executed.

(2) *Trustee with only administrative functions*. Under this type of arrangement the trust department will perform all of the functions previously listed except investment management. Investment management is usually performed by an independent investment adviser or individual trustees.

(3) *Agent*. This type of arrangement is common for multiemployer plans. The bank may function either *as a full trustee* or like a trustee with only administrative functions. The *bank is not a trustee* because of the requirements for joint union-management trustees.

(4) *Custodian*. Under this type of arrangement the bank does not serve as a trustee or as an investment manager. Some or all of the other functions previously listed may be performed.

[b] Types of Trusts

There are several variations in the form of trust utilized by benefit plans. A majority of trusts are maintained exclusively for the benefit of participants and beneficiaries of a single plan; however, common trusts and pooled trusts are also used.

(1) *Common trust*. A common trust is a trust used to accumulate assets of several unrelated plans. They provide a greater diversification of investment opportunies for smaller plans as well as cost reductions through lower brokerage commission fees and administrative expenses. A plan's investment in a common trust is stated in terms of units or shares. Common trust funds can offer a trustee considerable flexibility in the choice of investments. Separate common trust funds are available to provide fixed income and equity investments.

(2) *Pooled trust*. A pooled trust is similar to a common trust in that it combines the assets of several plans. A pooled trust, however, is generally sponsored by one employer and used to accumulate the assets of different plans of the employer and its subsidiaries.

[2] Insured Plans

Insured plans are plans where the funding agency is an insurance company. Contributions are generally paid to the insurer, who pays all the benefits to eligible participants in accordance with the terms of the insurance contract. Insurance contracts range from those providing fully guaranteed retirement benefits to those representing only investment vehicles which provide no guaranteed benefits.

Insurance companies offer complete facilities for administration of pension plans. Employers make the deposits required under a plan and insurance companies will maintain required records, including complete records of individual employee contributions in a contributory plan, file necessary reports, and make disbursements to retirees. The role of an insurance company in plan administration will vary according to the type of plan.

Insurance companies offer a range of pension plan insurance products, each having a unique mix of guarantees and investment alternatives. Not all insurance products contain a provision that in consideration for the premiums paid the insurance company will guarantee the payment of the scheduled (i.e., level of retirement annuity purchased) pension benefit. Accordingly, the distinction between an insured plan with guaranteed and nonguaranteed pension benefits is important. Oftentimes, "insured" is interchanged in error with "guaranteed" by those not familiar with insurance company terminology. Insured relates to the funding agency (i.e., insurance company) not to the guarantee, if any, relating to the pension benefits.

Insured plans can be categorized according to the methods by which assets are maintained and benefits are provided. In allocated plans the insurance premiums are used to provide benefits for specific participants. The plan assets (i.e., insurance policies) are allocated to the benefit of each specified participant. Allocated plans usually contain a guarantee regarding the pension benefits. Examples of allocated plans are:

(1) Individual policy plans;
(2) Group permanent contract plans; and
(3) Deferred group annuity plans.

This contrasts with plans wherein contributions are accumulated in unallocated funds to provide benefits for all participants. Upon a participant's retirement, the unallocated funds can be used to either purchase a life-time annuity for the benefit of the participant or pay the pension benefits as they become due. Examples of these types of unallocated insured plans are:

(1) Deposit administration group annuity contracts; and

(2) Immediate participation guarantee contracts.

Unallocated insured plans usually do not contain guarantees that the assets accumulated will be adequate to fund all retirement payments.

[a] Individual Policy Plans

As the name implies, individual insurance contracts are purchased for each participant covered by the plan. The contracts may either be annuities or ordinary life insurance contracts. If the funding instrument is an ordinary life insurance contract, the cash surrender value at the participant's retirement date is normally used to purchase a retirement annuity. Policies that combine the life insurance and annuity features are referred to as retirement income policies. Since an individual policy is purchased for each employee, the cost of this type of retirement plan is higher than others. In practice, the use of individual policy plans is usually confined to employers with a limited number of employees.

Individual policy plans may be combined with a side or conversion fund. Under this type of arrangement, contributions are used to purchase insurance policies and the excess is put into a conversion fund. At retirement, the cash surrender value plus a portion of the conversion fund are used to purchase a retirement annuity.

[b] Group Permanent Contracts

A group permanent plan is practically identical to an individual policy retirement income plan. The major difference is the reduction in cost due to reduced expense rates charged by the insurance company. A master contract is entered into between the insurance company and the plan sponsor. Participants receive certificates indicating their benefits and conditions of coverage as specified in the master contract rather than having individual policies issued. Group permanent contracts can also be used in conjunction with a conversion fund.

[c] Deferred Group Annuity Contracts

Under deferred group annuity contracts, contributions are used to purchase individual single-premium deferred annuities. The deferred annuities purchased are equivalent to the pension benefits earned (i.e., accrued benefits) by each participant. This type of plan is fully insured and generally is not designed to provide life insurance protection. There is little flexibility in the cost of this type of plan since units for each participant must be purchased as they accrue.

[d] Deposit Administration (DA) Group Annuity Contracts

Under DA contracts, the employer's contributions are not allocated to specific employees covered under the plan, but are instead held for the benefit of all participants. Under this type of arrangement, there is a reduction in the guarantees by the insurance company. The insurer will guarantee an interest rate on funds being accumulated in contractual or "active life funds," and specific rates at which retirement annuities may be purchased. It is the employer's responsibility, however, to see that the contributions to the fund are adequate. Accordingly, the insurance company is not insuring that each participant will receive his pension benefits as specified in the plan.

Contributions to the fund are based upon actuarial valuations rather than at premium rates specified by the issuer. This provides greater employer flexibility in funding through the choice of the actuarial valuation method. The various actuarial valuation methods that may be utilized are discussed in Chapter 8.

In addition to providing greater flexibility in funding, a DA contract provides a large amount of flexibility in designing a pension plan's benefits. A single premium to purchase an annuity is withdrawn from the fund at the time of each participant's retirement. Because retirement income annuities are not purchased until the employee's actual retirement, more complex benefit formulas can be readily implemented under deposit administration contracts. In addition, benefit features such as termination, death, early retirement, and disability are easily incorporated into a plan.

As noted previously, the insurance company will guarantee an interest rate on funds being accumulated in contractual or "active life" funds (also referred to as deposit administration, deposit, deposit account, or purchase payment funds). Such funds become part of an insurance company's general assets for investment purposes. The plan's balance in the DA fund is decreased as amounts are used to purchase benefits and increased with the amount of interest guaranteed in the contract and any dividends declared. Dividends are based on actual investment experience of the insurance company and are not guaranteed.

In computing the dividends, an internal record account is maintained by the insurance company for each contract. This account is a cumulative record of the actual income and expense under the contract and is used to compute the allocation of investment income under the contract. Favorable investment experience is allocated as dividends by average rates or over a period of time in order for the insurance company to build up contingency reserves.

Many insurance companies also have contracts wherein a portion of a plan's DA fund can be allocated to "separate accounts." The assets in "separate accounts" are not commingled with the general assets of the insurance company and may be invested without regard to restrictions imposed on the insurer's general account investments. The selection of the type of separate account, equity (common stocks, etc.), real estate, or fixed dollar (bonds, etc.) account, provides an employer with substantial investment flexibility. Separate accounts were developed by insurance companies to compete with bank trust funds in making unlimited equity investments available. The insurance company will not guarantee any principal amounts deposited in separate accounts or any income relating thereto. A contract holder's share of a separate account is usually determined on a unit-value basis. Unit values are determined based upon fair market values of the investments as of a given valuation date.

[e] Immediate Participation Guarantee (IPG) Contracts

An IPG contract has all the aspects of flexibility in plan design, funding through the choice of reasonable actuarial valuation methods and investing through the use of separate accounts, as does a deposit administration contract. There is a further reduction in the insurance company's guarantees with an IPG. With a DA contract, an insurance company is able to provide certain guarantees as a result of its control, such as dividends reflecting investment experience. However, with an IPG, there is an immediate reflection of actual experience in the plan's account.

Immediate participation guarantee contracts generally provide for payment of interest on fund accumulations, with expenses charged directly to the fund as incurred. Monthly retirement payments are made directly from the fund so that the contract holder (i.e., employer) will immediately participate in excess of interest and mortality gains. Because individual annuities are not actually purchased at time of retirement (as is the practice with deposit administration contracts), the insurance company will usually require a minimum balance in a retired life reserve fund sufficient to purchase annuities for all retirees.

[f] Other Types of Insurance Contracts

There are insurance contracts which combine features of both immediate participation and deposit administration contracts. These are generally referred to as modified immediate participation contracts or direct-rated deposit administration contracts. For example, a direct-rated deposit administration contract will have an "active life" fund which is maintained on an immediate participation basis with the amount required to purchase a single premium annuity withdrawn from the fund at the time of a participant's retirement. Whether or not an IPG makes annuity payments directly from the fund, as previously discussed, or is modified to provide for the purchase of annuities at retirement, an insurance company's guarantee will generally be limited to the payment of annuities to those participants who have actually retired. A relatively new insurance product is the investment contract which is more flexible than the IPG in that no minimum reserves are required to be established for retired participants. Only amounts sufficient to pay benefits during the next year must be maintained in the general assets of the insurance company.

[3] Combination Plans

Pension benefit plans which have features of both insured and trusteed plans are commonly referred to as "combination plans." This term is used both for insured plans where a "conversion fund" is held by the insurer and where a trust fund arrangement is used in conjunction with group permanent contracts or individual insurance and annuity contracts. The term "conversion fund" refers to assets of a plan which are separately invested and are then used to purchase a guaranteed life annuity at the time of participant's retirement. A conversion fund can be administered by the insurance company or a trustee.

Insurance contracts can be used by a trustee to provide supplemental benefits, as previously discussed, to take advantage of investment opportunities, and to provide a means of guaranteeing annuity payments to retired participants.

¶ 1.05 MULTIEMPLOYER BENEFIT PLANS

The foregoing material on types of benefit plans relates primarily to single-employer plans. Many of the concepts are equally applicable to multiemployer plans; however, there are differences and unique features which should be noted.

[1] Description of Multiemployer Plans

Multiemployer plans are plans which cover employees of two or more employers and are established pursuant to the terms of a collective-bargaining agreement. The Labor Management Relations Act of 1947 (also known as the Taft-Hartley Act) requires such plans to be administered under a declaration of trust providing for administration by a joint board of trustees composed of an equal number of employer and union representatives. Furthermore, Taft-Hartley also required that multiemployer plans be audited.

Under ERISA, a multiemployer plan is a plan maintained pursuant to one or more collective-bargaining agreements between an employee organization and more than one employer, and under which the amount of contributions made for a plan year by each employer making such contributions is less than 50 percent of the aggregate contributions made under the plan for that year by all employers making such contributions. Once a plan qualifies as a multiemployer plan for any plan year, the percentage test is raised to 75 percent. All employers who are members of an affiliated group are considered as one employer for purposes of qualifying as a multiemployer plan. An additional requirement for a multiemployer plan is that it must be established for a "substantial business purpose," and regulations have been proposed describing factors to be considered in determining whether a "substantial business purpose" exists.

The most distinguishing factor between multiemployer plans and single-employer plans is their administration. As indicated earlier, multiemployer plans are established pursuant to a collective-bargaining agreement and are jointly administered by employer and union representatives. The plan is normally negotiated between an associated group of employers (such as in the construction trades) and the union representing the employees. By contrast, single-employer plans are established by the management of one employer either unilaterally or through collective bargaining. Thus, ultimate responsibility for such plans rests with the sponsoring employer, whereas responsibility for multiemployer plans rests in a joint employer/union board of trustees.

Multiemployer plans were generally developed in industries characterized by skilled craftsmen, numerous small employers, intense competition, high level of employee mobility, and a high rate of business failure. Employers participating in multiemployer plans have a common industry bond usually through a trade association. The most common industries utilizing multiemployer plans are food, printing, apparel, construction, transportation, mining, and wholesale and retail trade. Participating employers in such plans are usually not financially related. Thus, multiemployer plans were developed to meet the needs of specific industries in a geographical area. The advantages of such plans to the industry include:

(1) Availability of pension benefits within a specific industry for the mobile employee;
(2) Standardization of pension costs for competing employers;
(3) Stabilization of experience for pension plans;
(4) Utilization of the economies of large-scale operations.

[2] Operating Characteristics of Multiemployer Plans

The types of pension and welfare benefits offered by multiemployer plans are similar to those offered by single-employer plans. In collective bargaining, it is common for unions to negotiate a total "benefit package" with employer associations. Such packages create separate plans for each type of benefit to be provided. For example, separate plans would be established for retirement benefits, health benefits, vacation benefits, etc. Normally, a separate board of trustees, composed of employer and union representatives, is established to administer each plan; however, "joint boards" which manage the affairs of all plans within the "benefit package" may be utilized.

A unique feature of multiemployer plans with regard to pension benefits is the makeup of the plans. Multiemployer plans commonly use a variation of the traditional defined contribution plan. This variation is composed both of a fixed contribution and a fixed benefit. Thus, the plans have the characteristics of both a defined contribution and a defined benefit plan.

This is a result of the union negotiating a fixed contribution rate with employer associations and the establishment of a uniform benefit formula for eligible employees even though funds are received on a defined contribution basis. Actuarial assumptions and a valuation method are needed to determine the level of contributions needed to maintain a given level of benefits. An additional assumption that must be considered in multiemployer plans, which is not found in single-employer plans, is that of expected future contributions. This is basically due to the frequent adjustments made to employer's contribution rates.

Trustees of multiemployer plans have the same responsibilities as those of single-employer plans; however, in general, the delegation of responsibilities is done in a more formalized manner. In this regard, most multiemployer plans utilize professional administrators to advise the board, maintain plan records, and comply with regulatory requirements.

Another concept unique to multiemployer plans is that of reciprocity. A reciprocity agreement is an agreement entered into by two or more multiemployer plans which allows an employee participant to accumulate credited service as long as he works within a participating plan. The primary objective of reciprocity is to extend the geographical area in which an employee may work without endangering his pension eligibility.

There are several basic types of reciprocity agreements. First, the pro rata method is an agreement under which each participating plan pays a proportionate share of the employee's pension benefit. The second is the money-transfer, or collection agency, agreement under which employer contributions are transferred currently, or at retirement, to the employee's home plan, which pays the benefit upon retirement. The second method is basically an arrangement in which participating plans act as a collection agent for each other. There are basically two advantages to this approach:

(1) The employee's benefits do not change from one plan to another as may occur in the pro rata method.

(2) There is no need to exchange eligibility data between two plans.

Another method of reciprocity occurs when accumulated contributions follow the employee to another plan, and benefits are provided by the new plan. This method is commonly referred to as the "money follows the man" plan. The concept of being able to physically transfer accumulated credits and monies to a new plan is known as "portability" of credits.

A serious problem associated with multiemployer plans is the liability related to accumulation of eligibility credits that exists for employees who change employment or stop working. It is difficult for plans to determine whether the employee will return to work. This is basically due to the seasonality of certain industries. As a result, multiemployer plans have favored provisions which determine benefits based upon service more than earnings.

Multiemployer plans are generally noncontributory plans, thus being financed almost entirely by employer contributions. Single-employer plans, on the other hand, use both contributory and noncontributory plans extensively. Contributions made to the multiemployer plan by participating employers are usually at uniform rates based upon the number of hours or days worked or gross earnings of the employee. Contributions from employers are made on a self-assessed basis and are generally remitted to the plan with a preprinted, detailed contribution report indicating employee participants, hours worked, etc. In the employer self-assessment method, contributions are usually made in the month following the month they accrue. The month the contribution is received by the plan is usually referred to as the "deposit month," and the month in which contributions are based is commonly known as the "work month." Due to seasonal employment and employee mobility, some plans have adopted provisions which allow employee participants who lack sufficient hours to meet minimum eligibility requirements to make self-payments to the plan to meet the minimum eligibility requirements.

Most multiemployer welfare benefit plans are funded. In addition, many welfare plans, such as health plans (which are normally insured plans in single-employer situations), are not fully insured. In these plans, insurance companies are frequently retained to handle claims for a fee.

¶ 1.06 AUDIT SIGNIFICANCE OF PLAN CHARACTERISTICS

ERISA has greatly expanded the role of the auditor with respect to employee benefit plans. In addition to auditing and reporting on plan financial statements, auditors may be called on as consultants in the areas of tax qualification, taxation of benefits, record-keeping, internal controls and procedures, and compliance with Department of Labor and Securities and Exchange Commission reporting and disclosure requirements.

All of the above areas are discussed in the subsequent chapters of this manual. An understanding of the various characteristics of plans, and how they affect a plan's operations and the regulatory requirements for specific plans, is fundamental to providing effective service to a plan.

Chapter 2

ERISA

¶ 2.01 LEGISLATIVE HISTORY

There has been a relatively short legislative history in the United States with respect to employee benefit plans. The Social Security Act of 1935 was the first major employee benefit legislation. Prior to the Social Security Act, old-age, survivor, and disability insurance benefits were primarily limited to governmental pension plans and a relatively few voluntary private plans. The major growth in private employee benefit plans occurred during the 1940s. This was influenced in part by wage restrictions imposed by the government and in part by the existence of a highly competitive labor market which resulted in companies offering pension plans and other employee benefits as a means of recruiting and retaining employees.

The growth of unions has also had a significant impact on the development of private employee benefit plans. In 1947, the Taft-Hartley Act amended prior legislation concerning the conduct of labor-management negotiations. A section of that legislation specifically addressed itself to union-negotiated employee benefit plans. It provided for such matters as the equal joint administration of benefit plans by management and union representatives, annual audits of the plans, and restrictions on the use of plan contributions.

In 1958, Congress passed the Welfare and Pension Plans Disclosure Act which required filing of a plan description form (Form D-1) and an annual report form (Form D-2) for employee benefit plans. As stated by one of the sponsors of the bill, Congressman Ralph Metcalf (D-Ill.), the legislation was an "attempt at self policing of employers and employees without establishing a centralized investigative agency and complex reporting, accounting, and registration procedures in addition to the disclosure."

¶ 2.02 OVERVIEW OF ERISA

In 1974, the Employee Retirement Income Security Act (ERISA) vastly expanded governmental involvement in employee benefit plans. While ERISA does not require an employer to establish or maintain employee benefit plans, it provides for certain minimum standards for participation, vesting and funding, expanded fiduciary responsibility, and disclosure requirements and termination insurance for such plans. In addition, it provides for governmental agencies to interpret and enforce the Act.

Prior to ERISA, an employer was able to design a pension or profit-sharing plan with very strict eligibility and vesting provisions. Generally, the Internal Revenue Service (IRS) rules concerning antidiscrimination and regulations concerning qualifying a plan for tax-exempt status were the main influence in these areas. Technically, vesting was not required prior to normal retirement age; however, IRS antidiscrimination rulings and collective bargaining generally resulted in vesting at an early retirement age and upon termination after an extended period of service. ERISA establishes minimum age and service requirements for participation in plans and minimum formulas for vesting benefits; it also defines credited service for the purpose of determining eligibility for participation and vesting.

ERISA also set forth certain minimum funding standards for pension plans. Prior to enactment of ERISA, unfunded plans were allowed to exist. The benefits from these "pay as you go" plans were contingent on the continued existence of earnings of an employer. Such unfunded plans are now limited to plans that provide for deferred compensation for selected groups of management and highly compensated employees, or to benefits in excess of the limitations on benefits and contributions imposed under ERISA.

Employer contributions to defined benefit and certain defined contribution plans are generally based upon actuarial valuations of the plan. Prior to ERISA, there was wide flexibility in the choice of actuarial assumptions used in such valuations and in the method used to amortize past service liabilities over future years of plan operation; consequently, employers had quite a bit of flexibility in funding plans. The minimum contribution required by the IRS was the amount necessary to keep the unfunded past service liability from increasing beyond its initial level. ERISA now provides for minimum funding standards which require amortization of past service liabilities and experience gains and losses over specific periods of time. In addition, ERISA provides that actuarial assumptions on which plan costs are determined and the method of asset valuation used must be reasonable, and it establishes means by which these matters can be monitored.

The minimum funding standards discussed above and the plan termination insurance provision of ERISA resulted from congressional studies which found that certain terminated plans had insufficient assets to pay promised benefits. They also determined that some plans were not accumulating assets fast enough to provide for future pension obligations.

Prior to ERISA, the sole source of benefits was the plan fund, and the liability was limited to fund assets. ERISA established the Pension Benefit Guaranty Corporation which will make up deficiencies, subject to certain limitations, if a plan terminates with insufficient assets to pay benefits that are vested. Furthermore, employers are now contingently liable up to 30 percent of their net worth for any deficiency in the assets of a terminated plan.

ERISA also contains broad guidelines and specific rules on fiduciary conduct and prohibited transactions and provides for significantly expanded reporting and disclosure requirements as compared to the Welfare and Pension Plans Disclosure Act. It is the expanded reporting and disclosure requirements which are of primary interest to the auditors. However, in order to fulfill their responsibilities under these provisions, the auditors need to be aware of the other provisions of the ERISA Act since they can have a direct effect on financial statements.

¶ 2.03 STRUCTURE OF ERISA

The Employee Retirement Income Security Act of 1974 is comprised of four titles:

Title I, *Protection of Employee Benefit Rights*, establishes minimum reporting and disclosure requirements, minimum participating and vesting standards, minimum funding standards, fiduciary responsibilities, and certain administrative and enforcement matters.

Title II, *Amendments to the Internal Revenue Code Relating to Retirement Plans*, conforms provisions of the Code to the new standards and procedures required under Title I.

Title III, *Jurisdiction, Administration, Enforcement; Joint Pension Task Force, Etc.*, gives the Secretary of Treasury certain administrative responsibilities and provides for coordination between the Department of the Treasury and the Department of Labor. In addition, it establishes a Joint Pension Task Force to study certain provisions under the Act and to make recommendations in certain areas that the Act does not cover, such as providing portability of pension rights.

Title IV, *Plan Termination Insurance*, establishes the Pension Benefit Guaranty Corporation and the procedures for disposition of a terminated pension plan, including the payment of benefits to covered employees and fixing the employer liability in connection with a termination.

At the present time, there is considerable activity in Congress concerning proposed amendments to ERISA. The principal thrusts of this activity are to eliminate, to the extent possible, the dual jurisdiction of the Department of Labor (DOL) and the Internal Revenue Service and to simplify the reporting and disclosure requirements, particularly for smaller plans. H.R. 4340, introduced by Representatives John Dent (D-Pa.) and John Erlenborn (R-Ill.), would create a new independent agency to regulate employee benefit plans, while S. 901, introduced by Senator Lloyd Bentsen (D-Tex.), would divide responsibility for administration of ERISA between the DOL and the IRS.

The major provisions of ERISA as well as regulations issued to date governing their application are discussed below.

¶ 2.04 EMPLOYEE PARTICIPATION AND VESTING (ERISA SECTIONS 201-211)

The provisions of both Title I (DOL) and Title II (IRS) are virtually identical in the areas of participation and vesting. The Internal Revenue Code also imposes group coverage requirements which have no parallel under the DOL requirements. Under ERISA, the DOL was given the responsibility to develop regulations governing joint enforcement of the participation standards. Regulations covering minimum standards for determining service for purposes of participation eligibility, vesting, and benefit accrual were issued by the DOL in December 1976.

[1] Participation

Generally, an employee cannot be excluded from a plan because of age or service if he is at least twenty-five years old and has completed at least one year of service. However, it is possible to exclude employees or groups of employees on other bases, provided the plan meets the IRS coverage requirements. These requirements, which are discussed in more detail in Chapter 3, provide for meeting a percentage of employees test or what is commonly known as the "fair cross section test."

As an alternative to the age 25 and one year of service requirement, a plan may delay participation until an employee has completed three years of service if it provides for immediate 100 percent vesting of the employee's accrued benefit as determined under the plan. Another alternative exists for plans maintained exclusivly for employees of a tax-exempt educational organization which provides full and immediate vesting for all participants. In this limited situation, a plan may require an employee to attain both age 30 and complete one year of service in order to begin participation in the plan.

In addition, a defined benefit plan or a target benefit plan may exclude any employee from participation who is within five years of the normal retirement age stated in the plan when he or she is hired.

It is the accrued benefit under the plan to which the vesting percentages apply. ERISA requires that a plan meet one of the following three minimum vesting rules:

(1) *Ten-Year Service Rule*—100 percent vesting after ten years of service.

(2) *Graded 5- to 10-Year Service Rule*—25 percent vesting after five years of service; then 5 percent additional vesting for each year of service from years six through ten, then 10 percent additional vesting for each year of service from year eleven through year fifteen, so that an employee is 100 percent vested after fifteen years of service.

(3) *"Rule of 45"*—50 percent vesting when the sum of an employee's age and years of service total forty-five, if he has completed at least five years of service, and 10 percent additional vesting for each year of service thereafter. Additionally, a participant under the "Rule of 45" must be 50 percent vested after ten years of covered service, such percentage increasing by 10 percent for each additional year of covered service, so that an employee is at least 50 percent vested after ten years and 100 percent vested after fifteen years regardless of his age.

A fourth, less used, vesting alternative is applicable to a class year plan. A class year plan is defined as a profit-sharing, stock bonus, or money-purchase plan which provides that nonforfeitable rights to benefits derived from employer contributions are determined separately for each plan year. The minimum vesting requirement for this type of plan is satisfied if the plan provides 100 percent vesting for an employer contribution no later than five plan years after the plan year for which the contribution was made. However, employees excluded under this provision are still counted for purposes of meeting the IRS coverage requirements. Also, for a defined benefit or target benefit plan to exclude employees on the basis of age, it must have a readily determinable normal retirement age defined in the plan.

[2] Vesting

Vested benefits are benefits that are not contingent on a participant continuing in the service of an employer. In other words, vesting means that an employee's right to his accrued benefit is not forfeitable, even if he terminates employment.

The minimum vesting schedules established by ERISA are stated in terms of a percentage of a participant's accrued benefit. For defined contribution plans (profit-sharing plan, savings plans, etc.), a participant's accrued benefit is the balance in his plan account. In a defined benefit plan, a particpant's accrued benefit is the benefit determined under the terms of the plan expressed in the form of an annual benefit commencing at normal retirement age. A defined benefit plan's benefit-accrual provision is usually contained in the plan as a formula or schedule that specifies the rate at which employees' benefits are accumulated. For example, some plans specify that employees accumulate a fixed dollar (e.g., $20 a month) benefit to be paid at age 65 for each year of service. Other plans determine benefits based on both service and salary. One example of this type of benefit-accural provision would be one which provides for a benefit of 1½ percent of final (or average) annual compensation per year of service.

In addition, the Act requires that defined benefit pension plans must meet one of the following three rules for the computation of accrued benefits to which the above above-determined vesting percentages are applied:

> (1) *The 3 Percent Rule.* For each year of service (up to 33⅓ years), an employee must accrue at least 3 percent of the benefit that would be payable under the plan if he began par-

ticipation at the earliest possible age and retired at normal retirement age.

(2) The *33⅓ Percent Rule*. The annual rate of which a participant may accrue benefits payable at normal retirement cannot exceed 1⅓ times the rate for any prior year. This rule against "backloading" would not permit, for example, a benefit-accrual rate of 2 percent for a year if the rate for any prior year was less than 1½ percent, since the 2 percent rate would be more than 1⅓ times the lower rate.

(3) *Fractional Rule*. The benefits accrued for any year of service are equal to the employee's projected benefit at normal retirement prorated on the basis of his actual years of participation as compared with his projected years of participation to normal retirement. For example, after twenty years of participation, an employee would have accrued benefits equal to two-thirds of his projected benefits, if he would have participated thirty years by his normal retirement date.

[3] Minimum Standards Regulations

The participation and vesting requirements of ERISA include a number of complex rules for determining when a year of service must be credited for those purposes. Particularly complex are the rules covering breaks in service and when and to what extent pre- and post-break service must be considered.

The application of the participation and vesting rules is dependent upon the measuring tools used in this area. Primary among these tools are the concepts of a year of service and a break in service. ERISA defines a "year of service" as a twelve-consecutive month period during which an employee has accumulated at least 1,000 hours of service with the employer. A "one-year break in service" is a twelve-consecutive-month period during which an employee has not accumulated more than 500 hours of service with the employer.

The purpose of the minimum standards regulations is to prescribe standards for determining hours of service and the measuring period used to accumulate hours of service in order to properly determine years of service. An "hour of service" is defined as any hour worked for which an employee is paid or entitled to payment, hours not worked, such as due to vacation, holiday, illness, incapacity, layoff, jury duty, military, or other leave of absence, for which an employee is compensated, and hours for which backpay is awarded. The regulations also provide a number of equivalencies which may be used to eliminate the necessity of accumulating all hours. For example, 870 hours actually worked are equivalent to 1,000 hours, including vacations, illness, and other paid nonworking time.

For purposes of *initial* eligibility to participate, the twelve-consecutive-month period used must begin with the employment date (or the beginning of the month in which employed). Subsequent computation periods of participation may be based on the plan year or the calendar year. Similarly, the employer may designate a computation period for vesting and benefit-accrual purposes.

¶ 2.05 MINIMUM FUNDING STANDARDS (ERISA SECTIONS 301-306)

Prior to ERISA employers had quite a bit of flexibility in funding defined benefit pension plans and certain defined contribution plans through the selection of actuarial assumptions and policies with regard to past service cost. ERISA requires that employers meet certain minimum standards in funding pension plan obligations, and sets more rigid criteria for the selection of actuarial assumptions.

[1] Role of the Accountant in Determining Funding Requirements

The primary responsibility for determining a plan's funding requirements and compliance with the minimum funding standards is that of the actuary. These determinations are made through an actuarial valuation using complex actuarial concepts and methods. However, the funding requirements also have a direct effect on a plan's financial statements (e.g., contributions receivable) and on the operations of a plan. Accordingly, the accountant needs to have a basic understanding of these requirements and of actuarial theory and concepts.

The following paragraphs describe briefly the minimum funding requirements of ERISA. Part II of this manual discusses actuarial concepts and theory in detail.

[2] Required Annual Contributions

All pension plans subject to the minimum funding standards are required to make annual minimum contributions equal to normal cost plus amortization over thirty years (for single-employer plans) or forty years (for multiemployer plans) of unfunded accrued liabilities. Single-employer plans in existence on January 1, 1974 may amortize unfunded accrued liabilities existing at the effective date of the new funding standards over a period of forty years. Normal cost is the annual cost of future pension benefits and administrative expenses assigned under an actuarial cost method to years subsequent to a particular pension plan valuation date.

Actuarial valuations involve assumptions concerning such matters as anticipated plan expenses and investment return. Actual experience seldom coincides with estimates concerning the future. Accordingly, experience gains and losses are likely to result. The Act provides that such experience gains and losses must be amortized over a period of fifteen years (twenty years in the case of multiemployer plans) from the time they are determined. The funding of both the experience gains and losses and unfunded accrued liabilities is to be in level annual installments including both principal and interest.

[3] Funding Standard Account

Plans must maintain a minimum funding standard account to keep track of the required annual contributions as determined above. If an "accumulated funding deficiency" (excess of the total charges to the account over total credits applied to the account) exists, plan sponsors are subject to certain non-tax-deductible excise taxes.

Items to be reflected in the funding standard account are as follows:

Charges

(1) Normal cost of the plan for the plan year.
(2) Annual amortization of:
    (a) The unfunded past service costs over forty years if the plan was in existence on January 1, 1974 or is a multiemployer plan, or thirty years if the plan came into existence after January 1, 1974 and is a single-employer plan.
    (b) The net increase, if any, in unfunded past service costs under the plan arising from plan amendments adopted in each year, over forty years for multiemployer plans and thirty years for other plans.
    (c) The net experience loss, if any, for each plan year over

twenty years for multiemployer plans and fifteen years for other plans.

   (d) The net loss, if any, resulting from changes in actuarial assumptions used for each plan year, over a thirty-year period.

(3) Amount necessary to amortize each waived funding deficiency over a period of fifteen years.

(4) Amount necessary to amortize over five years an amount credited to this account from the alternative minimum funding standard account.

Credits

(1) The amount contributed by the employer.

(2) Annual amortization of:
   (a) The net decrease, if any, in unfunded past service costs arising from plan amendments adopted in each year, over forty years for multiemployer plans and thirty years for other plans.
   (b) The net experience gain, if any, for each plan year, over twenty years for multiemployer plans and fifteen years for other plans.
   (c) The net gain, if any, resulting from changes in actuarial assumptions used for each plan year, over thirty years.

(3) The amount of waived funding deficiency for the plan year.

(4) Excess of debit balance in funding standard account (before allowing this credit) over debit balance in the alternative minimum funding standard account, if the accumulated funding deficiency was determined under the alternative minimum funding standard account for preceding plan year.

Additionally, the funding standard account is to be charged or credited with interest consistent with the rate of interest used to determine costs under the plan.

[4] Alternative Funding Standard

An alternative funding standard is available for plans using funding methods which provide contributions at least equal to the contributions required under the "entry age normal method." Under the entry age normal method, costs are reflected in two parts: (1) the "normal cost," which is the annual contribution which would have been necessary had the plan always been in effect; and (2) a single amount, the so-called past service or supplemental cost, which is the amount which presently would have been in the fund had the plan always been in existence.

Once a plan elects the alternative funding standard for any plan year, both an alternative funding standard account and the basic funding standard account described earlier must be maintained. The basic funding standard account will be credited for the excess of the accumulated funding deficiency under the basic account over such deficiency computed under the alternative account. The plan's minimum funding requirement will be the lesser of the minimum required contribution under either account.

Under the alternative funding standard, the minimum amount to be contributed to a defined benefit plan is (1) the excess, if any, of the present value of accrued benefits over the fair market value of plan assets, plus (2) normal cost determined pursuant to the funding method used under the plan or as determined under the unit credit method.

If a corporation switches from the alternative funding standard to the basic funding standard, it ceases to maintain the alternative funding standard account. In such a case, there is generally a five-year amortization period for the excess charges over credits that were built up in the basic funding standard account during the plan years when the alternative standard was in effect.

[5] Full Funding Limitation

ERISA also provides for a "full funding limitation" where the excess of accrued plan liabilities (including current normal cost) over the value of plan assets is less than the minimum funding requirement otherwise determined under the funding standard account. This situation may occur when plan assets have increased substantially and unexpectedly in value. ERISA recognizes this situation by providing that the maximum amount to be "charged" to the funding standard account and to be contributed to the plan is to be limited to the difference between the total accrued liabilities under the plan and the lesser of the fair market value of the plan's assets or the value of the plan's assets determined on the basis of the actuarial method of valuation normally used by the plan.

[6] Alternative Funding Method for Collectively Bargained Plans

In addition, temporary and proposed regulations issued by the IRS on July 25, 1977 (42 C.F.R. § 39382) authorize use of another alternative funding method for collectively bargained plans. This method is called the "shortfall method" and allows collectively bargained plans to elect to determine charges to the funding standard account on the basis of an estimated number of units of production or service for a certain period. The difference between the net amount charged or credited under the shortfall method and the net amount that would otherwise have been charged or credited is the shortfall gain or loss to be amortized over fifteen years.

[7] Enforcement and Waivers

To enforce the minimum funding standards, Section 1013 of ERISA (amending I.R.C. Section 4971) provides for a 5 percent excise tax to be imposed on the plan sponsor if the funding standards are not met. The initial tax of 5 percent is to be imposed on the so-called accumulated funding deficiency, which means, generally, the excess of charges over credits in the "funding standard account" for all plan years.

Any accumulated funding deficiency must be corrected within ninety days from the date a deficiency notice is mailed by the IRS with respect to the initial 5 percent excise tax. The ninety-day period may be extended if the IRS determines that the extension is reasonable and necessary. If the deficiency is not corrected within the specified period, an additional 100 percent tax may be imposed. Neither the 5 percent tax nor the 100 percent tax is deductible by the employer.

However, if an employer demonstrates "substantial business hardship" and shows that the application of the minimum funding requirements would be adverse to the interests of the plan participants in the aggregate, the IRS may waive all or part of the minimum funding requirements for a plan year. The term "waived funding deficiency" means the portion of the minimum funding standard which is waived by the IRS. In determining whether there is substantial business hardship, several factors are to be considered. For example, the IRS will consider whether the employer is operating at an economic loss or whether it is reasonable to expect that the plan will be continued only if the waiver is granted.

The amount of the entire waived funding deficiency for a plan year is credited to the funding standard account. This amount is then amortized in equal installments over fifteen plan years beginning with the next plan year. The amortized amount is treated as a charge against the funding standard amount. The IRS may not waive all or part of the funding requirements for more than five of any fifteen consecutive plan years.

ERISA also authorizes the Secretary of Labor to extend the amortization period for unfunded past service costs and experience gains and losses. An amortization period may be extended up to an additional ten years if a substantial risk exists that the plan might be terminated or that pension benefit levels or employee compensation might be adversely affected. To grant such an extension, the Secretary of Labor must also find that

- The extension would carry out the purpose of the Act;
- The extension would provide adequate protection under the plan for participants and their beneficiaries; and
- Not granting the extension would be adverse to the interests of the plan participants in the aggregate.

¶ 2.06 FIDUCIARY RESPSONSIBILITY (ERISA SECTIONS 401-414)

Under ERISA, a person is a fiduciary (whether or not so designated in the plan) to the extent he (1) exercises discretionary authority or control over a plan or the disposition of its assets; (2) renders investment advice to a plan for a fee; or (3) has any discretionary authority or responsibility in administration of a plan. To help guarantee that plans will be maintained exclusively for the benefit of participants, the Act contains broad guidelines and specific rules on fiduciary conduct and makes fiduciaries personally liable for losses due to breaches of these statutory duties.

It is anticipated that regulations will be issued defining more precisely the broad guidelines concerning fiduciary conduct. Such guidelines include the following:

(1) The "prudent man rule" requires that "care, skill, prudence and diligence under the circumstances then prevailing that a prudent man acting in a like capacity and familiar with such

matters would use in the conduct of an enterprise of a like character with like aims." This includes matters such as selection of co-fiduciaries, delegation of duties, and periodic performance reviews.

(2) A fiduciary is required to diversify the investments of a plan so as to minimize the risk of large loss. The degree of investment concentration which would violate this rule is not set forth in the Act.

[1] Prohibited Transactions

An auditor performing an examination of an employee benefit plan should be aware of the following specific rules.

(1) Defined benefit pension plans cannot invest more than 10 percent of plan assets in employer securities and/or employer real property. Employer real property means real property (and related personal property) which is leased to an employer of employees covered by the plan. There is a transitional rule which permits plans to reduce existing investments over a ten-year period. Defined contribution plans do not have this restriction with respect to qualifying employer securities if such plans explicitly provide for such investments. The exemption from the restriction does not apply to real property.

(2) Fiduciaries are prohibited from engaging directly or indirectly in certain specified transactions with a party-in-interest. A party-in-interest includes employers and unions of plan participants, persons rendering services to a plan and its officers and agents, officers, fiduciaries and employees of a plan and relatives, agents, and joint venturers of any of the foregoing. The prohibited transactions are summarized below:

- A sale, exchange, or lease of property between the plan and a party-in-interest;
- A loan or extension of credit between the plan and a party-in-interest.
- The furnishing of goods, services, or facilities between the plan and a party-in-interest;
- A transfer of plan assets to a party-in-interest or a transfer for the use or benefit of a party-in-interest;
- Use by a fiduciary of the income or assets of a plan in his own interest or for his own account;

- Receipt of any consideration by a fiduciary for his personal account from any person dealing with a plan in connection with a transaction involving income or assets of the plan (e.g., kickbacks).

[2] Exceptions and Exemptions for Certain Transactions

There are certain exceptions dealing with party-in-intrerest transactions which do not prevent a plan fiduciary from receiving reasonable compensation for services to a plan or receiving benefits from a plan as a participant or beneficiary as long as such benefits are in accordance with the terms of a plan as applied to all other participants and beneficiaries. In addition, such matters as payments to parties-in-interest for reasonable compensation for office space and legal, accounting, and other services necessary for the operation of a plan are permitted.

Transactions granted permanent exemptions under Section 408(b) of ERISA are as follows:

(1) Loans made by a plan to parties-in-interest who are participants in, or beneficiaries of, the plan, if such loans (a) are authorized by the plan, (b) are made available to all participants and beneficiaries on a reasonably equivalent and nondiscriminatory basis, and (c) are adequately secured and bear a reasonable rate of interest.

(2) A contract or reasonable arrangement to provide office space and legal, accounting, or other services necessary to establish and operate a plan, if no more than reasonable compensation is paid by the plan.

(3) A loan to an employee stock ownership plan, if the loan is primarily for the benefit of participants and beneficiaries of the plan and is at a reasonable rate of interest, and if the only collateral for the loan is qualifying employer securities.

(4) Investment of plan assets in interest-bearing deposits of a bank or similar regulated financial institution which is a plan fiduciary, if such deposits are expressly authorized by the plan or by a fiduciary (other than such institution) expressly empowered to instruct such investment, or if the plan covers only employees of the fiduciary.

(5) Contracts for life or health insurance or annuities for plan beneficiaries, if the plan is for employees of the insurer, or if the insurer is a wholly owned subsidiary of an employer whose employees

are covered by the plan. This exemption is applicable only if the plan pays a reasonable amount for the coverage and all amounts paid to the insurer do not exceed 5 percent of all insurance and annuity premiums received by the insurer during the year.

(6) Ancillary services provided by a bank or similar regulated financial institution which is a plan fiduciary, if reasonable compensation is paid, and if such ancillary services are regulated by adequate internal safeguards to prevent any harm to the plan. A non-interest-bearing checking account with a reasonable balance is an example of services covered by this provision.

(7) Exercise by a plan of a privilege to convert employer securities, if the plan receives adequate value in the exchange.

(8) A purchase or sale of interests between a plan and a common or collective trust fund or pooled income fund maintained by a fiduciary which is a regulated bank, trust company, or insurance company, if authorized by the plan and if the party maintaining the fund does not receive excessive compensation.

(9) A distribution of plan assets in accordance with the provisions of the plan and, in the case of a pension plan, a distribution of assets in accordance with the plan termination insurance provisions.

(10) Receipt by a party-in-interest of any benefits to which he may be entitled as a participant or beneficiary of the plan, so long as his benefits are determined on the same basis as those applicable to all other participants and beneficiaries consistent with the terms of the plan.

(11) Receipt by a fiduciary or a party-in-interest of reasonable compensation for services rendered to the plan (including reimbursement of necessary expenses), unless he already receives full-time pay from the employer maintaining the plan.

(12) Service as a fiduciary in addition to being an officer, employee, agent, or other representative of a party-in-interest or a disqualified person.

(13) Acquisitions, sales, and leases of qualifying employer securities and qualifying employer real property by an eligible individual account plan, if the transactions are for adequate consideration, and if no commission is charged. This exemption also applies to any other plan to the extent the transaction does not result in the plan's investment in qualifying employer securities and qualifying employer real property exceeding the 10 percent limitation. An example of this type

of exempted transactions would be the sale of employer stock to a stock bonus plan by a controlling shareholder. In addition, there are transitional exemptions until June 30, 1984 for loans and leases of real property between a plan and a party-in-interest that were in effect on July 1, 1974, if the transactions were equivalent to arm's-length transactions, and for transactions involving the undoing of such loans and leases.

In addition to the statutory exemptions, the DOL and the IRS have the authority to and have established procedures for granting administrative exemptions for specific transactions or classes of transactions.

Transactions that have been granted administrative exemptions include certain security transactions with broker-dealers and banks, rendering of investment advice and broker-dealer services, loans from employers to stock bonus plans, notes to cover delinquent employer contributions to multiemployer plans, construction loans made by multiemployer plans to participating employers, and furnishing of facilities and services by a multiemployer plan.

[3] Excise Taxes

ERISA provides for non-tax-deductible excise taxes to be levied on persons engaging in prohibited transactions with a plan. An initial tax of 5 percent of the amount of the transaction is imposed in all cases. An additional tax of 100 percent of the amount of the transaction can be imposed if the transaction is not corrected within a specified period.

¶ 2.07 PLAN TERMINATIONS—PENSION BENEFIT GUARANTY CORPORATION (ERISA SECTIONS 4001-4082)

The Pension Benefit Guaranty Corporation (PBGC) was established under Title IV of ERISA to administer a program to guarantee the timely and uninterrupted payment of limited amounts of vested benefits to participants and beneficiaries upon the termination of a plan. Most of the provisions of Title IV are not applicable to on-going plans and, therefore, are not of primary concern to plan auditors in most situations. Further, the plan termination provisions are applicable only to defined benefit pension plans. The more significant provisions of Title IV are summarized in the following paragraphs.

[1] Benefits Guaranteed

In general, the PBGC guarantees the payment of all nonforfeitable basic benefits to which a participant is entitled under the terms of the plan, at termination, on the basis of credited service to date, subject to certain limitations. The overall guaranteed monthly benefit (in the form of a life annuity commencing at age 65) may not exceed the actuarial equivalent of the lesser of (1) 100 percent of the average monthly wages during the individual's highest five years of participation in the plan, or (2) $750 adjusted for changes in the Social Security compensation base. The adjusted amount for 1977 is $937.50.

In the case of new plans (and increases in benefits under plan amendments) the maximum limitation is to be phased in generally for all individuals at the rate of 20 percent per year so that the benefit (or the increase) will be fully covered after the benefit has been in effect for five years.

[2] Premium Payment and Rates

Premiums for termination insurance may be paid by the plan or by the sponsoring employer. Currently, premiums are to be paid within thirty days of the beginning of the plan year using the Premium Declaration Form PBGC-1. Premium rates are currently $1.00 per participant for single-employer plans and $.50 per participant for multiemployer plans. It is anticipated that the premium rates for single-employer plans will be increased in 1978.

[3] Employer Liability

ERISA also established a contingent liability for employers to reimburse the PBGC for benefit payments made by it on the termination of an employer's plan. The employer's liability is an amount equal to the lesser of (1) the excess of the current value of the plan's guaranteed benefits over the current value of the plan's assets allocable to such guaranteed benefits or (2) 30 percent of the employer's net worth as determined within 120 days prior to termination, computed without regard to the subject liability.

ERISA also requires the PBGC to offer contingent liability insurance to employers to cover the potential 30 percent of net worth liability. To date, the PBGC has made no proposals regarding this requirement.

Chapter 3

QUALIFICATION UNDER THE INTERNAL REVENUE CODE

¶ 3.01   INTRODUCTION

Employee retirement benefit plans and related trusts intended to qualify as tax-exempt have been subject to specific provisions of the Internal Revenue Code for many years. The principal tax benefits of a qualified plan are:

(1) Current deductibility of contributions by the employer (subject to certain limitations);

(2) Deferment of income to the participants until the benefits are distributed or otherwise made available to them;

(3) Exemption of the trust from income tax, other than any tax on unrelated business taxable income;

(4) Favorable income tax treatment of lump-sum distributions; and

(5) Favorable estate tax treatment under certain conditions.

The Employee Retirement Income Security Act of 1974 (ERISA) includes many provisions similar to those of the Code and extends them to plans not intended to be qualified plans. At the same time, ERISA amends the provisions of the Code to conform in most instances to the Department of Labor (DOL) provisions.

Chapter 2 of this manual discusses the participation, vesting, and funding requirements of ERISA which are common to both the Labor Department and the Code. This chapter covers matters specific to tax-qualified plans and summarizes certain provisions, such as Social Security integration and joint and survivor annuity election, common to both the DOL and Code.

¶ 3.02   PROCEDURE TO OBTAIN QUALIFICATION—GENERAL

The statutory and administrative rules governing qualified retirement plans are very complex. To meet the initial qualification requirements, it is necessary that the plan satisfy these rules in a precise manner. Neither the Code nor the regulations thereunder require a pension, profit-sharing, or stock bonus plan to obtain advance approval (i.e., a determination) from the Internal Revenue Service; however, it is advisable to seek a specific ruling for qualification and most plans will have received a determination letter.

A request for advance approval of a plan is generally to be submitted to the Office of the District Director of the IRS for the district in which the employer's principal place of business is located. An employer can reasonably rely on a favorable determination letter and assume that the form of the plan is satisfactory. A determination letter, however, does not protect a plan from disqualification if it is not operated in conformity with the statutory and IRS administrative rules. Furthermore, a new determination letter should generally be requested when any material amendment is made to a plan.

Applications for plan determinations are filed on IRS forms. The basic forms are Form 5300 for defined benefit plans and Form 5301 for defined contribution plans. In many cases the auditor will be asked to assist in preparing or to prepare the determination application.

¶ 3.03   NOTIFICATION TO INTERESTED PARTIES

Section 3001 of ERISA requires an applicant for a determination letter to provide the IRS with satisfactory evidence that he has notified each employee who is an "interested party." In general, interested parties include present employees and terminated employees with vested benefits.

When the notice is given in person or by posting, it must be given not less than seven days nor more than twenty-one days prior to the date the application for a determination is made. Notice should be given not less than ten days nor more than twenty-four days prior to the date of application for a determination letter when such notice is given by mailing. The notice must be in writing and must include:

(1) A brief description of the interested parties;

(2) The name of the plan, the plan identification number, and the name of the plan administrator;

(3) The name and taxpayer identification number of the applicant;

(4) A statement that an application for a determination letter is being made to the IRS, identifying the District Director's Office, and whether the application relates to initial qualification, a plan amendment, or a plan termination;

(5) A description of the plan's requirements for participation;

(6) A statement as to whether the IRS has issued a previous determination letter on the qualified status of the plan;

(7) A statement that any person receiving notification is entitled to submit, alone or with a group of employees, or request the Department of Labor to submit, a comment as to whether the plan satisfies the requirements for qualification. Comments made by employees must be received by the District Director on or before the forty-fifth day after the application for determination is received by the District Director. In Revenue Procedures 75-31, specific deadlines for comment are also provided where the Department of Labor is involved in the com-

ment process. Furthermore, the Revenue Procedure describes the requirements for properly commenting to the District Director, and provides a sample notice for interested parties.

¶ 3.04 SUBSTANTIVE REQUIREMENTS FOR QUALIFICATION

Section 401(a) of the Internal Revenue Code establishes the requirements for qualification of retirement benefit plans under which employer payments are held in trust (or are held by an insurer) for future distribution to participants. This does not include profit-sharing plans of the cash-bonus type, where payments are made during the taxable year or soon after the end of the taxable year when the amount payable can be determined. Also excluded are dismissal wage or supplemental unemployment benefit, sickness, accident, hospitalization, medical expense, recreation, welfare, and similar benefit plans. The provisions of the Code are applicable only to the qualification of trusteed or insured pension, profit-sharing, and stock bonus plans. Some custodial accounts, however, are treated as qualified trusts and are subject to the same requirements.

[1] Exclusive Benefit Rule

Under a qualified trust, no part of the corpus or income may be used for, or diverted to, purposes other than the exclusive benefit of employees or their beneficiaries. In the case of profit-sharing and stock bonus plans, there may be no reversion of trust funds to the employer corporation after a plan is initially qualified by the Internal Revenue Service. For a retirement plan trust to qualify, the trust instrument must make it impossible for the nonexempt use or diversion to occur.

[2] Participation and Coverage Requirements (I.R.C. Section 410)

Participation standards for age and years of service are the same for the Code as under the DOL. Conditions for participation based on factors other than age and years of service (e.g., the exclusion of employees at facilities located within one state) are permissible, provided the alternate coverage tests for qualification are satisfied. Furthermore, employees can be excluded from a plan and from being counted under the coverage tests if they are covered under a collective-bargaining agreement in which pension benefits have been bargained for in good faith (whether or not they were provided).

Since a qualified plan must be primarily for the benefit of employees, there must be a reasonable proportion of the total employees as participants in the plan. Accordingly, consideration must be given to the number of employees who are to be included in the plan and those employees who may be eliminated from participation.

To satisfy the percentage test for coverage a plan must cover at least: (1) 70 percent of all employees, or (2) 80 percent of all eligible employees as long as 70 percent or more of all the employees are eligible for participation. In determining who are "all employees," certain employees may be excluded. Employees who have not satisfied the minimum age and years of service requirements under the plan are not counted.

It is important to note that an employer may designate several retirement benefit plans as constituting parts of a total plan which he intends to qualify. Where all of the designated plans cover a sufficient proportion of all employees, there is no requirement that a definite proportion of the employees be included in any one plan. The plans as a total unit, however, must meet the coverage requirements. Considering several plans of the employer as part of a total plan may, however, present other problems. (See the pertinent discussion below at ¶ 3.04[3].) The concept of treating several plans of an employer as a "single plan" may be especially important for a controlled group of corporations since all members are treated as a single employer. Thus, the coverage tests are based on the total employees of the controlled group.

An employer may establish eligibility requirements for employee participation in the plan as long as the requirements do not discriminate in favor of officers, shareholders, or highly compensated employees ("prohibited group"). For example, a plan may qualify where participation is limited to employees who are within designated departments provided the effect of covering only such employees does not discriminate in favor of the prohibited group. Other conditions for participation may be established as long as the minimum participation standards (which only relate to age and years of service) are satisfied along with the coverage requirements. Furthermore, an eligibility requirement is not considered discriminatory merely because it excludes hourly employees, or is limited to salaried or clerical employees.

The basic test to determine whether discrimination in coverage exists because of a "salaried-only" or other classification is the "fair cross-section of employees" test. Under this test, the total percentage of all company employees covered under the plan, generally is unimportant if the plan covers a varied cross-section of employees determined by compensation levels. A plan which is limited to a small portion of a company's total employees can still qualify if the covered employees are predominantly those outside the prohibited group. The IRS considers all employees of the company, whether within or without the plan, to determine if a "fair cross-section of employees" are participants.

The application of the "fair cross-section of employees test" is discussed in Revenue Ruling 66-12. In that ruling, an employees' pension plan, intended to qualify under Section 410(a) of the Code, limited participation to salaried employees and excluded hourly paid employees. Eleven of the twenty-six participants were either officers, shareholders, or highly compensated employees. The compensation of each of the remaining fifteen participants was substantially the same as that of the eighty-three excluded hourly paid employees. Under these facts, it was held that the coverage requirements were satisfied regardless of whether the excluded employees were covered under a similar or comparable plan. In making the determination, the IRS compares the compensation levels of the plan participants with the compensation levels of the excluded hourly paid employees.

To determine whether participants in a plan are predominantly those outside of the prohibited group, the participants in the prohibited group must be determined. It has been held that an assistant secretary-treasurer who acts in a nominal capacity and exercises his officership functions on only a few occasions is not an "officer" for purposes of the discrimination test. Nominal stock holdings in a large corporation also would not place an employee within the prohibited group. Less than a 5 percent stock ownership will generally exclude an employee from the category of "stockholder."

A determination of participants who are "highly compensated" within the meaning of Section 410(b)(1)(B) of the Code is more difficult. The IRS has broad discretion in determining which employees are highly compensated and thereby included in the prohibited group. This discretion is subject to judicial review, although the IRS's determination is given substantial weight. In making this determination, the IRS considers the compensation levels of employees within and without the plan. The break point of compensation to determine which participants are "highly compensated" is generally the dollar figure where the plan participants are more highly compensated than substantially all of the excluded employees.

[3] Discrimination in Contributions or Benefits and Comparability (I.R.C. Section 401(a)(4))

For a plan to be qualified, there must not be discrimination in contributions or benefits in favor of employee-participants who are officers, shareholders, or highly compensated. A clear example of prohibited discrimination would occur where a profit-sharing plan provides for the allocation of employer contributions among participants to the extent of 20 percent of compensation for highly compensated employees but only 10 percent for other employee-participants.

In certain instances, however, there may be variations in contributions or benefits if the plan as a whole benefits the employees in general and does not discriminate in favor of the prohibited group. An example of a permitted variation occurs under a money-purchase pension plan or a profit-sharing plan where an allocation formula takes into account years of service. Such a formula could, for example, provide for an allocation of employer contributions with one unit granted per $100 of compensation and two units per year of service. The ratio of a given participant's units to the total units of all participants times the total employer contribution will be the amount allocated to the participant's account. Such a weighted allocation formula may not, in operation, result in prohibited discrimination as measured by the ratio of benefits to compensation.

As discussed earlier, the qualification of a retirement plan depends in part upon acceptable coverage. Often, employers maintain separate plans for salaried and hourly paid employees. Where the hourly plan is not under a collective-bargaining agreement, the salaried plan standing alone may have difficulty satisfying the coverage requirements unless the plan covers a "fair cross-section" of employees. Separate plans for salaried and hourly paid employees may be considered as a unit to satisfy the coverage requirements. Once the plans are considered a unit, it should not be difficult to satisfy the percentage tests. This, however, does not necessarily mean that both plans will be qualified. To obtain qualification for both plans, contributions and benefits of both plans must be comparable. In making a determination of whether the two plans are comparable, several factors must be considered. Among the more important factors in testing comparability are provisions in both plans relating to participation, and contribution or benefits.

Where the separate plans are not comparable, the plan which causes the unit to fail qualification is held not to be qualified. The other plan, however, may still maintain its qualified status. For example, if the overall benefits of the salaried plan are greater than the hourly plan, the salaried plan will be disqualified where both were treated as a single unit. The hourly paid employees' plan may, however, continue as a qualified plan.

[4] Minimum Vesting Standards (I.R.C. Section 411)

In addition to the three vesting standards contained in both the DOL and IRS provisions of ERISA (See ¶ 2.03), the IRS may impose more stringent vesting—up to 40 percent after four years of service, an additional 5 percent for the next two years, and 10 percent additional vesting for the next five years—where the IRS believes that the plan's selected vesting provisions would otherwise result in an accrual of benefits or forfeitures tending to discriminate in favor of the officers, shareholders, or highly compensated employees.

[5] Treatment of Forfeitures (I.R.C. Section 401(a)(8))

Under the Code, forfeitures arising from severance of employment, death, or for any other reason must not be applied, in the case of a defined benefit pension plan, to increase the benefits of the remaining participants in the plan. Rather, the forfeited amounts must be used as soon as possible to reduce future employer contributions under the plan. This contrasts with the Code's treatment of a profit-sharing or stock bonus plan. The Code allows such plans to use the forfeitures to reduce future required employer contributions or to increase benefits for the remaining participants. Although forfeitures may be reallocated to increase benefits for remaining participants, no prohibited discrimination may result from such an allocation. The most common method for treatment of forfeitures in a profit-sharing plan is to reallocate the forfeitures to increase the benefits of the remaining participants in the same manner as employer contributions are allocated.

[6] Integration With Social Security Benefits (I.R.C. Section 401(a)(4))

In determining whether a plan discriminates in contributions and benefits in favor of the prohibited group, consideration may be given to the Social Security benefits. Where the combined benefits the employer provides under Social Security and the private plan are not more favorable for the prohibited group than the lower-paid individuals, the private plan will not be discriminatory. Accordingly, a plan is not discriminatory merely because it provides no benefits or lesser benefits with respect to compensation covered under the Social Security Act. Plans which are designed in this manner are referred to as "integrated plans." The Treasury Department has provided specific rules (Reg. § 1.401-3(e)) to determine whether such integrated plans meet the statutory requirements of nondiscrimination.

Integrated plans generally exclude employees who earn less than a specified amount or provide proportionately lesser benefits for such employees. To qualify, an integrated plan must provide benefits under the plan which integrate properly with those provided under Social Security or a similar program, such as the Railroad Retirement Act. The compensation level selected for classification purposes is called the "integration level." Guidelines have been established limiting the percentage of contributions or benefits above the integration level. Where contributions or benefits exceed the limit of such guidelines, the plan will fail to qualify. In addition, for an integrated plan to qualify, it must prohibit using an increase in the Social Security benefit level to reduce the retirement benefits provided for terminated participants. In other words, the integration level cannot be increased for participants who are already retired and receiving integrated plan benefits. Social Security integration is discussed in more detail at ¶ 7.09.

[7] Timing Requirement for Payment of Benefits (I.R.C. Section 401(a)(14))

For a plan to qualify under the Code, it must provide that, unless the participant elects otherwise, payment of benefits will commence within sixty days after the close of the plan year in which (1) the participant attains age sixty-five, or any earlier normal retirement age specified in the plan, (2) the tenth anniversary of the time the participant commenced participation in the plan, or (3) the time the participant terminates his service with the employer, whichever is later.

[8] Joint and Survivor Annuity Requirement (I.R.C. Section 401(a)(11))

If a qualified plan provides payment of retirement benefits in the form of an annuity, it must generally provide for a joint and survivor annuity. In the case of an employee who retires, or who attains the normal retirement age, the joint and survivor provision must apply unless the employee elects otherwise.

All participants must be given a reasonable period before the annuity starting date to elect in writing not to take a joint and survivor annuity. This election can only be made after the participant has been supplied with a written explanation of the joint and survivor provision, including the practical (dollars and cents) effect on him (and his spouse) of making an election not to take the joint and survivor annuity.

A plan is not required to subsidize the cost of providing such a joint and survivor annuity; rather, the benefit payable can be reduced to make it comparable in cost to a single-life annuity.

In the case of an employee who is eligible to retire (and receive benefits) prior to normal retirement age (e.g., under an elective early retirement provision) and who does not retire, the joint and survivor annuity need not be provided unless the employee makes an affirmative election. Moreover, this option need not be made available until the employee is within ten years of normal retirement age or reaches the date of the earliest optional retirement age under the plan, whichever is later.

[9] Provision Required Which Prohibits Alienation of Benefits (I.R.C. Section 401(a)(13))

The Code requires a qualified plan to contain a provision, effective by the beginning of the first plan year after 1975, that a participating employee's benefits generally may not be assigned or alienated. An exception is made for assignments to secure loans from the plan if such loans do not constitute prohibited transactions.

[10] Protection of Participants Where There Is a Merger, Consolidation, or Other Transfer of Plan Assets or Liabilities (I.R.C. Sections 401(a)(12) and 414(1))

The Code provides that in the event plan assets are merged after September 2, 1974, every participant must be entitled to receive a benefit which is not less than the benefit he would have been entitled to immediately before the merger. This is also a condition for qualification. This determination is to be made as if the plan were terminated as of the date of merger. Furthermore, a participant's accrued benefits must be funded as adequately as prior to the merger. ERISA provides that a plan administrator must give at least thirty days' notice to the IRS prior to the merger, including an actuarial statement, indicating that the requirements of the Act have been satisfied. These rules also apply to a consolidation or transfer of assets or liabilities of a plan to another qualified plan.

[11] Termination of a Qualified Plan (I.R.C. Section 411(d)(3))

For a plan to be qualified, it must be a permanent and continuing program. The fact that a plan contains provisions for its termination or curtailment at the discretion of the employer will not deprive it of qualification at inception. An employer has the right to provide for discontinuance or curtailment of a plan since conditions may arise in the future which leave the employer with no alternative.

Under the Code, all qualified plans must expressly provide that in the case of their termination the rights of each employee to benefits accrued to the date of termination are fully vested to the extent the plan is funded. This is not a requirement of ERISA or of the DOL, nor does it affect the amount of PBGC-guaranteed benefits determined without regard to termination vesting. In addition, profit-sharing and stock bonus plans must provide for full vesting where a plan has a complete discontinuance of contributions. Once a plan is terminated, there may be no discrimination in payment of benefits, or the plan will be treated as disqualified prior to any distributions. Accordingly, special termination rules have been established for the distribution of employer contributions to an employee who is among the twenty-five highest paid at the time the plan is established and whose anticipated annual pension exceeds $1,500. This special rule, however, is not applicable to profit-sharing, stock bonus, and money-purchase pension plans. Accordingly, these limitations are applicable only to defined benefit plans.

Upon termination of a defined benefit plan, an employer is still obligated for the required amount of funding through the date of termination. In addition, full and immediate vesting is required in the case of a partial termination of any qualified retirement plan. A partial termination is where a sizable reduction in benefits occurs under the plan. Note that the termination insurance provisions of ERISA are also applicable to defined benefit plans.

[12] Incidental Benefits—Insurance and Death Benefits (I.R.C. Section 401(L))

The primary purpose of a qualified pension plan must be to provide for retirement benefits at termination of employment. A qualified pension plan may not provide for benefits in the case of layoff or sickness, accident hospitalization, or medical illness, except for hospitalization and medical expenses for retired employees under certain circumstances. Where life or accident and health insurance features are incidental to the primary benefit of a qualified plan, they may be included to a limited extent. Where an annuity or pension plan is funded with insurance contracts, life insurance benefits are deemed to be incidental if a preretirement death benefit is no greater than 100 times the monthly annuity, i.e., $1,000 of life insurance for each $10 of monthly retirement benefit. Post-retirement death benefits are deemed incidental if they are equal to or less than 50 percent of the base salary in effect in the year preceding retirement, requiring less than 10 percent of the cost of the plan exclusive of the death benefit.

In the case of a profit-sharing trust providing for the use of trust funds to pay premiums on ordinary life insurance contracts when employer contributions have not been accumulated for at least two years, the insurance feature is deemed incidental if: (1) aggregate life insurance premiums for each participant are less than one-half the aggregate of contributions allocated to the credit of the participants, and (2) the plan requires the trustees to convert the entire value of the life insurance contract at or before retirement into cash, or provide periodic income so that no portion of such value may be used to continue life insurance protection beyond retirement. Similarly, in profit-sharing trusts where employer contributions have not been accumulated for at least two years, such amounts are treated as incidental if they are used to pay premiums for accident and health insurance, and if the aggregate premiums do not exceed 25 percent of the funds allocated to the account of the participant for whom the insurance is acquired. Where the funds are used to purchase both ordinary life and accident and health insurance, the amount expended for accident and health insurance plus one-half of the premiums paid for ordinary life insurance may not, in the aggregate, exceed 25 percent of the funds allocated to that participant's account.

¶ 3.05   CONTRIBUTIONS AND BENEFITS

Prior to ERISA, the Code contained limits on the deductibility of employer contributions to employee benefit plans. These provisions continue to apply with certain amendments. ERISA additionally imposed limits on the amount of benefits from and contributions to qualified pension plans. The ERISA provisions affect plan qualification, while an excess contribution under prior rules simply postponed the deductibility of the expense. This section explains the limits on deductibility of employer contributions to qualified employee pension benefit plans and discuss the limits on benefits from or contributions to qualified plans. The auditor's knowledge in these areas will be of primary benefit in auditing the employer's financial statements.

[1] Deductibility of Contributions

Employer contributions to qualified retirement benefit plans are deductible only to the extent of the limitations contained in Section 404(a) of the Code. In addition, contributions must satisfy the requirements that all expenses be ordinary and necessary (I.R.C. §§ 162 and 212), and must meet the payment tests under Section 404(a)(6) of the Code.

Prior to ERISA, only accrual-basis taxpayers were allowed to make contributions after year-end. However, ERISA now allows all taxpayers to make a deductible contribution if made before the date prescribed for filing the tax return (including extensions) for the taxable year if:

(1) The contribution is treated by the plan in the same manner as if it had been actually received on the last day of the year; and

(2) Either (a) the employer designates in writing to the plan administrator or trustee that the contribution is for the preceding year, or (b) the employer claims the contribution as a deduction on his tax return for such preceding year.

[a] Defined Benefit Plans

Deductible contributions to defined benefit plans are limited to:

(1) *"Normal Cost"* Method: An amount equal to the normal cost of the plan plus the amount necessary to amortize the past service or other supplementary pension credits in equal annual payments over ten years; or

(2) *"Level Funded"* Method: The amount necessary to provide the required benefit for each participant if spread evenly over each participant's remaining employment period. (If the remaining unfunded cost of any three participants is more than 50 percent of the total remaining unfunded cost, the cost attributable to those participants must be distributed over at least five years.)

However, if the minimum funding standard requires a greater contribution than otherwise allowable under the plan's funding method, such amount shall be allowed as a deduction. Consequently, an employer will never be denied a deduction for an amount which is required to be contributed to the plan under another Code provision. In no event, however, may the deductible contribution exceed the full funding limitation provided under the minimum funding rules.

Any amount paid in excess of the maximum deductible limitation will be a carryover to succeeding taxable years. Such excess may then be deducted to the extent of the difference between the amount paid and the maximum amount deductible for such year.

[b] Defined Contribution Plans

Deductible contributions to a defined contribution plan are generally based on a percentage of compensation test. The primary limitation on the employer's deduction is 15 percent of covered compensation. Compensation includes all amounts otherwise paid or accrued during the year to employees who are participants in the plan. The IRS has ruled that the proper class of employees is that which is allocated employer contributions under the plan. Consequently, terminating employees are not included, unless contributions are made on their behalf; but newly eligible employees are included.

It should also be noted that the plan's definition of "compensation" is not controlling, insofar as the employer's deduction is concerned. The limitation is based on actual compensation regardless of the base the plan uses to compute the employer's contribution.

If in any year an employer does not make the full 15 percent contribution, the corporation is permitted to make a larger deductible contribution in a succeeding year. The maximum deductible amount in such succeeding year is the *lesser* of:

(1) 15 percent of covered compensation plus the excess of the sum of primary limitations for prior years over the amounts deducted ("credit carryover"); or

(2) 25 percent of covered compensation.

Any amount contributed in excess of the 15 percent primary limitation may be carried over to subsequent years and deducted when combined with the current year's contribution to the extent of the primary limitation (i.e., 15 percent of covered compensation). Consequently, an employer is not allowed to contribute the maximum 15 percent currently and deduct an excess contribution carryover against any credit carryover.

Example:

Year	Contri- bution	Primary Limitation (15% of Compensation)	Amount Deductible	Credit Carryover	Contri- bution Carryover
1976	$15,000	$50,000	$15,000	$35,000	$ -0-
1977	90,000	30,000	50,000*	15,000	40,000
1978	-0-	20,000	20,000	15,000	20,000

Note: The credit carryover applies only to current contributions. Thus, any current contribution in 1978 of less than $20,000 will still result in the same deduction ($20,000).

In addition to the general limitations applicable to defined contribution plans, some special rules also apply to profit-sharing plans of affiliated groups. Any contribution to such a plan must come out of the current or accumulated profits of the employer. However, where a plan involves members of an affiliated group, it is permissible for profitable members of the group to "make up" a contribution for the loss members. This type of contribution may only occur when a member is in a tax-loss situation. It is not allowed if the member is profitable but simply has a liquidity problem. If the group does not file a consolidated return, an allocation of the contribution must be made among the profitable members of the group.

[c] Combination Plans

If an employer maintains both a defined benefit plan and a defined contribution plan in which any employee is a beneficiary under both plans, a separate, additional limitation is provided. This limit is the greater of:

(1) 25 percent of covered compensation; or

---

* The deductible amount for 1977 represents 25 percent of current year covered compensation.

(2) The amount necessary to satisfy the minimum funding standard.

This limitation is in addition to the other limitations already described. In no way does this limitation allow a greater deduction than the sum of the separate limitations on each plan. Any amount disallowed by this limitation may also be carried over to future years subject to the same limitation. This combined limitation does not apply, though, if no employee is simultaneously covered under both plans.

[2] Limitations on Contributions and Benefits (I.R.C. Section 415)

A plan will not be qualified if it provides for benefits or contributions in excess of the prescribed limitations. Generally, defined benefit plans may not provide benefits greater than $75,000 (adjusted for cost of living increases) a year or 100 percent of the employee's average compensation for his three consecutive highest years, whichever is less. Annual additions to a participant's account in a profit-sharing plan or other defined contribution plan are limited to the lesser of $25,000 (adjusted for cost of living increases) or 25 percent of compensation.

For purposes of these limitations, all defined contributions plans and all defined benefit plans of the same employer are combined. However, if an employee participates in both a defined contribution plan and a defined benefit plan of the same employer, ERISA provides for a combined limitation which is described at ¶ 3.05 [2] [c].

[a] Defined Benefit Plans

Generally, in the case of a defined benefit plan, the projected annual benefit of a participant may not, at any time within the limitation year, exceed the *lesser* of:

(1) $75,000 as adjusted for cost-of-living increases ($84,525 in 1977); or

(2) 100 percent of the participant's average compensation for his highest three consecutive years of service.

A participant's projected annual benefit is computed by assuming that all relevant factors (e.g., compensation and benefits) will remain constant until the date of his normal retirement. However, in projecting his annual benefit under the plan, the following adjustments (to the $75,000 amount only) are made:

(1) Benefits attributable to rollover contributions are not considered.

(2) If the benefit is payable in a form other than a straight-life annuity or a qualified joint and survivor annuity, the projected annual benefit must be adjusted to an actuarial equivalent benefit in the form of a straight-life annuity. However, ancillary benefits (e.g., preretirement death benefits) not directly related to retirement benefits are disregarded.

(3) Benefits attributable to mandatory employee contributions are disregarded. Voluntary employee contributions are considered a separate defined contribution plan for this purpose.

(4) If a retirement benefit is payable before age fifty-five, such benefit must be adjusted to an actuarial equivalent commencing at age fifty-five.

Despite the $75,000 or 100 percent of compensation limits, if the annual benefit payable under the plan(s) does not exceed $10,000 and the participant has ten years of service, the general limitations are waived. Thus, an employee could always qualify for at least a $10,000 annual benefit. As a condition of this de minimis rule, however, the participant cannot ever have participated in any defined contribution plan maintained by the employer.

[b] Defined Contribution Plans

Generally, in the case of a defined contribution plan, the annual addition to a participant's account in any limitation year may not exceed the *lesser* of:

(1) $25,000 as adjusted for cost-of-living increases ($28,175 in 1977); or

(2) 25 percent of the participant's compensation.

The annual addition is defined as the sum of:

(1) Employer contributions;

(2) The *lesser* of:
  (a) The employee's contributions (both mandatory and voluntary) in excess of 6 percent of compensation,
  (b) One-half of the employee's contributions; and

(3) Forfeitures.

[c] Combination Plans

In addition to the separate limitations on benefits and contributions, a further limitation is imposed in cases where an individual is a participant in both a defined benefit plan and a defined contribution plan maintained by the same employer. In such a case, the sum of the defined benefit plan fraction and the defined contribution plan fraction for any limitation year may not exceed 1.4.

The *defined benefit plan fraction* is a fraction in which the numerator is the participant's projected annual benefit under the plan and the denominator is the participant's maximum annual allowable benefit. The *defined contribution plan fraction* is a fraction in which the numerator is the sum of *all* annual additions to the participant's account and the denominator is the maximum amount of *all* annual additions which could have been made. It is worth emphasizing that the defined contribution plan fraction is based on the current year plus all prior limitation years.

> *Example*: E is paid $100,000 per year from Corporation X. X has had a defined benefit pension plan in existence for a number of years, which provides for a benefit equal to 50 percent of the participant's average compensation for his highest three years. In addition, X established a defined contribution plan this year to which it contributes 20 percent of each participant's compensation. Under these plans, E's defined benefit plan fraction and defined contribution plan fraction is determined as follows:

Defined benefiit plan fraction:

$$\frac{\text{Projected benefit at year-end}}{\text{Maximum benefit permitted}} \qquad \frac{\$50,000}{\$84,525^*} = .59$$

Defined contribution plan fraction:

$$\frac{\text{Total annual additions to employee's account at year-end}}{\text{Maximum annual additions possible since date of employment}} \qquad \frac{\$20,000}{\$200,000} = .10$$

---

* See ¶ 3.05 [2] [a].

In computing the denominator for the defined contribution plan fraction, an annual addition is allowed for *each year of service with the employer*. Service with the employer differs from participation in the plan, so it does not matter whether the plan was in effect or the employee was a plan participant in determining this segment of the fraction.

A grandfather provision, for individuals who were participants in both a defined benefit plan and a defined contribution plan on September 2, 1974, allows the sum of the fractions to continue to exceed 1.4 if:

(1) The defined benefit fraction is not increased; and

(2) No further contributions are made to the defined contribution plan.

¶ 3.06 TAXATION OF BENEFITS

In general, distributions made to beneficiaries of qualified trusts are taxable in the year the distributions are paid or made available. The most common form of benefit payment is an annuity, and annuities are subject to specific taxation rules. There are also special rules for the taxation of lump-sum distributions and for rollovers to other qualified plans or an individual retirement account (IRA).

[1] Annuities (I.R.C. Section 72)

If the annuity rules apply to the distribution, each payment is deemed to consist of: (1) a nontaxable portion representing a recovery of the retiree's own contributions, and (2) a taxable portion to be included in gross income. Thus, all payments from a noncontributory plan are taxable to the beneficiary as ordinary income when received since the beneficiary has not made any contributions. For a contributory plan, the nontaxable amount is determined by multiplying the amount received by the ratio (termed "exclusion ratio") of the total employee contributions (termed "investment in the contract") to the "expected return." The term "expected return" means the total payments which would be received if a beneficiary (or beneficiaries) lived for the average length of time expected for persons of his (or their) age and sex or for such other stated time described in the plan.

The time factor used to compute "expected return" is generally derived from the tables supplied in Section 1.72-9 of the Treasury Regulations. The "exclusion ratio" is determined at the time the periodic distributions begin and is not subsequently modified.

The exclusion recovery rule may be illustrated by the following example:

> *Example*: *X* is to receive from a qualified pension plan an annuity for life of $100 per month starting at age sixty-five. The life expectancy for *X* is 15.0 years. Therefore, the expected return from the annuity is $18,000 ($100 x 12 x 15.0). Assume now that *X* made contributions of $4,000 under the plan. This represents his "investment in the contract." The exclusion ratio is the ratio of the investment in the contract to the expected return ($4,000 ÷ 18,000 = 22.2%). Thus, *X* will exclude from his gross income 22.2 percent of the $1,200 annual payment, or $266.40 per year.

When a retiree will recover all his own contributions to the plan within the three-year period beginning on the annuity starting date, no amounts are includable in his gross income until he has fully recovered those contributions. After recovery of the total employee contributions (if within the three-year period), all additional annuity amounts received are includable in income by the retiree.

> *Example*: *G*, an anesthesiologist with the University of Michigan Hospital in Ann Arbor, retired at age sixty-five on January 1, 1977. As a hospital employee, *G* made contributions to the Public Employees' Retirement Plan amounting to $35,000 through the date of his retirement. *G* will receive an annuity for life from this plan of $975 per month starting January 31, 1977. Because *G*'s contributions will be recovered within three years from the annuity starting date ($975/month × 36 months = $35,100, which is greater than the sum of *G*'s contributions), no amounts are includable in his gross income until the contributions have been recovered.

[2] Lump-Sum Distributions (I.R.C. Section 402(e)(4))

In order to qualify for lump-sum distribution treatment, the distribution must meet certain requirements. These requirements are:

> (1) The distribution or payment must be made within one taxable year of the recipient.

(2) The entire balance to the credit of the employee in all plans of the same type must be paid or distributred.

(3) The employee must have been a participant in the plan (or plans) for at least five or more tax years prior to the year in which the distribution is made. (This does not apply to capital gain treatment.)

(4) The distribution or payment must be made from a plan qualified under Section 401(a) of the Code.

(5) The distribution must be made on account of the employee's
   (a) Death;
   (b) Attainment of age 59½;
   (c) Separation from service with the employer; or
   (d) Total and permanent disability.

The tax on a lump-sum distribution falls into two categories:

(1) Capital gain treatment for a portion of the lump-sum distribution; and

(2) A separate tax on the remaining portion (ten-year averaging).

An election may be made to forgo the capital gain treatment and subject the entire distribution to the ten-year averaging rules. This election was added by the Tax Reform Act of 1976.

[a] Capital Gain Treatment

In general, long-term capital gain treatment of lump-sum distributions to beneficiaries applies to pre-1974 plan participation. The following formula applies:

$$\text{Capital gain portion} = \frac{\text{Total taxable}}{\text{amount}} \times \frac{\text{Calendar years of active participation before 1974}}{\text{Total calendar years of active participation}}$$

Total taxable amount is defined as the amount by which the distribution exceeds the sum of

(1) Amounts considered contributed by the employee reduced by any amounts previously distributed to him which were not includable in gross income; and

(2) The net unrealized appreciation of employers' securities so distributed.

The capital gain portion of a lump-sum distribution is included in taxable income subject to the usual capital gain treatment. In computing the distributee's tax liability, the alternative tax, ordinary income averaging, and the maximum tax are all available.

[b] Ten-Year Averaging

The tax calculation for the non-capital gain portion of the lump-sum distribution is a complex ten-year averaging procedure. A separate tax is determined using the tax tables for a single individual by computing the tax on $2,200 plus one-tenth of the amount by which the total taxable amount of the lump-sum distribution exceeds the minimum distribution allowance. For these purposes, the beneficiary's income, other than the lump-sum distribution, is ignored. The minimum distribution allowance is:

(1) *The lesser* of $10,000 or one-half of the total taxable amount of the lump-sum distribution for the taxable year, reduced (but not below zero) by,

(2) 20 percent of the amount (if any) by which the total taxable amount exceeds $20,000.

After the above computations are made, the initial separate tax is determined by multiplying the result by ten. To arrive at the actual separate tax on the ordinary income portion, the initial separate tax is multiplied by a fraction, the numerator of which is the ordinary income portion of the distribution and the denominator of which is the total taxable amount of the distribution.

The following example illustrates the long-term capital gain and ten-year averaging treatment for a lump-sum distribution.

Example: On December 31, 1977, *A* terminates his services and receives a lump-sum distribution of $70,000 from a qualified plan. *A* has been participating in the plan since January 1, 1968. The plan is noncontributory. *A* is married; both *A* and his wife are fifty years old. Their only other income is *A*'s salary of $15,000 and his salary from a second job of $5,000. Their itemized deductions are $3,000.

Without electing to treat the entire distribution as ordinary income, the tax on the portion of the distribution which is not treated as a long-term capital gain is computed as follows:

Total taxable lump-sum distribution		$70,000
Less: Minimum distribution allowance: lesser of $10,000 or one-half of total taxable lump-sum distribution	$10,000	
Reduced by: 20% of net distribution in excess of $20,000	10,000	-0-
DISTRIBUTION LESS ALLOWANCE		$70,000

The tax on $2,200* plus one-tenth of the distribution less allowance computed from the tax rate schedule for single taxpayers is $1,350.

Multiply this amount by 10: $13,500.

Then, multiply by the fraction,

$$\frac{\text{Years of participation in plan after 1973}}{\text{Total years of participation}} = \frac{4}{10} = 0.4$$

which yields $5,400.

Thus, the tax on the ordinary income portion of the distribution is $5,400.

The amount of the distribution taxed as long-term capital gains is the amount of the distribution multiplied by the fraction:

$$\frac{\text{Years of participation before 1974}}{\text{Total years of participation}} = \frac{6}{10} = 0.6$$

Distribution	$70,000
Capital gain element ($70,000 x 0.6)	$42,000

The capital gain element is taxed along with other income (exclusive of the ordinary income element) in the normal manner for determining an individual's tax liability. The tax on the taxable income of $39,500 ($15,000 salary from first job, plus $5,000 from second job, plus $42,000 capital gain element of lump-sum distribution, less

---

* This represents zero bracket amount for a single taxpayer.

$21,000 capital gain exclusion, less two $750 personal exemptions) is calculated using the tax rate schedule for married taxpayers filing joint returns.

Since the capital gain exclusion is a tax preference item, this transaction also triggers a minimum tax of $1,650 (($21,000 − $10,000) × 15%). Note that the separate tax may not be used to offset tax preference items.

Summary:

Tax on $39,500	$10,475
Separate tax on ordinary income portion of distribution	5,400
Minimum tax	1,650
TOTAL TAX	$17,525

[c] Election to Treat Pre-1974 Participation as Post-1973 Participation

The Tax Reform Act of 1976 substantially increased the minimum tax by raising the rate to 15 percent and by lowering the exemption and denying the carryover of tax paid in previous years. It is now possible to pay a higher combined tax on a lump-sum distribution by treating the distribution as a distribution subject to capital gain treatment. To alleviate this problem, the Tax Reform Act of 1976 added an irrevocable election to forgo the capital gain treatment on a lump-sum distribution, thus treating the entire distribution as ordinary income subject to the separate tax.

Example: Using the facts of the preceding example, if *A* elects to treat the entire distribution as ordinary income, subject to the ten-year income averaging, he computes his tax as follows:

Total taxable lump-sum distribution		$70,000
Less: Minimum distribution allowance: lesser of $10,000 or one-half of total taxable lump-sum distribution	$10,000	
Reduced by: 20% of net distribution in excess of $20,000	10,000	-0-
Distribution less allowance		$70,000

The tax on one-tenth of the distribution, less allowance, computed from the tax rate schedule for single taxpayers is $1,350.

Multiply this amount by 10: $13,500.

Since the election has been made to treat the entire distribution as ordinary income, the tax on the distribution is the entire $13,500.

The tax on the taxable income of $18,500 ($15,000 salary from first job, plus $5,000 salary from second job, less two $750 personal exemptions) is calculated using the tax rate schedule for married taxpayers filing joint returns.

Tax on $18,500	$ 3,085
Tax on distribution	13,500
TOTAL TAX	$16,585

Consequently, *A* would make the election to treat the entire distrribution as ordinary income. Using the ten-year averaging, *A* has a tax liability of $16,585 for 1977.

A taxpayer who wishes to use the ten-year averaging and capital gain treatment for a lump-sum distribution must use this treatment for the aggregate of the lump-sum distributions he receives in the same taxable year. In addition, for purposes of determining the tax rate on the last distribution, ERISA requires that the lump-sum distributions received by an individual during a taxable year be aggregated with all lump-sum distributions to that recipient during his five prior taxable years.

[d] Net Unrealized Appreciation on Employer Securities

Section 402 of the Code also provides special tax benefits for the distribution of employer securities. If a qualified trust distributes employer securities, part or all of the "net unrealized appreciation" is deferred until the distributee sells or otherwise disposes of the stock.

[3] Rollovers

The Tax Reform Act of 1969 added a new opportunity to defer the taxation of distributions from qualified plans—a rollover. In general, if certain statutory provisions are met, it is possible to defer tax on a distribution from a qualified plan if the distribution is transferred to another qualified plan.

The required statutory provisions are as follows:

- The balance of the credit to the employee must be paid to him in one or more distributions made within one taxable year of the employee.
- The distribution constitutes a lump-sum distribution or is made on account of either a termination of a pension plan or a complete discontinuance of contributions to a profit-sharing or stock bonus plan.
- On or before the sixtieth day after the employee receives the property, he transfers it to an individual retirement account (IRA), a qualified plan, or a qualified annuity plan.

To avoid taxation, the same property that was distributed must be transferred to the new plan. Also, the amount rolled over must be *equal* to the amount received less the amount of any employee contributions. (The employee must have a zero basis in the assets rolled over.) In addition, since an IRA can be used as a conduit from one qualified plan to another qualified plan only if the assets of the IRA consist solely of assets transferred from a qualified plan, a separate IRA should be set up to receive the assets rolled over from a qualified plan.

Part II

ACTUARIAL VALUATIONS

Chapter 4

ACTUARIAL VALUATIONS AND THEORY–OVERVIEW

¶ 4.01 INTRODUCTION

As described in Chapter 1, "Types of Employee Benefit Plans," the cost of a defined contribution pension plan is readily determinable; by contrast, the cost of a defined benefit pension plan can only be determined from actuarial valuations. The valuations are designed to determine the contributions required to accumulate sufficient assets to pay the pension benefits as they become due. The chapters of this section discuss in detail actuarial present values, assumptions, valuation methods, and gains and losses. The practical aspects of an actuarial valuation are also discussed. The purpose of this section is to provide a basic understanding of actuarial science as it relates to defined benefit pension plans. At the present time, there is considerable uncertainty as to the involvement accountants will have in auditing such determinations. There is no uncertainty, however, as to the significance of such determinations to defined benefit plans. A basic understanding of the actuarial valuation process is necessary for all professionals involved in services to these plans.

The actuarial valuation process involves measuring pension benefits, measuring the actuarial present value of these benefits, and selecting an actuarial valuation method to determine the sponsor's annual contributions. In performing a valuation, the actuary must make assumptions as to how many participants will eventually receive benefits, the amount of the benefits, and how much of the benefits paid will be provided from investment earnings, participant contributions (in the case of a contributory plan), and sponsor contributions.

Once the assumptions have been chosen and the pension benefits have been valued, the actuary selects a valuation method designed to provide a pattern for funding the plan. Valuation methods differ primarily in how the incidence of cost is assigned to future periods. Actuarial valuation methods are similar to methods of depreciation. The selection of the depreciation method will determine the incidence of cost (i.e., provision for depreciation) assigned to future periods. The incidence of cost will vary significantly based upon the method selected (e.g., the pattern under the straight line will be significantly different than under the double-declining balance method). Accordingly, the selection of the valuation method will determine the incidence of the cost assigned to future periods.

All actuarial valuation methods utilize assumptions as to the future. Since these assumptions are only forecasts of future events, actual experience is expected to differ. Periodic actuarial valuations take account of the variation of actual experience from the assumed experience. These variations are referred to as experience gains and losses, and they result in modifications of subsequent funding estimates. Under many actuarial valuation methods, the experience gains and losses are identified separately and explicitly adjusted. Other actuarial methods do not separately identify experience gains and losses; however, implicit adjustments in funding estimates result.

The actuary may provide the sponsor of a pension plan with the following basic services:

(1) Performing an annual actuarial valuation to determine the contribution needed to satisfy the Employee Retirement Income Security Act of 1974 (ERISA) minimum funding, the pertinent federal income tax deduction, limitations, and the accounting cost pursuant to Accounting Principles Board (APB) Opinion No. 8;

(2) Evaluating the cost of proposed changes to an existing plan;

(3) Performing certain administrative service, such as computing accrued or vested benefits for individual participants;

(4) Projecting cash flow requirements of the plan, to assist the trustee in tailoring investment decisions; and

(5) Assisting in preparation of required reports and employer brochures.

This chapter analyzes the procedures followed by the actuary in performing the first type of service, an actuarial valuation. The other services are important to the sponsor, but are not necessary for an understanding of the actuarial valuation process and, accordingly, are not discussed.

¶ 4.02 ACTUARIAL VALUATION PROCESS

Actuarial firms typically utilize computerized procedures for performing the detailed mathematical calculations required in a valuation. These involve computer programs reflecting the specific technique the actuary believes will result in a reasonable valuation. The actuarial valuation process can generally be divided into five steps:

(1) Obtaining reliable participant data from the plan administrator;

(2) Selecting the most reasonable mix of assumptions and coding the parameters needed to describe the plan benefit;

(3) Entering these (two) "data sets" into the computer;

(4) Reviewing the output from the computer valuation; and

(5) Preparing an actuarial report discussing and analyzing the results.

[1] Participant Data

The first step in this process is to obtain an accurate listing of the participants covered by the plan (active, inactive with vested benefits, retired, etc.). The basic data needed for each participant are:

- Name;
- Sex;
- Social Security or other identification number;
- Birthdate;
- Hired date.

Additional information may be required depending upon the benefit provisions in the plan or the actuarial valuation method selected. If the benefit formula credits a flat amount per participant per year or specifies a flat amount at retirement, no additional details may be required. When the benefit formula is based on compensation, appropriate salary data must be included. Ordinarily, the participant data received from the plan sponsor are entered on a preprinted employment data form or are supplied in a machine-readable data file.

Upon receiving this data, the actuary should be satisfied that it is reasonably accurate. The degree of view and testing is dependent on the actuary's judgment. Usually, the testing is limited to a comparison of the current year with the prior year data to assure consistency. To assure there are no obvious inconsistencies, a reconciliation should be performed such as:

| | *Number of Participants* | | |
	Active	*Inactive Vested*	*Retired*
Prior year	xxx	xxx	xxx
New participants	xxx		
Terminated participants	(xxx)	xxx	
Retired this year	(xxx)	(xxx)	xxx
Other activity (e.g., death)	(xxx)	(xxx)	(xxx)
CURRENT YEAR	xxx	xxx	xxx

In some valuations (generally smaller groups), the actuary may account for each individual either as continuing in the group, retired, terminated (vested), terminated (nonvested), or deceased. Based on the actuary's knowledge of the plan sponsor's business and the results of the tests performed, the actuary will determine if the data submitted are reasonable. Currently, the actuary will usually highlight in his report the fact that the valuation is based upon the participant data furnished by the sponsor. However, it should be noted that ERISA provides that the actuary may rely on the opinion of a "qualified public accountant" as to any accounting matter. In this regard, accounting may be requested to certify participant data submitted to the actuary.

For those plans required to be audited, the independent accountant should be involved in this process on a timely basis. The accountant, actuary, and plan sponsor are all concerned with the accuracy of the participant data submitted. In addition, the independent accountant will usually be auditing the participant data subsequent to the time the data are submitted to the actuary. These parties should meet prior to the submission date to discuss the sponsor's procedures for verifying the data, the accountant's procedures for auditing the data, and the actuary's procedures for reviewing the data. This communication process could avoid some of the duplication of "testing procedures" as well as establishing a timetable for the preparation, submission, verification, and actuarial valuation of the participant data. This could avoid later embarrassment if significant errors were found in the data subsequent to the valuation date.

[2] Actuarial Data

The actuary will review the results of the prior valuations, current experience, and any plan amendments occurring since the previous valuation to determine if there are any changes required in the current year's valuation process—either in the provisions of the plan being valued or in the actuarial assumptions being used in the calculations. Based on this review, the actuary will prepare a coding form specifying the actuarial parameters to be used in the current valuation. Unlike participant data (a separate record required for each individual or group of individuals), only one set of parameters is required to be used in performing the valuation. These parameters are usually divided into the following sets:

- General plan identification;
- Actuarial assumptions;

- Plan benefit formula;
- Ancillary benefit provisions;
- Vesting provisions.

Once the employee data and actuarial data are finalized, entering of these data sets into the computer is a mechanical task, usually performed by the support staff of the actuarial firm.

[3] Review of the Valuation

The form and content of the valuation output are based on the system designed by the actuary. This report could be one page—representing only the grand totals of the individual participant calculations—or several pages—representing a complete subsidiary listing of the calculations relating to each participant. Since the actuary is concerned with plan determinations in the aggregate, the content of the output is generally limited to the grand totals. An example of this output is:

XYZ Employer, Inc.
Cleveland, Ohio
January 1, 19X7

	Past Actives	New Entrants	Inactive Vested	Retired	Total
Number of participants					
Actuarial present value:					
Retirement benefits					
Withdrawal benefits					
Ancillary benefits					
Total projected benefits					
Supplemental actuarial value					
Normal cost					
Actuarial present value of vested benefits					
Actuarial present value of future normal costs					

xxx The ABC Actuarial Firm xxx

After reviewing these tabular results for reasonableness and consistency with prior years, and performing any additional manual computations, the actuary will prepare his report.

[4] Actuarial Report

The actuarial report should usually contain:

(1) A narrative summary of the valuation results (including the range of the allowable Internal Revenue Service deduction);

(2) Financial statements and supporting schedules analyzing the results;

(3) An outline of the principal provisions of the plan;

(4) A description of the actuarial valuation method and assumptions; and

(5) A comparison of actual experience with assumptions.

The form and content of the report varies between as well as within actuarial firms; however, the data as outlined above are generally included.

¶ 4.03   ACTUARIAL PRESENT VALUE

This concept of actuarial present value is the cornerstone of the actuarial valuation process and must be understood prior to any review of actuarial data. The interprofessional Pension Actuarial Advisory Group in an Exposure Draft (October 1, 1977) titled "Pension Terminology Report" has defined actuarial present value as:

"The present amount equivalent to an amount or series of amounts payable or receivable in the future that results from applying actuarial assumptions; with the amount(s) referred to being adjusted where appropriate to reflect expected changes from the present date to the date of future expected payment or receipt by reason of expected salary changes, cost of living adjustments, or other changes; and adjusted to reflect the time value of money (through discounts for interest) and the probability of payment (by means of decrements such as for death, disability, withdrawal or retirement) expected to occur between the present date and the expected future date of payment or receipt."

The definition is similar to that of "present value." The primary difference is that present value usually means adjusting a future amount to reflect only the time value of money. Actuarial present value contains additional adjustments to the future amount to reflect various probabilities. Both concepts are concerned with measurement of a future amount valued as of the current valuation date.

[1] Discount for Interest

The definition of "actuarial present value" stated that a future amount was "adjusted to reflect the time value of money and the probability of payment." The adjustment for the time value of money (i.e., discount for interest) is similar to the accounting concept of present value. In performing a valuation, the actuary is concerned with discounting cash flows of future amount(s) (e.g., pension benefit payments) in determining the annual contribution required to the plan. In the simplest circumstances, the plan could provide that a lump-sum payment will be made to each participant at retirement. If the payment was $5,000 and the participant was one year from retirement, the present value of this pension benefit could be measured once the discount rate for interest was selected. Assuming a rate of 6 percent per annum, the computation required to compute the present value of the lump-sum payment would be:

$$\text{Present value} = \frac{\text{Lump-sum payment}}{(1 + \text{interest rate})}$$

$$= \frac{\$5,000}{(1 + .06)}$$

$$= \frac{\$5,000}{1.06}$$

$$= \$4,716.98$$

Therefore, the present value of $5,000 needed in one year, discounted for interest at 6 percent is $4,716.98. If the sponsor wanted to "fully fund" this pension benefit, he could deposit $4,716.98 in a savings account providing a 6 percent per annum yield. At retirement in one year, the lump-sum benefit payment would be provided by:

Sponsor's contribution	$4,716.98
Interest earnings	283.02
AMOUNT NEEDED AT RETIREMENT	$5,000.00

[2] Discount for the Benefit of Withdrawals

As previously noted, actuarial present value reflects adjustments for other variables (e.g., probability of payment) in addition to the time value of money. The effect on the valuation of these adjustments is similar to the discount for interest. While the discount for interest represents the anticipated investment earning rate, the discounts for the probability of payment of retirement benefits represents the anticipated probability that the participant will stay to retirement. Since this probability of payment is related to the withdrawal rate, it will be referred to as the benefit of withdrawals. The effect on the valuation can be demonstrated by assuming there is an 80 percent probability that each of five participants will stay to retirement and collect a lump-sum payment of $5,000. Without regard to the time value of money, the sponsor would only have to contribute $20,000 to the plan to fully fund these benefits. This contribution would be calculated by:

Lump-sum payment	$ 5,000
Number of participants	× 5
Payments required	$25,000
Probability of payment	× .80
CONTRIBUTION NEEDED	$20,000

If the assumption (80 percent) concerning this probability of payment is correct, then only four of the five currently active participants will stay to retirement to collect $5,000. Accordingly, only four $5,000 payments will be needed. In this example, each participant's lump-sum payment would be provided by:

Sponsor contribution	$ 4,000
Benefit from withdrawals	1,000
	$ 5,000

The benefit from withdrawals does not represent an additional benefit to each remaining participant because the benefit was anticipated in the calculation of the sponsor's contribution to the plan.

The actuary selects the benefit from withdrawal rates based upon the anticipated forfeitures of retirement benefits by terminating participants. Unlike the interest rate, the benefit from withdrawals varies according to the attained age of the participant at each valuation date. This represents the probability that the nearer the participant is to retirement, the less likely he will withdraw. In addition, the longer the participant's credited service under the plan, the less he forfeits (due to vesting) upon terminating prior to retirement. The actuary will evaluate these probabilities and other factors (e.g., turnover rates) and construct a benefit from the withdrawal rate table by age (demonstrated at ¶ 7.10). To simplify the mathematical calculations made in this section, a level 2 percent per annum benefit from withdrawals has been selected. Discounting future amounts by a level rate permits the use of published present value tables and avoids the sophisticated calculations needed in the valuations where the benefit from withdrawal varies.

[3] Combined Effect of the Discounts for Interest and Benefit From Withdrawals

Even though the discounts for interest and benefit from withdrawals are separate assumptions in the valuation process, the effect of each on the valuation is similar. To eliminate the need for complex mathematical calculations, a 2 percent level discount for the benefit from withdrawals was selected. The mathematical calculations can be further simplified by combining the two "level" discount factors into one overall annual rate. This can be demonstrated by comparison of these discounts to a certificate of deposit account. For example, assume the interest provisions of a certificate of deposit are:

- 6 percent per annum interest will be paid; and
- 2 percent per annum bonus interest will be paid on the principal and interest earnings if not withdrawn for a three-year period.

Assuming the certificate of deposit remains in effect for three years, the effective annual yield of these two "interest" rates would be computed as:

$$\text{Effective Yield} = \text{Interest Earnings plus Bonus Earnings}$$
$$= .06 + .02\,(1.06)$$
$$= .0812$$

The combined effect of these two provisions is equivalent to an 8.12 percent per annum yield. In the examples presented in Chapter 5, the actuarial interest assumption was selected as 6 percent per annum. The discount for the benefit from withdrawals, having an effect on the actuarial valuation similar to the bonus interest provision, was established as a level 2 percent per annum. Accordingly, the effects of these two assumptions in determining actuarial present value is equivalent to 8.12 percent per annum in the examples presented.

The use of a combined rate representing the effects of the discount for interest and discount for the benefit from withdrawals greatly simplifies the calculations required in demonstrating the actuarial valuation process. In actual practice, there would not be one overall rate (e.g., 8.12 percent). Instead, the actuary would select one rate for interest and use a table (i.e., turnover table) for the benefit from withdrawals.

[4] Present Value of a Future Amount

The ultimate cost of the benefits provided under a pension plan is a function of many variables since payments will not begin until the participant retires—which could be decades into the future. At retirement, the fund needed to provide for the estimated annual retirement benefits is referred to as "the amount needed at retirement." Once the actuary has determined the *amount needed at retirement*, it must be discounted to its actuarial present value as of the *current valuation date*. This procedure is necessary in order to measure the funding requirements of the plan. The actuarial present value of the amount needed at retirement to fund the total anticipated retirement benefit is referred to as the actuarial present value of projected benefits. Actuarial present value is a function of the discounts for interest and for benefit from withdrawals as previously defined, and the length of time between the current valuation date (e.g., present date) and retirement date (e.g., future date). If the combined effect of these discounts is level (i.e., 8.12 percent per annum), the calculations required are identical to those needed to determine the present value of $1, when the discount factor is 8.12 percent per annum. For example, for each $1 in a savings needed in three years which will accumulate earnings at 8.12 percent per annum, the saver would have to deposit:

$$\text{Deposit required} = \text{Future value divided by the annual yield for 3 years}$$
$$= \$1 \div (1 + .0812)^3$$
$$= 1 \div 1.2631957$$
$$= \$.7912$$

Accordingly, $.7912 deposited today will grow to a future value of $1 in three years assuming an effective yield of 8.12 percent per annum. Conversely, the present value of $1 needed in three years and discounted at 8.12 percent per annum is $.7912. Applying this concept to the actuarial valuation process, the actuarial present value "discount rate" is 8.12 percent per annum in these situations. Therefore, the actuarial present value of $1 needed at retirement in three years is $.7912, which represents the combined discount factor in this example. To compute the appropriate combined discount factor used in other examples in this section, the following equation should be solved:

Combined discount factor = $1 ÷ $(1.0812)^n$

Where: n is equal to the number of years between the current valuation date and the future date.

[5] The Present Value of a Series of Future Payments

Once the value of the pension benefits for each participant has been determined, costs are allocated to future periods. Actuaries have developed a variety of valuation methods to perform this task. These valuation methods are similar to depreciation methods for the cost of fixed assets in that the method determines the annual incidence of cost—not the level of ultimate cost. In arriving at the annual incidence of cost (i.e., normal cost), the actuary divides the value of the benefits by a "factor" which is a function of the number of years cost is being allocated and the pattern of recognition desired. Assuming that normal cost is recognized in a level amount per year, the calculation of this "factor" is similar to the factor used to discount a series of equal payments made at the beginning of each year (i.e., annuity due). For example, the present value of an annuity due of $1 for a three-year period dscounted at 8.12 percent per annum is:

Present value of annuity due = Payment for first year

plus

Payment for second year
discounted for one year

plus

Payment for third year
discounted for two years

$$= \$1 + \frac{\$1}{(1.0812)} + \frac{\$1}{(1.0812)^2}$$

$$= \$2.7803$$

Therefore, the present value (discounted at 8.12 percent per annum): of an annuity due of $1 (for three years) is $2.7803. Conversely, if the current balance of the savings account was $2.7803 earning 8.12 percent per annum, the saver could withdraw $1 at the beginning of each year for three years. In this calculation, the annuity due factor was 2.7803.

Since the combined discount factor is 8.12 percent per annum, the combined annuity due factor in the examples contained in this section is equivalent to:

Combined annuity due factor =

$$1 + \frac{1}{1.0812}^1 + \frac{1}{1.0812}^2 + \ldots + \frac{1}{1.0812}^n$$

Where: n is equal to the number of years normal cost is assigned.

In an actual valuation, the calculation of the factor is much more complicated than presented herein and is discussed at length in Chapter 7.

¶ 4.04   SUMMARY

These examples demonstrate the basic mathematical concepts used in an actuarial valuation. Accountants initially confronted with actuarial data are often thrown into a state of confusion because:

(1) The terminology used is extremely confusing; and
(2) The formulas used to describe the valuation are quite complex.

The remaining chapters of this section describe actuarial valuation in more detail, but do not introduce any additional mathematical concepts. Terminology is introduced and explained through the use of examples to define actuarial present value, actuarial present value of projected benefits, supplemental actuarial value, and normal cost. This approach is followed to enable the reader to obtain additional insight in the actuarial valuation process without requiring an extensive mathematical background.

Chapter 5

ACTUARIAL PRESENT VALUE DETERMINATIONS

¶ 5.01 ACTUARIAL PRESENT VALUE OF PENSION OB-LIGATIONS

Under formal pension plans, benefits will be payable to participants if certain conditions are met. In the simplest circumstance (disregarding the provisions of the Employee Retirement Income Security Act of 1974 (ERISA)), a plan could provide that a lump-sum payment will be made to each participant at retirement, only if he has remained a member of the group continuously until his normal retirement date.

Since the plan's obligation to each active participant is contingent on that participant remaining in the employment group until reaching retirement age, mathematical techniques are required to reflect this probability. If, additionally, the amount of the payment is to be based on some factors that are not presently known (e.g., his average salary over his working career), projection techniques need to be utilized to estimate the retirement benefit. Finally, because each participant's lump-sum payment will be made at his normal retirement date, the estimated retirement benefit must be discounted at a suitable interest rate.

A similar analysis can be made for a plan providing a series of monthly payments, commencing at the participant's normal retirement date and continuing during his lifetime. Each monthly retirement payment can be evaluated separately in terms of the projected amount, probability of payment, and interest discount in the same manner as the lump-sum payment.

The foregoing characterizes the techniques used to determine the actuarial present value of a pension plan's obligations. There are various levels of measurement of the actuarial present value (henceforth referred to as actuarial value) of these obligations, which include:

- Accrued benefits;
- Vested benefits;
- Termination benefits;
- Projected benefits.

The *actuarial value of projected benefits* represent the estimated value of all future benefits; it is used in assigning cost to future periods by actuarial valuation methods. The *actuarial value of accrued benefits* represent the estimated value of benefits earned to date. The *actuarial value of vested benefits*, on the other hand, represent only that portion of the *actuarial value of accrued benefits* to which participants already have a nonforfeitable interest. The soundness of an *on-going* plan (i.e., its ability to meet its obligations) depends on the relationship of its assets to these actuarial present value measurements. If the plan or a group of participants (via merger, spin-off, layoff, etc.) is being terminated, special actuarial calculations must be performed to determine each participant's *termination benefits*.

The plan sponsor, the actuary, the accountant, the government regulator, and the plan participant are concerned with valuing the plan assets and obligations in order to measure the soundness of the plan. Accordingly, these different categories of actuarial values have been defined and developed to assist these interested parties in performing this evaluation.

¶ 5.02   ACCRUED BENEFITS

The pension plan agreement normally contains provisions describing the method of calculating retirement benefits. The various types of formulas used are discussed in Chapter 1, "Types of Employee Benefit Plans." A participant's accrued benefit represents the level of annual (or monthly) retirement benefits he has earned to date. For example, the calculation of the accrued benefits for a participant age 58 and covered under the plan for three years would be:

- Benefit formula—Accrued benefit payable annually is equal to 1½% of each year's compensation.

- Participant's earning history—$30,000 at age 55, $31,500 at age 56, and $33,076 at age 57.

For a participant who has completed three years of service *as of the current valuation date*, the accrued benefits earned would be:

Salary	Benefit Formula	
$30,000	1½%	$ 450
31,500	1½%	473
33,076	1½%	496
	ACCRUED BENEFIT	$1,419

The participant has earned to date an annual benefit of $1,419 *commencing* on his normal retirement date. As demonstrated, the calculation of the accrued benefit does not require sophisticated mathematical techniques. Rather, the calculation requires historical salary data and the specific benefit formula of the plan.

The actuary must compute the amount needed to fund the accrued benefit of $1,419 payable annually during retirement. This calculation is a function of the assumed interest earnings during the retirement period and the probability that the retiree lives to receive each retirement payment. Actuaries have developed standard tables containing annuity factors to be multiplied by the accrued benefit to determine the amount needed at retirement, which give appropriate recognition to the probable number of payments required (mortality assumption) and the effect of assumed earnings (interest assumption). Using the 1951 Group Annuity Table* (Ga-1951) projected to 1970 (Ga-1970) with a 6 percent interest rate, we get:

Accrued benefit	$ 1,419
Ga-1970 factor with 6% interest	× 9.465
AMOUNT NEEDED AT RETIREMENT	$13,431

Therefore, the plan should have accumulated $13,431 by the retirement date of the participant to fund fully the accrued benefit earned to date, provided the post-retirement interest and mortality assumptions are accurate.

If the participant will retire at a future date, the amount needed at retirement must be discounted to its present value. Assuming the participant will retire in seven years (at age 65) and 6 percent will be earned annually from the current valuation date to retirement date, the calculation of the actuarial value of accrued benefits would be:

Amount needed at retirement	$13,431
Present value of $1 needed in 7 years	× .665057
ACTUARIAL VALUE OF ACCRUED BENEFITS	$ 8,932

At the current valuation date (seven years prior to retirement date), a fund of $8,932 is required to provide fully for the participant's benefits earned to date if:

(1) The participant stays in employment to satisfy the vesting provisions;

---

* See ¶ 7.03 for a discussion of these tables.

(2) The fund earns 6 percent annually; and

(3) The post-retirement mortality assumption is accurate.

The actuarial value of accrued benefits, as defined, represents one measurement of the plan's obligation. The basis for the calculation is the accrued benefits earned to date; accrued benefits earned in subsequent years or possible forfeiture of accrued benefits recognized (via termination prior to complete vesting) are not considered in this valuation. Accordingly, this special-purpose valuation represents the measurement of the plan's obligations if (1) the plan terminated as of the current valuation date (hence, additional benefits could not be earned), and (2) each participant became 100 percent vested (hence, no forfeitures of accrued benefits recognized).

¶ 5.03 VESTED BENEFITS

Vested benefits are accrued benefits to which a participant is entitled regardless of whether he continues to work for the sponsoring employer. Vested benefits are generally expressed as a percentage of accrued benefits under the plan. The vesting and benefit accrual requirements of ERISA have been previously described at ¶ 2.02 [1] [b]. The actuarial value of vested benefits is computed based upon the participant's accrued benefit and the vesting provisions of the plan.

Continuing with the previous example, the participant with three years of service earned an accrued benefit of $1,419. Assuming the vesting provisions of the plan provided 10 percent cumulative vesting per year of service, the vested benefits are:

Accrued benefit	$1,419
Vesting percentage	× .30
VESTED BENEFITS	$ 426

The actuarial value of vested benefits at the current valuation date would be computed as:

Accrued vested benefit	$ 426.00
Ga-1970 factor with 6% interest	× 9.465
AMOUNT NEEDED AT RETIREMENT	$4,032.00
Present value of $1 needed in 7 years	÷ .665057
PRESENT VALUE OF VESTED BENEFITS	$2,682.00

The actuarial value of vested benefits can be viewed as the fund required as of the current valuation date to provide a retirement benefit of $426 per annum, and represents another measurement of the plan's obligation. The basis for the calculation is the accrued benefits earned to date which are not subject to forfeiture. Accordingly, this special-purpose valuation represents the measurement of the plan's obligation if (1) the plan terminated as of the current valuation date (hence, additional benefits would not be earned), and (2) each participant's benefits were limited to those vested (hence, no opportunity to become completely vested through continued service).

¶ 5.04   TERMINATION BENEFITS

The actuarial values of accrued benefits and vested benefits, as previously defined, measure the plan's obligations on the implicit basis of termination. "Termination" is assumed because the effect of the participants' continued service on accrued and vested benefits is not anticipated. These valuations, even though useful in evaluating the soundness of a continuing plan (i.e., overall relationship of the plan's assets to obligations), do not measure the security of each participant with respect to the soundness of his individual benefits. For example, assume a plan was terminating and:

- Participants—the plan has three participants, each covered since age 55; at the termination of the plan, X participant was age 65 and retired, Y participant had five years of service, and Z participant had one year of service.

- Benefit formula—Accrued benefit earned is equal to 1½ percent of each year's compensation.

- Vesting—Cumulative 10 percent per year of covered service.

- Participant's historical earning—For each participant at age 55, $30,000 per year which increased 5 percent per annum.

- Normal retirement—Age 65.

- Fair market value of plan assets—$55,000.

At the plan termination date, the actuarial value of accrued benefits is:

Partic- pant	Accrued Benefits*	Ga-1970 Factor	Discount Factor for 6% Interest Until Age 65	Actuarial Value of Accrued Benefits
X	$5,660	9.465	1.00000	$53,572
Y	2,487	9.465	.747258	17,590
Z	450	9.465	.591898	2,521
				$73,683

At the plan termination date, the actuarial value of vested benefits is:

Participant	Actuarial Value of Accrued Benefits	Percent Vested	Actuarial Value of Vested Benefits
X	$53,572	100%	$53,572
Y	17,590	50%	8,795
Z	2,521	10%	252
			$62,619

If the participants reviewed the actuary's report prepared on a continuing plan basis, they might surmise that their "pension benefits" were 75 percent secure (assets divided by accrued benefits) or were 88 percent secure (assets divided by vested benefits)—depending on their perception of the most appropriate test of soundness. In the case of actual termination, neither valuation (actuarial values of accrued and vested benefits) would be the appropriate measurement. Upon plan termination, soundness would be measured by the level of asset allocated to each participant.

If the assets in the plan are less than the actuarial value of accrued benefits, the order of priorities for allocation of plan assets specified in ERISA is generally as follows:

(1) Voluntary participant contributions;

(2) Mandatory participant contributions;

(3) Benefits of participants who have retired or are eligible to retire;

---

* See the table at ¶ 5.05 for calculation.

(4) Vested benefits;

(5) All other benefits.

Therefore, the value of the vested benefits, primarily as defined in the plan, becomes the means to determine asset allocation on plan termination. In the above example, this would result in the following allocation, since the value of the assets ($55,000) is less than the actuarial value of vested benefits. The plan assets would be allocated to priority grouping No. 3 prior to any distribution to grouping No. 4:

Partic- ipant	Value of Vested Benefits	Priority Grouping	Asset Allocation Percentage	Assets Allocated
X	$53,572	3	100%	$53,572
Y	8,795	4	15.8%	1,388
Z	252	4	15.8%	40
	$62,619			$55,000

Compared to the actuarial value of accrued benefits, the "security of each participant's benefits" differed significantly from the 75 percent measurement of the overall soundness of the plan:

Participant	Actuarial Value of Accrued Benefits	Assets Allocated	Ratio of Assets to Accrued Benefits
X	$53,572	$67,541	100.0%
Y	17,590	1,388	7.9%
Z	2,521	40	1.6%

Accordingly, upon plan termination the relationship of the plan's assets and accrued benefits bears little relationship to each participant's share in assets.

In addition to setting requirements for the vesting of benefits, ERISA established the Pension Benefit Guaranty Corporation (PBGC) to guarantee that participants receive certain benefits in plan terminations. Guaranteed benefits by the PBGC are vested benefits as defined in the plan subject to prescribed limitations, which are discussed at ¶ 2.07[1]. In addition, the guaranteed benefits are phased in at 20 percent per year until the plan or benefit (arising from plan amendment) has been in effect for five years.

ERISA also provides that, in the event of plan termination, the sponsoring employer is liable to the PBGC for the lesser of:

- The excess, if any, of the actuarial present value of guaranteed benefits over the current value of the plan's assets; or
- 30 percent of the sponsoring employer's net worth.

As a result, the two participants in this example might be entitled to obtain their lost vested benefits from the PBGC if the benefit provision satisfies the five-year phase-in rule and the prescribed limitations as to maximum benefits.

The accountant providing services to the pension plan should consider the effect of plan termination on asset allocation when discussing the soundness of a particular plan. Soundness (i.e., relationship of the aggregate plan assets to the aggregate plan obligations) should not be equated with a participant's security as demonstrated in this example. The plan's assets represent unallocated funds held for the benefit of all participants and are only allocated upon partial or complete plan termination pursuant to specific rules and regulations. If the plan sponsor is considering termination or partial termination (e.g., spin-off of division or subsidiary), the accountant should consider the impact to the participants affected to determine if financial statement disclosures are adequate.

¶ 5.05   PROJECTED BENEFITS

The actuarial value of projected benefits is determined at the current valuation date to measure the total estimated cost of the plan. In determining projected benefits, the actuary is concerned with the ultimate retirement benefit, including the accrued benefits to be earned subsequent to the current valuation date. The term "projected" is used because prior to retirement certain assumptions have to be made. The calculations of the projected benefit for a recently hired participant age 55 covered under the plan can be demonstrated by assuming:

- Participant's earning—Starting salary of $30,000 a year, which is expected to increase 5 percent a year;
- Benefit formula—Accrued benefit equal to 1½ percent of each year's compensation.

Based upon this date, the projected benefit upon retirement at age 65 would be:

Age	Future Earning Assuming 5% Annual Increase	Plan's Benefit Formula	Benefit Accruing in Current Year	Accrued Benefit	Cumulative Vesting
55	$30,000	1½%	$ 450	$ 450	10%
56	31,500	1½%	473	923	20%
57	33,076	1½%	496	1,419	30%
58	34,728	1½%	521	1,940	40%
59	36,466	1½%	547	2,487	50%
60	38,288	1½%	574	3,061	60%
61	40,202	1½%	603	3,664	70%
62	42,214	1½%	633	4,297	80%
63	44,324	1½%	665	4,962	90%
64	46,540	1½%	698	5,660	100%

PROJECTED BENEFIT $5,660

Since the plan's benefit formula was based on a percentage of annual compensation, the assumption required for this calculation was the future earnings of the participant.

[1] Amount Needed at Retirement

Since $5,660 represents the annual projected benefit, the *amount needed at retirement* is the actuarial present value of the future series of annual projected retirement payments measured at the retirement date. This value should reflect an assumed interest rate and the probability that the retired participant lives to receive each payment in the series. Using the 1951 Group Annuity Table projected to 1970 (Ga-1970) with a 6 percent interest rate, we get:

Annual projected retirement benefit	$ 5,660
Ga-1970 factor with 6% interest	× 9.465
AMOUNT NEEDED AT RETIREMENT	$53,572

Therefore, the pension plan should accumulate assets equal to $53,572 by the expected retirement date of the participant to provide fully for his anticipated retirement benefits. This fund should be sufficient to satisfy the participant's retirement benefits if:

(1) The actuary's projection of the retirement benefits is accurate;

(2) The assets accumulated at retirement will earn 6 percent per annum; and

(3) The actuary's post-retirement mortality assumption retirement is accurate.

The actuarial value of projected benefits represents the present actuarial value at the current valuation date of the amount needed at retirement. The length of time between the current valuation date and the expected retirement date affects the level of this value.

[2] Determination of the Discount Factors

Assuming the amount needed at retirement is $53,572 and the *current valuation date* is at age 55 (ten years prior to expected retirement at age 65), the actuarial value of projected benefits can be calculated after the discount factors relating to interest and probability of staying to retirement are computed.

The discount factor for interest will be based upon the value of $1 required ten years from the current date assuming an interest rate of 6 percent per annum. The present value of $1 discounted at 6 percent for ten years would be:

$$\text{Interest discount factor} = 1 \div 1.06^{10}$$
$$= (.943396)^{10}$$
$$= .558395$$

Therefore, $.558395 invested at 6 percent per annum, will have a value of $1 in ten years.

The discount factor for the probability of staying to retirement adjusts for those participants at age 55 who will not stay to retirement and who will forfeit accrued benefits earned (but not vested). These lost benefits will be shared by those participants who remain. In actual practice, the actuary will use published tables or construct a table that will assign different probabilities of staying by each succeeding year by age groupings, which is discussed in detail at ¶ 7.10.

To simplify our illustration, a 2 percent per annum benefit from terminations was assumed. Accordingly, the present value of $1 discounted at 2 percent over a ten-year period (representing the probability of a participant at age 55 will stay to retirement) would be:

$$\text{Probability factor} = 1 \div 1.02^{10}$$
$$= (.980392)^{10}$$
$$= .820348$$

Therefore, there is a .820348 probability that a participant age 55 will stay ten years to retirement.

[3] Calculation of the Actuarial Value of Projected Benefits

The calculation of the actuarial value of projected benefits would be:

Amount needed at retirement	$53,572.00
Discount factor for interest	× .558395
Discount factor for probability of staying	× .820348
ACTUARIAL VALUE OF PROJECTED BENEFITS AT CURRENT VALUATION DATE	$24,540.16

The combined effect of a 6 percent per annum interest assumption and a 2 percent per annum benefit from termination is equivalent to 8.12 percent per annum. Therefore, the combined discount factor used in this chapter would be:

$$\text{Combined discount factor} = 1 \div 1.0812^{10}$$
$$= .458078$$

The calculation of the actuarial value of projected benefits would be:

Amount needed at retirement	$53,572.00
Combined discount factor	× .458078
ACTUARIAL VALUE OF PROJECTED BENEFITS AT CURRENT VALUATION DATE	$24,540.16

[4] Assumption of the Probability of the Participant Staying to Retirement

The probability of the participant staying to retirement is an important assumption in the actuarial valuation. This can be demonstrated by assuming the plan's sponsor decided to fund fully projected benefits for 100 participants (age 55) who will retire in ten years. The contribution to the pension fund would be:

$2,454,016 (100 contributions of $24,540.16).

These funds would earn interest at 6 percent per annum resulting in a total pension fund of:

$4,394,769 ($2,454,016 plus compound interest).

Since the actuary assumed the probability of a participant at age 55 staying to retirement at age 65 is .820348, the number of participants expected to retire under the plan would be:

82.0348 (100 participants times probability of staying).

Thus, each participant retiring will have a share of the assets at retirement of:

$53,572 (pension fund divided by 82.0348).

The $53,572 represents the amount needed at retirement from the example. The level of the actuarial value of projected benefits for each participant will increase at each succeeding valuation date until the current valuation date is also the actual retirement date (in this example, at age 65); since the probability of staying to retirement and the present value of a dollar increase annually—reaching 1.0 at retirement. The increase in the level of projected benefits for succeeding valuation dates is demonstrated in Graph 5-1.

¶ 5.06 SUPPLEMENTAL ACTUARIAL VALUE

Supplemental actuarial value does not represent an actuarial valuation of a future pension obligation (e.g., accrued, vested, termination, or projected). This value represents the difference between the actuarial values of future pension obligations and future normal costs. This term has frequently been referred to as accrued liability, past service cost, actuarial liability, net actuarial deficiency, and supple-

GRAPH 5-1. ACTUARIAL VALUE OF
PROJECTED BENEFITS

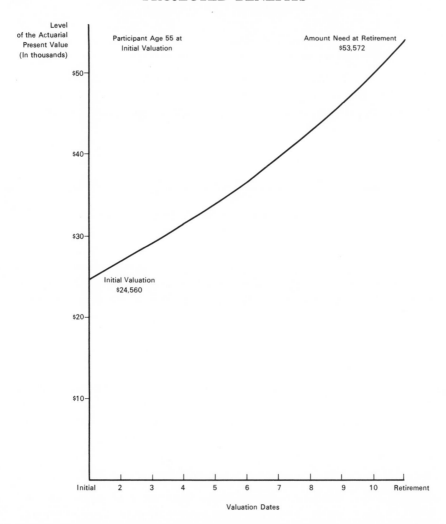

mental liability. Supplemental actuarial value represents the actuarial value of normal cost assigned to prior periods and is similar to the accountant's concept of accumulated depreciation, as demonstrated in the following example.

Continuing with the example contained at ¶ 5.05, the sponsor would need to provide retirement benefits starting in ten years of $5,660 per annum. Assuming the plan will not earn any income and the participant will stay to retirement, normal cost would be:

Amount needed at retirement	$53,572.10
Active service period	÷ 10 years
NORMAL COST	$ 5,357.20

From a retrospective approach, the supplemental actuarial value represents the summation of normal cost assigned to prior periods. Accordingly, at the end of the second plan year, the supplemental actuarial value would be:

Normal cost, year 1	$ 5,375.20
Normal cost, year 2	5,357.20
	$10,714.40

In this simple example in which normal costs were assigned on a "straightline" basis over the active service career, the similarities with the accountant's accumulated depreciation concept are apparent. However, the actuarial concept differs in two important respects

(1) The actuary primarily views the concept from a prospective approach; and

(2) The actuarial calculations are based upon discounting future amounts.

[1] Prospective Approach

The supplemental actuarial value is defined from a prospective approach (i.e., represents the difference between a future amount and future normal costs). From this viewpoint, the supplemental actuarial value computed by the actuary at the end of the second plan year would be:

Actuarial value of projected benefits	$53,572.00
Sum of future normal costs (8 years times $5,357.20)	42,857.60
	$10,714.40

The results under either the retrospective or prospective approach would be identical. However, the use of the prospective approach facilitates several of the more complicated actuarial calculations required in the valuation.

[2] Effects of Discounting

In the previous example, the discount factor for the time value of money and the probability of staying to retirement was 1.00 (i.e., no discount assumed). To demonstrate the effects of these discounts assume:

- Participant's entry age — 55
- Expected retirement age — 65
- Amount needed at retirement — $53,572.00 (age 65)
- Actuarial value of projected benefits — $24,540.16 (age 55)
- Discount for interest — 6% per annum
- Discount for probality of staying — 2% per annum
- Actuarial valuation method — Level normal cost over active service career

Normal costs would be calculated by the following formula:

NORMAL COST = Actuarial value of projected benefits at age 55 divided by actuarial present value of 10 annual payments of $1 discounted at a 6 percent interest rate *and* by the probability of staying to retirement;

or, given the assumptions selected in this example:

NORMAL COST = Actuarial value of projected benefits at age 55 divided by the combined annuity due factor representing 8.12 percent per annum discount over a 10-year period.

The calculation of the combined annuity due factor (as demonstrated at ¶ 4.03[5]) is equivalent to the present value of an annuity due of $1 received at the beginning of each year (for ten years) which earns 8.12 percent per annum, or 7.215838.

Actuarial value of projected benefits $24,540.16

Combined annuity due factor
(8.12%—10 years)   ÷7.215836

NORMAL COST $ 3,400.88

Under this prospective approach, the steps necessary to compute the supplemental actuarial value at the end of the third year are:

(1) Actuarial value of projected benefits

Amount need at retirement $53,572.00

Combined discount factor
(8.12%—7 years)   × .578972

$31,016.69

(2) Actuarial future normal cost

Normal cost $ 3,400.88

Combined annuity due factor
(8.12%—7 years)   × 5.60610

$19,065.67

(3) Supplemental actuarial value

Actuarial value of projected benefits $31,016.69
Actuarial value of future normal costs   −19,065.67

$11,951.02

The supplemental actuarial value at the end of the third year of active service is $11,951.02. Since the calculations seem quite complex to the nonactuary, the supplemental actuarial value in this example calculated under the more traditional retrospective approach would be:

Retrospective Calculation

Valu-ation Year	Begin-ning of Year	+	Current Year's Normal Cost	×	Earnings Accumu-lation Factor	×	Benefit From Terminated Employees	=	End of Year
1	$ 0		$3,400.88		1.06		1.02		$ 3,677.03
2	3,677.03		3,400.88		1.06		1.02		7,652.63
3	$ 0		$3,400.88		1.06		1.02		$ 3,677.03

As previously stated, the calculation of the supplemental actuarial value under either approach is identical.

[3] Relationship to Actuarial Value of Projected Benefits

The supplemental actuarial value for a participant increases each year until the expected retirement date. At retirement, the supplemental actuarial value is equal to the actuarial value of projected benefits because the accumulated value of future normal cost is zero. This relationship is graphically shown for each succeeding valuation date on Graph 5-2.

The supplemental actuarial value is equal to the actuarial value of projected benefits less the actuarial present value of future normal costs. At the initial valuation date for a new participant, the supplemental actuarial value is zero; therefore, the actuarial value of future normal cost must equal the actuarial value of projected benefits. At the retirement date for a participant in this example, there are no future normal costs to be accrued; therefore, the supplemental actuarial value must equal the actuarial value of projected benefits.

¶ 5.07   SUMMARY

The actuarial value of projected benefits and supplemental actuarial value are determinations related to the assignment of normal cost over the prospective service career of the participants. The actuarial values of accrued, vested, and termination benefits are special-purpose determinations used by various professionals in evaluating and reporting upon the plan. In the example provided in this chapter, the relationships of these measurements are depicted in Graph 5-3. In evaluating the plan's obligations, there is considerable debate concerning which measurement is most appropriate. In the example noted,

GRAPH 5-2. RELATIONSHIP OF ACTUARIAL VALUE OF PROJECTED BENEFITS, SUPPLEMENTAL VALUE, AND FUTURE NORMAL COST

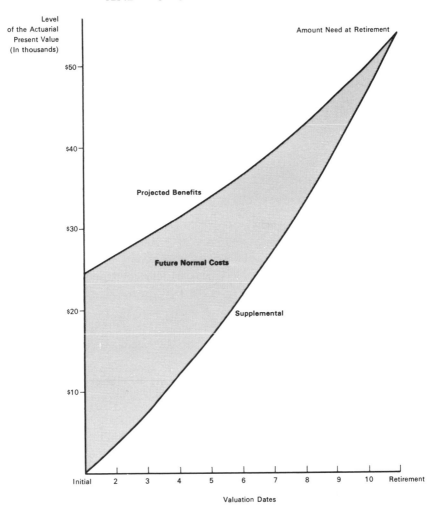

the supplemental actuarial value was greater than the actuarial values of accrued and vested benefits. This may or may not be true when graphing these measurements for a particular plan. The level of the supplemental actuarial value is a function of the actuarial valuation method selected. As in the case of plotting accumulated depreciation patterns for a fixed asset, the pattern of the incidence of cost determines the line. These patterns fluctuate widely depending on the depre-

GRAPH 5-3. RELATIONSHIP OF ACTUARIAL VALUE OF PROJECTED BENEFITS, SUPPLEMENTAL VALUE, ACCRUED BENEFITS, AND VESTED BENEFITS

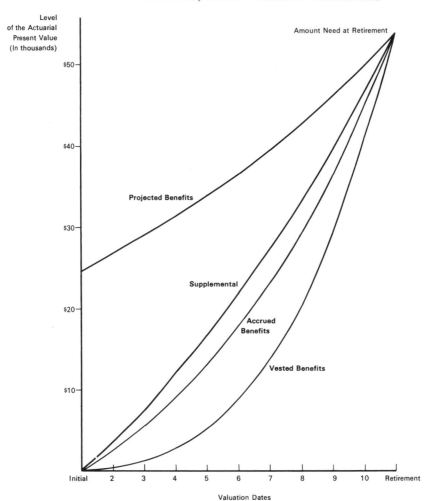

ciation method selected (e.g., straight line vs. double-declining balance).

Accordingly, it is extremely difficult to make generalities concerning the most appropriate measurement to be used in evaluating the plan's obligation; however, the purpose of this section was to make the reader more aware of the nature of these measurements.

Chapter 6

ACTUARIAL DETERMINATIONS OF ASSET VALUES, UNFUNDED SUPPLEMENTAL VALUE, AND ANNUAL PENSION COST

¶ 6.01   ACTUARIAL VALUATION OF PLAN ASSETS

The soundness of an on-going pension plan is partially a function of the value of a plan's assets. Since actuaries are primarily concerned with the long-range soundness of a plan, they have developed special methods to value plan assets. These methods range from historical cost to current market value. In between these extremes, the actuaries have developed methods which attempt to avoid significant year-to-year market fluctuations. While the asset valuation method selected has no effect on the actuarial value of projected benefits, it does affect the level of current contributions to the plan.

A plan is funded through contributions from the sponsor, from the participants (in contributory plans), and through interest earnings on plan assets. Included in the definition of "interest earnings" are investment income (i.e., dividends, interest, rent, etc.) and investment gains and losses. In the actuarial valuation process, a long-term interest assumption is selected in order to forecast the portion of the ultimate retirement payments to be funded from this source. Obviously, any variance between assumed and actual interest income will directly affect the amount and incidence of the sponsor contributions, since this is the only other source of funding in a noncontributory plan. The actuary attempts to assign long-range values to the assets in order to maintain a level and systematic funding pattern.

[1] Sponsor's Annual Contribution

The sponsor's annual contribution to the plan represents the sum of the normal costs and the supplemental cost. Supplemental cost is a function of the supplemental actuarial value and the value of the plan assets. Supplemental actuarial value (as discussed in Chapter 5) represents the theoretical level of assets the plan should have accumulated through the current valuation date pursuant to the actuarial valuation method selected. If the actual level of assets is less than the supplemental actuarial value, this will result in unfunded supplemental actuarial value. The plan sponsor's contribution toward the unfunded supplemental actuarial value is referred to as supplemental cost. The relationship of normal and supplemental cost is depicted in Graph 6-1.

The value of the assets determined by the actuary has a direct effect on the unfunded supplemental actuarial value and on the determination of supplemental costs. As a result, the actuarial value of assets is significant to the sponsor in contribution determinations; however,

GRAPH 6-1. RELATIONSHIP OF NORMAL AND SUPPLEMENTAL COSTS

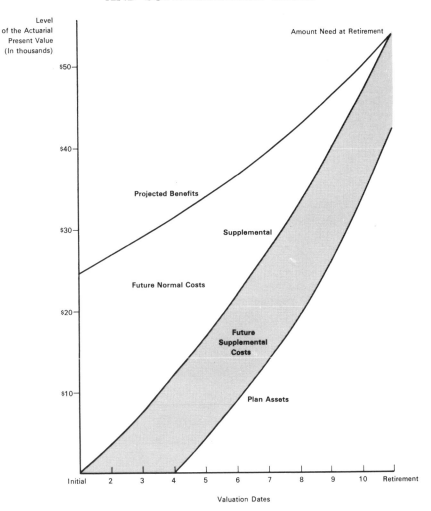

from the plan's viewpoint, the asset value assigned is important only as it affects the contribution received from the sponsor. The assets in the plan's "balance sheet" are valued at current market value as required in the Employee Retirement Income Security Act of 1974 (ERISA). Accordingly, symmetry between the valuation of plan assets used in the "balance sheet" and used in the actuarial valuation is not currently required.

[2] Special Considerations

In reviewing an actuarial report on the valuation of a plan, the reader should be careful to ensure that actuarial present value determinations and assets are compared *as of the same date*. The typical actuarial valuation is performed *as of* the beginning of the plan year. In this evaluation, the actuarial value of projected benefits, supplemental actuarial value, and actuarial value of vested benefits are computed as of the beginning of the year. The normal cost (pension cost assigned to each year under the actuarial valuation method in use, excluding any amortization of unfunded supplemental actuarial values) calculated is for the coming year and is not included in these determinations.

For each active participant, the supplemental actuarial value will increase during the plan year because of the addition of normal cost for the year and the accumulation of assumed interest earnings, and the benefits from withdrawals. Assuming the current valuation date is January 1, 19X4, the value of the plans assets of December 31, 19X4 is not an appropriate basis for comparison to the actuarial values contained in the 19X4 actuarial report. Either the January 1, 19X4 assets should be used or the actuarial values as of December 31, 19X4 (i.e., January 1, 19X5) should be estimated or determined.

Before proceeding with a description of some of the more common asset valuation methods, it should be noted that under ERISA the historical cost valuation method will no longer be acceptable for purposes of complying with the *minimum funding standards*. ERISA provides that "the value of the plan's assets shall be determined on the basis of any reasonable actuarial method of valuation which takes into account fair market value. . . ." ERISA also provides that the plan can elect to carry bonds at amortized cost. These provisions are concerned with the purpose of determining minimum sponsor contributions and do not affect the method of carrying investments in the plan's financial statements prepared in accordance with generally accepted accounting principles, or in accordance with the methods permitted in filings to the Department of Labor.

Accountants providing services to plan sponsors and the pension plan should review the actuarial report and plan financial statements to determine the method of valuing the plan assets used in the determination of:

• The sponsor's annual contribution;

- The sponsor's annual pension expense required by Accounting Principles Board (APB) Opinion No. 8 and Financial Accounting Standards Board (FASB) Interpretation No. 3;
- The sponsor's unfunded vested benefits;
- The sponsor's unfunded past service liability as required by Regulation S-X for Securities and Exchange Commission (SEC) registrants; and
- Financial statement amounts in filings required by the Department of Labor.

If the method used to value the plan assets varies significantly from current value, disclosure of the variance should be considered, especially in those situations in which the sponsor is considering terminating the plan. The FASB has placed the issue of pension accounting and reporting by plan sponsors on its technical agenda to clarify the accounting for the cost of pension plan covered by ERISA. (The final statement is not expected until 1980.)

[3] Types of Asset Valuation Methods

Usually, the asset valuation methods other than historical cost or market are applied only to equity securites. They are designed to recognize a portion of market appreciation (depreciation) while avoiding the dramatic fluctuations that using actual market values could produce. Some of the more common valuation methods are described below:

- *Long-Range Appreciation Method.* The adjusted book value of common stocks is increased each year by a specified percentage representing the anticipated long-term appreciation. For conservatism, the total adjusted value is normally limited to a percentage (e.g., 80 or 90 percent) of market value. Under this method, realized gains and losses are usually recognized separately.
- *Long-Range Yield Method.* The adjusted book value of common stocks is increased each year by an amount necessary to bring realized investment yield (i.e., dividends and realized gains and losses) up to the assumed investment yield.
- *Percentage Difference Method.* A specified percentage (e.g., 20 percent) of the difference between book value and market value is added to the adjusted book value each year. Specific adjust-

ments for realized gains and losses may or may not be made under this method.

- *Average Ratio Method*. The ratio of market value to book value is determined each year. The average of these ratios for some period (e.g., five years) is then used to adjust current book value. Realized gains and losses are included in book value, but their effect is smoothed by the averaging process.

In addition to affecting the level of the unfunded supplemental actuarial value, the asset valuation method can have an indirect effect on the actuarial valuation. The interest assumption used in the valuation should reflect the long-term anticipated investment yield. In selecting this assumption, consideration should be given to historical investment yield, portfolio mix, and future expectations. Some of the asset valuation methods previously described may reflect an improper view of historical investment yield. To the extent improperly measured, historic yield is considered in determining an interest assumption; that assumption may also be improper. For example, the historical cost valuation method does not consider unrealized investment gains and losses. An interest assumption developed from historical investment yield without including unrealized gains and losses may not be appropriate.

¶ 6.02 UNFUNDED SUPPLEMENTAL ACTUARIAL VALUE

The difference between the supplemental actuarial value and the actuarial value of plan assets is equal to the unfunded supplemental actuarial value. An actuarial balance sheet of a pension plan would consist of:

Assets	*Liabilities*
Supplemental actuarial value	Actuarial value of projected benefits
Actuarial value of future normal costs	

By substituting the relationship of the plan assets and unfunded supplemental actuarial value for supplemental actuarial value, this actuarial balance sheet is expanded to:

Assets	*Liabilities*
Actuarial value of plan assets	Actuarial value of projected benefits
Unfunded supplemental actuarial value	
Actuarial value of future normal costs	

The actuarial value of future normal costs, actuarial value of plan assets, and actuarial value of projected benefits have been discussed. The unfunded supplemental actuarial value represents the portion of the normal costs assigned through the current valuation date which have not been funded and consists of:

(1) Unfunded past service cost arising from the adoption of the plan;

(2) Unfunded prior service cost (as defined under APB Opinion No. 8) arising from plan amendment;

(3) Unamortized experience gains and losses;

(4) Unamortized actuarial revaluation gains and losses; and

(5) Unfunded normal costs accrued since the adoption of the plan.

[1] Unfunded Past Service Cost

The sponsor could decide to give pension credits for the past service of existing participants when the plan was adopted. Under several actuarial valuation methods, normal cost will be calculated as though the plan was in existence during the period of this past service, resulting in an initial supplemental actuarial value. For example, continuing with the example used in the supplemental actuarial value section (¶ 5.06), assume that

(1) The plan was adopted giving credit for a participant's past service.

(2) The participant has completed three years of service (hired at age 55).

GRAPH 6-2. UNFUNDED PAST SERVICE AT ADOPTION OF PLAN

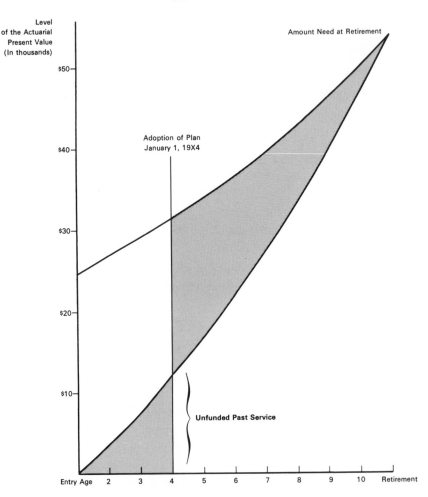

Therefore, the supplemental actuarial value at the end of the third year of service was $11,951.02 (as previously calculated in ¶ 5.02[2]). Since the sponsor has not funded the normal costs for the three years prior to the adoption of the plan, the unfunded supplemental actuarial value is equal to this unfunded past service cost demonstrated by Graph 6-2.

Retrospectively, the initial supplemental actuarial value represents the accumulated value of normal costs assigned to years prior to the adoption of the plan. Since there are no assets in the plan when adopted, the initial supplemental actuarial value is unfunded. The term "past service cost" is a misnomer because the unfunded past service cost is a function of the actuarial valuation method selected rather than of the accrued benefits given credit. The unfunded supplemental actuarial values are determinations made pursuant to the actuarial valuation method selected.

[2] Unfunded Prior Service Cost

Subsequent to the adoption of the plan, the sponsor could decide to retroactively as well as prospectively improve the benefits by amending the plan. This decision could be a gratuitous decision or the result of collective-bargaining negotiations. If the actuarial valuation method selected gives retrospective recognition to this increased cost, the actuary will recalculate the level of the supplemental actuarial value as of the date of the amendment. The difference between the original supplement actuarial value and the *recalculated* supplemental actuarial value is referred to as the prior service cost, which is demonstrated in Graph 6-3.

[3] Unamortized Experience Gains and Losses

The actuarial valuation of a plan involves several assumptions, such as interest earnings and termination prior to retirement. If the assumptions are not accurate (i.e., actuarial experience is different than assumed), experience gain or loss results. For example, if 4 percent was earned on the investments during the year and the actuary used 6 percent in the actuarial valuation, an experience loss equal to the "lost earnings" would occur. The reasons for actuarial gains and losses as well as measurement are discussed in Chapter 9.

[4] Unamortized Actuarial Revaluation Gains and Losses

Actuarial valuations require the selection of many assumptions such as the rates of investment earnings and withdrawal. If the actuary changes either the actuarial valuation method or actuarial assumption(s), actuarial revaluation gain or loss results. The actual determination of these gains and losses is identical to that described under unfunded prior service cost.

GRAPH 6-3. INCREASE IN PRIOR SERVICE COST ARISING FROM PLAN AMENDMENT

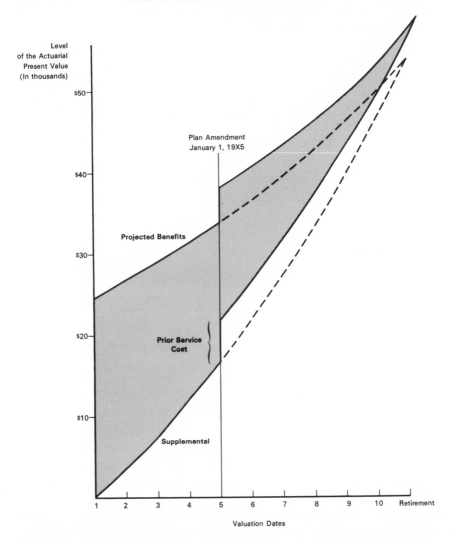

[5] Unfunded Portion of Any Normal Cost Accruing Since Adoption of the Plan

The actuarial valuation assumes that the normal costs are funded as accrued. If the sponsor fails to contribute the normal cost for any year subsequent to the plan's adoption, unfunded supplemental actuarial value is increased by the difference.

The level of the unfunded supplement actuarial value is a function of the actuarial valuation method and the actuarial value of plan assets. Given the identical set of participant data, assumptions, and portfolio, different valuation methods will result in different levels of the unfunded supplemental actuarial value, which is discussed in depth in Chapter 8.

¶ 6.03   ANNUAL PENSION EXPENSE

Normal cost and unfunded supplemental actuarial value are needed to determine the range of sponsor's contribution to the plan. The current year's contribution level should satisfy the tax deductibility requirements of the Internal Revenue Code and the minimum funding account provisions of ERISA. Included in the actuary's report are the contribution alternatives that will satisfy these requirements. Even though the actuarial valuation process is concerned with the funding of a plan, accountants have used the results to measure annual pension expense pursuant to APB Opinion No. 8. The Opinion permits two basic techniques to recognize supplemental cost in the annual computation of the sponsor's expense:

(1) The unfunded supplemental actuarial value is amortized with interest over a specified period(s); or

(2) The unfunded supplemental actuarial value is recognized as expense only to the extent of interest accrued thereon. Since the actuarial valuation assumes normal costs have been funded and will earn interest earnings, the lost earnings must be recognized by the sponsor as pension expense.

The recognition of pension expense as required by APB Opinion No. 8 provided no assurance that the cost accrued would be paid to the pension plan (i.e., funded). ERISA, unlike APB Opinion No. 8, defines the maximum acceptable funding period for each element of the unfunded supplemental actuarial value. Even though ERISA prohibits the "interest only" approach to funding and specifies different acceptable amortization period, APB Opinion No. 8 is still effective for determining the pension expense of the sponsor pending any action by the FASB. The differences between APB Opinion No. 8 and ERISA in this area are summarized below:

Unfunded Supplemental Actuarial Value Element	APB Opinion No. 8 Expense Recognition		ERISA Funding Requirement	
	Minimum*	Maximum	Minimum	Maximum
Past service	Interest only	10%	30 or 40** yrs.	10 yrs.
Prior service	Interest only	10%	30 or 40** yrs.	10 yrs.
Actuarial gains and losses	20 yrs.	10 yrs.	15 yrs.	10 yrs.

---

* Longer allowable amortization periods are specified for multiemployer plans. Past and prior service liabilities may be amortized over forty years, and actuarial gains and losses may be amortized over twenty years.

** Plans in existence on January 1, 1974 are allowed to amortize unfunded liabilities existing as of the beginning of the first plan year to which the funding requirements apply over a forty-year period.

Chapter 7

ACTUARIAL ASSUMPTIONS

¶ 7.01 GENERAL

The total cost of a pension for each participant is not known until the final benefit check has been paid, which could be decades into the future. Since provisions for funding and pension expense must be made before the total cost is known, assumptions are necessary in performing actuarial valuations. In selecting these assumptions, the actuary must take into account current economic factors (e.g., market conditions and potential investment returns), the special features of the plan sponsor (e.g., type of business, and employee turnover), and the special features of the plan (e.g., benefit options, death and disability provisions, and early retirement).

Under the Employee Retirement Income Security Act of 1974 (ERISA), the actuarial assumptions used must be "reasonable (taking into account the experience of the plan and reasonable expectations)" and must, "in combination, offer the actuary's best estimate of anticipated experience under the plan." The reasonableness of the assumptions used can be evaluated over a period of years by comparing the actual experience of the plan with that anticipated by the assumptions. More favorable experience than expected results in experience gains, while less favorable experience results in experience losses.

Regardless of the care with which chosen, assumptions will turn out to be "wrong." The probability that what actually happens will correspond precisely to what is assumed to happen is, for all practical purposes, nil.

The suitability of the assumptions chosen lies in how closely the actual results conform with the anticipated results. Actuaries must review periodically the pattern of experience gains and losses to determine if a change in any assumption is necessary. The more common actuarial assumptions are discussed in the following paragraphs.

¶ 7.02 INTEREST ASSUMPTION

The assumed interest rate represents the expected rate of investment return on the plan's assets. The actuary tries to estimate the long-range rate of return on the plan's assets since these earnings affect the amount that would otherwise be provided by contributions from the sponsor. The interest assumption considers investment earnings and, depending on the asset valuation method, should also consider realized and unrealized appreciation (or depreciation) of the investments. The interest assumption should reflect the total anticipated rate of investment return.

Neither economists, actuaries, accountants, bankers, nor plan sponsors have proven themselves particularly foresighted in projecting long-term investment return. The prediction of the long-term return for decades into the future is subject to severe error. Since the interest assumption is the primary factor used to discount pension benefits to their actuarial present value, errors in the interest assumption have a significant effect on the valuations.

The interest assumption is inversely related to the level of the sponsor's funding provisions (i.e., the greater the expectation of the investment earnings, the lower the contribution required from the sponsor).

The magnitude of the effect of a change in the interest assumption is a function of the mix of the various service careers of the covered participant. A one percent change in the interest assumption would probably have a significant impact on normal cost, which should be considered in selecting a reasonable interest rate. The choice of interest assumption involves (explicitly or implicitly) a judgment as to the rate of future inflation. Other actuarial assumptions, which may also be subject to inflation, should be made on a consistent basis. This is discussed in more depth at ¶ 7.14.

¶ 7.03 MORTALITY ASSUMPTION

The mortality assumption can be segregated into the rate of mortality among active participants and that among retired participants. Mortality among active participants is one of several factors affecting the probability of a participant staying to retirement. Mortality among retired participants reflects the probability that each payment in the future stream of payments will actually be made. In selecting the mortality assumption, there is a need for an element of conservatism over current mortality studies since there has been a trend toward increased longevity. Also, the mortality assumption should make provision for the greater life expectancy of female participants.

The mortality rate prior to retirement is frequently combined with expected rates of withdrawal from the plan for other reasons such as voluntary or involuntary termination or disability. The assumption as to mortality after retirement is normally combined with the interest assumption through the use of standard annuity tables.

The combination of death and turnover assumptions (multiple decrement approach) and the development of standard annuity factors are discussed at ¶¶ 7.10 and 7.12, respectively.

Because of the reliability of statistical data available to measure the probability of death, the mortality assumption by itself is normally one of the least sensitive assumptions in terms of its effect on the actuarial valuation.

The statistical probability of death has been expressed in standard tables in terms of the probability of a person of a specified age and sex living from one year to the next. Currently, the most widely used of these tables in pension valuations is the Group Annuity Table for 1951 (Ga-1951). This table is usually used with a projection scale, which was developed along with the table, to compensate for increased longevity since the development of the table.

Ga-1951 is generally used as projected to 1960 (Ga-1960) or later. A recent study being used with increasing frequency is the 1971 Group Annuity Mortality Table published by the Society of Actuaries.

Another method of updating mortality tables is the age "set back" method, which compensates for the greater life expectancy of females. In applying the "set back" method, the attained age for each participant is simply set back the selected period of years; three to five years is normally used (e.g., a female age 62 will be assumed to be 59 if a three-year setback is used). A one-year setback is approximately equivalent to a ten-year projection of the Ga-1951 table. As a rule of thumb, a one-year setback or a ten-year projection will have about a 3 percent impact on costs.

¶ 7.04 TURNOVER ASSUMPTION

Many eligible participants will not stay to retirement. One reason is death; however, the more common reason is voluntary or involuntary terminations (i.e., turnover). Turnover incidence varies between companies, industries, and age groups, and by length of service and type of work force (e.g., blue collar versus white collar). Because of these variables, the turnover assumption can vary widely between plans and has a substantial impact on the actuarial valuation. Many actuaries select a turnover assumption on an aggregate basis, which assigns different turnover rates by each age. A more sophisticated method is called the select and ultimate method, which varies turnover rates by both age and length of service. For example, a participant age 55 with ten years of covered service has a greater probability of staying to retirement than a participant age 55 with one year of covered service.

In determining the appropriate turnover rates, the specific experience of the employer as well as current economic conditions should be considered; however, this is not always done. In general, an average turnover rate of 2 to 3 percent is considered low, while 7 to 11 percent is considered high.

¶ 7.05   DISABILITY ASSUMPTION

Turnover as defined by Accounting Principles Board (APB) Opinion No. 8 is termination of employment for a reason other than death. Disability may be combined with turnover or be considered as a separate assumption, depending on the type of plan or the form of the disability benefit. For example, a separate disability assumption might be made in a plan for foundry workers, but not in a plan for office employees. A separate disability assumption might also be made where disability benefits are provided in the pension plan and are unrelated to the value of retirement benefits (e.g., a flat amount per week). Valuing disability benefits (as well as death benefits and deferred vested benefits for terminated employees) is discussed later in this chapter.

In most cases, a separate disability assumption will have a minor impact on the actuarial valuation.

¶ 7.06   SALARY SCALE ASSUMPTION

When the defined benefit is expressed as a function of salary, a salary assumption should ordinarily be used to project the retirement benefit expected to be paid to each participant.

The purpose of using a salary scale is to project the level of compensation that will exist during the years the pension benefit will be determined. The primary factors affecting the salary scales are increased productivity and inflation.

Salary scales, usually expressed in terms of an annual percentage increase, may be developed based on experienced productivity increases adjusted for anticipated inflation, or they may be set arbitrarily. More sophisticated salary scales may reflect career promotion and productivity patterns, used in the salary scale assumption, or they may vary depending on age, job, and length of service. The inflation factor, however, should be consistent with the inflation factor, if any, used in the interest assumption.

For plans in which the defined benefit is expressed as a function of salary, the salary scale assumption will have a substantial effect on the actuarial valuation, especially where the retirement benefit is computed based on an average of final or highest years compensation. For example, a participant age 25 earning $10,000 will be expected to earn $97,035 at age 64 if a 6 percent annual increase was assumed. When the retirement benefit is related to current as well as future earnings of the participant, a salary scale tries to predict the actual future level of earnings in order to project the level of the retirement benefit. In selecting the appropriate scale to be used, the actuary should evaluate the special features of the employee group and current economic conditions.

¶ 7.07 RETIREMENT ASSUMPTION

Pension plans usually specify a normal retirement age; however, plans frequently permit participants to retire prior to or work past the normal retirement age. Early retirement is a more common valuation problem, the extent of the problem depends on the provisions of the plan. If the plan provides for early retirement benefits reduced to their actuarial equivalent, the valuation problems are minor.

Some plans, however, have been modified to provide early retirement benefits greater than the accrued benefits earned to date. In these cases, the actuary should include an assumption as to the rate of participant electing early retirement. If no assumption or other compensating adjustment is made, significant losses could result when unanticipated early retirements occur which would probably not surface in the actuarial valuation results until several years into the future.

¶ 7.08   EXPENSE ASSUMPTION

Expenses of a plan (e.g., professional fees, trustee fees, and Pension Benefit Guaranty Corporation (PBGC) premiums) may be paid either by the plan or directly by the plan sponsor. If expenses are paid directly by the plan sponsor, there is no effect on the funding requirements of the plan. If expenses are paid by the plan, the actuary should include an assumption as to the amount of these expenses in the valuation.

¶ 7.09   SOCIAL SECURITY INTEGRATION ASSUMPTIONS

Many pension plans integrate the retirement benefits with Social Security retirement benefits. The purpose of integration is to eliminate the double charge to the sponsor for providing retirement benefits under plans with defined benefit formulas based upon compensation. Since the sponsor is paying Federal Insurance Contributions Act (FICA) taxes on all participants up to the FICA wage base limitation (i.e., the "break point"), the pension plan can be designed to exclude from the plan's retirement benefit the Social Security benefit provided through sponsor contributions. Integration is therefore designed to provide a total retirement benefit (Social Security and the pension plan), which is an *equal percentage of compensation* for all participants.

The Internal Revenue Service (IRS) has a complex set of rules and regulations concerning the integration of a pension plan with Social Security. These rules are designed to ensure that the final integrated formula results in a total retirement benefit which is, at a minimum, an equal percentage of compensation for all participants and, at a maximum, equal to the results of nonintegration. Accordingly, the rules are designed to prohibit providing greater retirement benefits (as a percentage of compensation) to higher-paid participants. Because of the complex and changing nature of the Social Security system, these rules and regulations are quite complex and beyond the scope of this presentation. The IRS permits two basic methods of integrating the pension plan: step-rate and offset.

[1] Step-Rate Integration

Under this method the retirement benefit is determined from two tiers of earnings. One defined benefit rate is applied to earnings up to the break point (covered earnings), and a higher defined benefit rate is applied to the excess. The determination of the "break point" for each participant is governed by integration rules; however, the sponsor has the option to specify in the plan a

(1) Fixed break point (e.g., $6,600);
(2) Scheduled break point (e.g., table indexed fixed by year of birth: 1936—$5,400; 1937—$6,000; 1938—$6,600; etc.); or
(3) Floating break point (e.g., similar to scheduled break point except adjustments are made to the table for increases in the Social Security maximum wage base as they occur).

In theory, the break point is based upon the average of the FICA wage bases (covered earnings) during each participant's service career. In order to simplify the determination of the covered earnings, the IRS has permitted these three options. Once the break point has been specified in the plan (e.g., fixed amount or scheduled amounts), changes must be made through plan amendment and must satisfy integration regulations.

The easiest way for the accountant to determine if the plan is integrated by the step-rate basis is to review the defined benefit formula (i.e., an explicit statement concerning integration is usually not made). For example, a plan's benefit formula incorporating a fixed break point would state:

The annual retirement pension is the sum of (1) 10 percent of your covered compensation, and (2) 37.5 percent of your covered compensation in excess of $6,600.

As a special case, if, under a step-rate plan, the benefit rate applicable to compensation below the break point is nil, the plan is known as an (pure) excess plan.

[2] Offset Integration

The other major integration method is offset integration, under which a portion of the participant's primary Social Security benefit (PIA) is substracted from (offset against) the retirement benefit. The applicable PIA may be either "fixed" at the Social Security law in effect at a point of time (e.g., the 1958 law) or based on the actual Social Security law in effect at time of retirement (i.e., floating offset). Examples of defined benefit formulas under this method are:

- Your normal retirement benefit is determined by (1) 60 percent of your final average monthly compensation less (2) 50 percent of your primary Social Security benefit you are entitled at age 65.
- Your normal retirement benefit is equal to (1) 1½ percent of your average final compensation multiplied by the number of years of credited service less (2) 1½ percent of your Social Security benefit multiplied by the number of years of credited service.

Obviously, if the offset was based upon the prospective Social Security benefit in effect at retirement instead of the current (or previous) benefit, the plan sponsor would recognize cost savings (i.e., future Social Security benefits will be higher, resulting in a greater offset to each participant's benefits under the plan).

[3] Effect on Valuation

If a plan's step-rate break point is fixed or scheduled, or if the offset is fixed, no projection of Social Security changes is necessary or appropriate in the normal valuation. Of course, it might be "known" that a scheduled step-rate plan will be reintegrated by amendment to keep pace with Social Security—the same as it is "known" that benefits will increase the next time the collective-bargaining agreement opens up. However, it would run afoul of ERISA minimum funding requirements to anticipate cost savings not yet part of plan provisions, and tax-deductible limits would be faulted in the event of advance funding for benefits not yet in the plan.

For either floating break points or floating offsets, provision should be made for change (presumably, increases) in the FICA wage base levels (i.e., maximum taxable wage base). If the salary scale assumption is considered to be a combination of productivity and inflation, at least the inflation component should bear on the projection of the FICA wage base(s), since the 1972 amendments to the Social Security law, is governed, albeit indirectly, by inflation. For example, if the assumed annual rate of salary increase is 6 percent, the FICA wage base might be considered to increase at 5 percent per annum. (The law provides for increases in steps of $300 per year, but that provision is immaterial for valuation purposes.)

The Social Security law provides not only for escalation of the FICA wage base, but also for changes in the Consumer Price Index (CPI)—of the benefit factors applied to the average covered compensation. This CPI escalator applies both to Social Security benefits in course of payment and to prospective benefits, which affects the funding of offset plans, but not step-rate plans.

It could be assumed that the CPI will increase at about one-half of the rate of increase of the FICA wage base. (The "official" government figures in 1972 were 2¾ percent—CPI, and 5 percent—FICA wage base). Alternatively, and more in keeping with recent experience, the CPI assumption could be nearer to that of the FICA wage base; however, the compound effect of these two assumptions can rapidly result in Social Security retirement benefits exceeding the plan's retirement benefit. Therefore, the common-sense actuarial approach to this possibility is to put a replacement ratio cap on the Social Security offset (i.e., regardless of the projected Social Security results, the offset will never exceed 50 percent).

Finally, it is possible in an actuarial valuation to understate the cost *impact* of future compensation increases (i.e., to use too low a salary projection scale) and to understate the cost *savings* of future increases in Social Security. Because of the balancing nature of these two understatements, such a valuation might produce reasonable costs for a given year. However, the measurement of the cost savings resulting from integration would, by itself, be totally unrealistic if decisions were to be made as to possible changes by a sponsor in his approach to, or degree of, integration.

¶ 7.10 MULTIPLE DECREMENT APPROACH TO ACTUARIAL ASSUMPTIONS

The assumptions as to death, disability, and turnover all represent factors affecting the probability of a participant staying to retirement. These factors are often called decrements and can be considered individually or in combination. Individual consideration of these decrements involves more sophisticated techniques than the combined approach, but may be necessary to value potential death, disability, and termination (i.e., deferred vested benefits) benefits provided in the plan. The multiple decrement factors may be developed from the plan's historical experience or from a standard published table. For example, withdrawal factors reflecting multiple decrements (i.e., turnovers, deaths, and disability) could be developed from a table, as follows:

Age Beginning of Year	Remaining in Service, Beginning of Year	Turnovers	Withdrawals		Total
			Deaths	Disability	
55	1,000,000	29,386	3,317	1,990	34,693
56	965,307	35,455	3,336	2,669	31,460
57	936,877	21,720	4,026	2,684	28,430

From this table, the actuary develops the withdrawal factors used in the valuation, such as:

Probability of staying from age 55 to 56:

= employees staying to age 56 ÷ employees age 55

= 965,307 ÷ 1,000,000

= .965307

Benefit from employees age 55 terminating during year:

= 1 ÷ probability of staying from age 55 to age 56

= 1 ÷ .965307

= 1.035940

Withdrawal factors are used to estimate the benefits lost by the terminated participants which are shared by the participants that stay. However, withdrawal factors do not take into account the fact that terminated participants are usually entitled to the vested portion of benefits that have been earned. Generally, actuaries have developed two methods to compensate for the effects of vesting. One method separately determines each participant's probability of withdrawing, and multiplies this by the value of the vested benefit earned to date. This is the more accurate but also the more complex method of adjusting for the cost of vested benefits of terminated participants. Adjusting the decrement table for withdrawals relating only to nonvested benefits is the more common method.

[1] Adjustments for Nonvested Withdrawals

Assuming that participants withdrawing because of death or disability receive separate benefits (ancillary benefits) in lieu of vested benefits (thus, zero vesting upon the occurrence of these events), the modifications to the table are:

Participant's Age Beginning of Year	Turnovers During the Year	Estimated Nonvested Rates	Estimated Nonvested Terminations
55	29,386	50%	14,693
56	25,455	45%	11,455
57	21,720	40%	8,688

This is not a precise method since the actuary has to estimate the value of vested benefits. Vesting is a function of provisions in the plan and the length of service of the participant. A participant age 55 with ten years of credited service could be 60 percent vested, while an employee age 55 with one year of credited srvice could be 10 percent vested. The decrement table adjusted for vesting would be:

Age Beginning of Year	Remaining in Service Beginning of Year	Nonvested Withdrawals			
		Turnovers	Deaths	Disability	Total
55	1,000,000	14,693	3,317	1,990	20,000
56	980,000	11,455	3,336	2,669	17,640
57	962,360	8,688	4,026	2,684	15,398

Expanding this table for a ten-year period for the participant age 55 would result in the following withdrawal factors:

Partic- ipant's Age	Participant Activity During Year			Withdrawal Factors	
	Beginning	Withdrawals	Ending	Probability of Staying	Benefit From Termination
	(1)	(2)	(1) − (2) = (3)	(3) ÷ (1) = (4)	(1) ÷ (3) = (5)
55	1,000,000	20,000	980,000	.98000	1.0204
56	980,000	17,640	962,360	.98200	1.0183
57	962,360	15,398	946,962	.98400	1.0163
58	946,962	13,257	933,705	.98600	1.0142
59	933,705	11,204	922,501	.98800	1.0121
60	922,501	9,225	913,276	.99000	1.0101
61	913,276	7,306	905,970	.99200	1.0081
62	905,970	5,436	900,534	.99400	1.0060
63	900,534	3,603	896,931	.99600	1.0040
64	896,931	1,794	895,137	.99800	1.0020

From this table the actuary would estimate that a participant age 55 has a probability of staying to retirement of 89.5137 percent (participants remaining at retirement ÷ participants beginning of current year). In the determination of the actuarial value of projected benefits, the "discount factor" for the probability for staying to retirement would be .895137.

Assuming the amount needed at retirement was $53,572.00, the actuarial value of projected benefits ten years prior to retirement would be:

Amount needed at retirement	$53,572.00
Interest discount factor—6%	× .558394
Probability factor—from above	× .895137
	$26,777.38

In the example of actuarial present value determinations in Chapter 4, a 2 percent annual benefit from termination was assumed. This assumption reduced the number of calculations required in determining normal cost. In practice, the actuary must perform more sophisticated calculations to give efffect to varying annual benefits from termination rates on the determination of normal cost.

[2] Effect of Decreasing Benefit From Withdrawals

The first step to determine normal cost in this example would be to calculate the combined annuity due factor (as defined at ¶ 4.03[4]). This calculation, normally performed by the computer, would be:

Participant's Age Beginning of Year	Present Value of $1 Received Each Year—6%	Probability of Staying at Age 55 to Each Succeeding Plan Year	Discount Factor Each Year
	(1)	(2)	(1) × (2) = (3)
55	1.00000	1.00000	1.0000
56	.94340	.98000	.9245
57	.89000	.96236	.8565
58	.83962	.94696	.7950
59	.79209	.93370	.7395
60	.74726	.92250	.6893
61	.70496	.91328	.6438
62	.66506	.90597	.6025
63	.62741	.90053	.5650
64	.59190	.89693	.5308
COMBINED ANNUITY DUE FACTOR			7.3469

The calculation of normal cost would be the actuarial value of projected benefits divided by the combined annuity due factor:

$$\text{Normal Cost} = \$26,777.38 \div 7.3469$$
$$= \$3,644.71$$

Prior to the "age of computers" the actuaries used a number of "shortcuts" (e.g., constant benefit from withdrawals, summarizing participant data within age groupings, etc.) to reduce the number of manual calculations required in the valuation. With the aid of sophisticated computer software, the actuary can design a package to perform these calculations using more realistic approaches than previously permitted.

Theoretically, the actuary should perform a study of the sponsor's historical employment data and develop a decrement table to be used in the valuation. Due to practical problems in obtaining this historical data and not having a large enough employment base to develop statistically valid withdrawal factors for each age, this is not often performed. Instead, the actuary reviews the nature of the sponsor's business (for example, turnover among workers in a service industry might be less than among workers in a foundry), the vesting provisions of the plan, and the available employment data and decides on one of the standard withdrawal tables.

The standard withdrawal tables are referred to as turnover tables. The tables reflect varying rates of turnover by age ranging from very high turnover at lower ages and low turnover at higher ages to a somewhat level turnover rate for all ages. In using these tables, the effects of vesting must be considered separately (e.g., using a turnover table which results in less tabular turnover than actually expected).

¶ 7.11   VALUING ANCILLARY BENEFITS

Pension plans frequently provide benefits other than retirement income to participants. The most common of these benefits, referred to as ancillary benefits, are death and disability. The nature of death or disability ancillary benefits determines whether separately preretirement mortality and disability probabilities are required to value the additional cost, if any, of these benefits.

If the benefits are unrelated to retirement benefits (i.e., a fixed dollar amount), separate identification and valuation are desirable. Provision should be made for the cost of the death or disability benefits by separate computations or other adjustment. One method of adjustment would include the actuary using an unstated technique to provide for the cost of the ancillary benefit (e.g., selecting a lower-than-assumed interest rate in which future experience gains from interest would offset the "pay as you go cost" of the ancillary benefit(s)). As previously mentioned, the use of unstated techniques or shortcuts could be caused by the lack of sophistication of the actuary's computer software package.

The cost of the death benefit is a function of mortality rate and benefit provided. The cost of the disability benefit is a function of the rate of disability, the value of the disability payments, and the rate of recovery. These costs should be measured during the actuarial valuation, not on a pay-as-you-go basis.

Early retirement benefits or joint and survivor benefits without actuarial equivalent reductions in the retirement benefits are other forms of ancillary benefits. Accordingly, an assumption should be made as to the probability of payment (i.e., the number of participants who will choose these options), and the ancillary benefit should be valued (i.e., normal cost determined). The calculations required are similar to those demonstrated in Chapter 5 for valuing retirement benefits.

¶ 7.12 STANDARD ANNUITY FACTORS

Upon retirement, the calculation of the actuarial value of retirement payments is affected by the interest and the mortality assumptions. To simplify the computation required for retired participants, actuaries have developed standard annuity factors for each age. Annuity factors are developed by combining the mortality rate (reflects probability of payment) with the present value factors (reflects the time value of money), and represents the discount factors for the series of retirement payments expected to be made. For example, the 1951 Group Annuity Table projected to 1970 (Ga-1970) with a 6 percent interest assumption includes the following factors:

Attained Age	Life Annuity Factor
65	9.465
66	9.186
67	8.905
68	8.872

At retirement, supplemental actuarial value is equal to the actuarial present value of projected benefits used to allocate normal cost during the active service life of the participant by the actuarial valuation method selected. The supplemental actuarial value for each year thereafter is reduced by the retirement payment and increased for interest and the benefit of survivorship. Therefore, the change from age 65 to 66 was caused by:

Supplemental actuarial value, age 65	$53,572	(9.465 × $5,660)
Retirement benefit paid	(5,660)	
Investment earnings	3,045	
Benefit of survivorship	1,036	
SUPPLEMENTAL ACTUARIAL VALUE, AGE 66	$51,993	(9.186 × $5,660)

¶ 7.13 ACTUARIAL EQUIVALENT

The actuarial equivalent is defined as having an *equal* actuarial present value under a selected set of assumptions. If alternatives are provided by the plan, no special valuation problems are encountered if these alternatives are actuarially equivalent. For example, the plan could specify that the retiree select a retirement payment alternative in which the payments are guaranteed for a ten-year period and for life thereafter. If this alternative is not selected, the payments will be made for life with no other guarantee. The alternative provides the retiree with ten years' guaranteed payments regardless of mortality; it also costs more than one contingent on only mortality. This would create no special valuation problem if the plan stated that the alternative retirement payment is reduced to its actuarial equivalent as demonstrated by:

(1) *Determination of amount needed at retirement with no actuarial equivalent reduction.* Assume the participant will retire at age 65, will have earned an annual benefit of $5,660, and that the 1951 Group Annuity Table projected to 1970 with 6 percent interest is used to obtain the appropriate actuarial factors.

Retirement payment earned	$ 5,660.00
Ga (1970) annuity factor	× 9.465
AMOUNT NEEDED AT RETIREMENT	$53,572.00

To provide a life-time retirement payment of $5,660, the plan needs to accumulate $53,572 by retirement.

(2) *Determination of the actuarial equivalent retirement payment.* The applicable actuaial factor for a payment for ten years certain and life thereafter is 10.271.

Amount needed at retirement	$53,572.00
Ga (1970) annuity factor	÷ 10.271
REDUCED RETIREMENT PAYMENT	$ 5,216.00

By selecting this retirement alternative, the annual retirement payment is reduced $444 per year; however, the retiree (or his beneficiary) will receive the payments for a minimum of ten years.

Since the plan provides for an actuarial equivalent reduction, no cost is involved in selecting this alternative.

[1] Plan Alternative Not Reduced to Actuarial Equivalent

If a plan that provides this type of retirement alternative does not require an actuarial equivalent reduction, an experience loss (determined at the date of retirement) could result. For example, assume that the plan provides that the annual retirement benefit will only be reduced one percent for selecting the alternative. The calculation of the experience loss is demonstrated as follows:

(1) Determination of the reduced retirement payment:

Retirement payment earned	$ 5,660
1% Reduction specified in plan	.9900
REDUCED RETIREMENT PAYMENT	$ 5,603

(2) Determination of the amount needed at retirement:

Reduced retirement payment earned	$ 5,603
Ga (1970) annuity factor	× 10.271
AMOUNT NEEDED AT RETIREMENT	$57,548

(3) Calculation of the experience loss at retirement:

	Amount Needed at Retirement
Life with ten years certain	$57,548
Life only	53,572
EXPERIENCE LOSS	$ 3,976

If the actuary did not value this additional benefit (e.g., alternative retirement payment greater than its actuarial equivalent), the experience loss as demonstrated in this example would not surface until participant's retirement. If alternatives are not reduced by their actuarial equivalents, the actuary should include the probability of alternatives being selected (i.e., probability of payment) as an assumption in his valuation to avoid these potentially significant experience losses arising at retirement.

¶ 7.14 EFFECT OF INFLATION ON INTEREST AND SALARY SCALE

In discussing the interest and the salary scale assumptions, reference was made to the effect of inflation. Interest rates are sometimes considered to consist of (1) compensation for the use of money and (2) the effect of inflation. If, for example, 3½ percent is considered normal compensation for the use of money, the difference between 3½ percent and an assumed interest rate would be the assumed effect of inflation. Thus, in the long run, an interest rate of 7½ percent would assume a 4 percent inflation factor.

Since salary levels are considered to be affected by increased productivity and inflation, the salary scale assumption should include a factor for inflation similar to that developed for the interest assumption. For example, if productivity increases are expected to be 2 percent, a reasonable and consistent salary scale would be 6 percent (2 percent productivity factor and 4 percent inflation factor).

In the past, many actuaries have ignored the effects of inflation on both the interest and salary scale assumptions on the theory that the effects were offsetting. In fact, the offsetting effects of inflation in these assumptions on pension costs vary depending on the funding level of the plan and the benefit formula. In addition, recent experience has shown that while the effects of inflation are *usually* consistent as to investment return and salary levels, they are *not always* consistent. Recent stock market declines coupled with salary inflation have produced larger experience losses in plans where the effects of inflation were considered to be offsetting than in those where they were separately provided in each assumption.

The American Academy of Actuaries release, "Recommendations Regarding Determination of Actuarial Present Values Under Pension Plans," expresses a preference for the explicit recognition of inflation in each applicable actuarial assumption, and requires disclosure in the actuarial report if explicit recognition is not given to inflation.

¶ 7.15 SUMMARY

This chapter has described a number of the assumptions normally made for an actuarial valuation. Other assumptions may be necessary depending on the specific provisions of the plan (e.g., if benefits are adjusted for cost-of-living increases, an assumption as to this factor should be made). Whatever assumptions are made, the guidance given in the American Academy of Actuaries "Recommendation Regarding Determination of Actuarial Present Values Under Pension Plans" should be considered. The publication states:

> "The actuarial assumptions selected should represent the actuary's best judgment of future events affecting the related actuarial present value. They should take into account the actual experience of the covered group to the extent information is available and applicable, but in recognition of the nature of a pension plan, they should reflect long-term trends rather than give undue weight to short-term volatility in recent experience.

> "The actuary should consider the impact of inflation and the method of valuing assets in selecting the actuarial assumptions to be used.

> "The actuary should give consideration to the reasonableness of

each actuarial assumption independently on the basis of its own merits and to the combined impact of all the assumptions.

"The actuary should give careful attention to changes in plan design which may significantly alter the level and trend of expected future experience. For example, a liberalization of early retirement benefits may make advisable a revision in the retirement assumptions."

Chapter 8

ACTUARIAL VALUATION METHODS

¶ 8.01 GENERAL

The actuarial valuation method selected has a direct effect on the level of normal cost recognized as well on the supplemental actuarial value. Actuarial valuation methods differ only as to the respective proportion of a participant's benefits that are allocated to each plan year. At anticipated retirement, the supplemental actuarial value is equal to the actuarial value of projected benefits for a participant regardless of the actuarial valuation method used. Actuarial valuation methods were designed to allow the sponsor flexibility in selecting a *funding pattern* for the plan. As previously discussed at ¶ 6.03, the results of these valuation methods are also used by accountants in measuring annual expense of the plan.

Actuaries are primarily concerned with determining the year-by-year progression of plan contributions to insure that the sponsor can afford the total cost of a pension plan. Their role is similar to a mortgage banker computing the monthly payment for a young family thinking about buying a house. If a low initial mortgage payment is present which will balloon in subsequent years, the family might not be able to afford the increased payments. Accordingly, if the family is not cognizant of the later higher payments, they would have a false sense of security because of their ability to meet the low initial payments.

Actuarial valuation methods can be classified into accrued benefit methods (unit credit) or projected benefit methods. The accrued benefit method allocates the cost to a given year based on what was actually accrued by the participant for that year's service. Each year's computation of cost is based upon the plan provisions as they relate to that year's accrued benefit, and the total retirement benefit is not projected to retirement. The projected method estimates the retirement benefit and allocates cost to each year of service in a level amount per year or as a level percentage of salary. This method does not necessarily result in periodic matching of the accrued benefit earned with the cost recognized.

¶ 8.02 UNIT CREDIT METHOD (ACCRUED BENEFIT METHOD)

The unit credit method assigns the cost of the benefits earned during the year by the participant to each year of service. Normal cost relating to one participant increases each year since the time to retirement decreases (which reduces the effect of the discounts for interest and probability of staying to retirement). Normal cost also increases if the benefit formula gives additional benefits in the later years or relates the benefit to salary (which would tend to increase over time due to inflation and increases in productivity). Accordingly, the unit credit method is not as popular as the projected benefit method.

[1] Normal Cost Under Unit Credit Method

Assuming a participant age 55 earned a retirement benefit of $450 during the year, normal cost for the participant retiring in ten years at age 65 would be:

(1) Normal cost first year at age 55:

Accrued benefit earned during year	$ 450.00
Ga (1970) annuity factor with 6% interest	× 9.465
AMOUNT NEEDED AT RETIREMENT	$4,259.25

Normal cost would represent the amount needed at retirement discounted to the current valuation date (ten years prior) for interest earnings and the probability of staying to retirement:

Amount needed at retirement	$4,259.25
Combined discount factor (8.12% for 10 years)	× .458078
NORMAL COST YEAR 1	$1,951.07

(2) Normal cost second year at age 56:

Accrued benefit earned age 56	$ 475.00
Ga (1970) annuity factor with 6% interest	× 9.465
AMOUNT NEEDED AT RETIREMENT	$4,495.88

Since the time between the current valuation date and retirement date has decreased by one year, the combined discount factor relating to interest and the probability of staying has increased:

Amount needed at retirement	$4,495.88
Combined discount factor (8.12% for 9 years)	$\times$ .495274
NORMAL COST, YEAR 2	$2,226.69

Normal cost increased in year 2 for this participant because:

(1) The accrued benefit (equal to 1½ percent of salary) earned increased because the participant's salary increased.

(2) The preretirement period decreased by one year resulting in an increase in the discount factor relating to the interest assumption.

(3) The participant's probability of staying was assumed to increase as he approached retirement, resulting in an increase in the discount factor.

[2] Use of Unit Credit Method

As a result of this annual increase in the participant's normal cost under the unit credit method, plan sponsors wanting a more level cost per year would probably adopt one of the projected benefit methods. However, in theory when a plan covers a large number of participants, total normal cost could remain relatively stable under the unit credit method since younger participants (with low initial normal cost) would replace retiring participants (with higher normal cost). However, unless the group has matured to the point where the average age remains stable, normal cost (as related to salary) will increase.

The unit credit valuation method is generally used in plans with a defined benefit formula that assigns a readily determined benefit to each year of service, such as a flat dollar amount or percentage of current salary. When the benefit formula defines the retirement benefit in terms of salary during some period of future service, such as the average salary for the five years prior to retirement, actuaries generally do not feel this valuation method is appropriate.

[3] Modifications to Unit Credit Method

Sometimes the unit credit method is modified to obtain the results of a project method; this is accomplished by:

(1) Using a projected salary in lieu of the current year's salary to

obtain a more stable normal cost per year on an individual basis; or

(2) Eliminating the probability of staying to retirement, which would generate higher normal cost in the early years, but would reduce the expected higher normal cost in later years by the benefits from withdrawals. Therefore, the use of the unit credit method does not necessarily provide assurance that the normal cost is being computed on a basis of accrued benefits. Additional clarification is required to determine if this method has been adjusted for any unstated techniques.

¶ 8.03 PROJECTED BENEFIT METHODS—GENERAL

Projected benefit methods can be classified according to the manner in which supplemental cost is recognized in future valuations:

(1) By arbitrarily amortizing the unfunded supplemental actuarial value over a specified time period;

(2) By adjusting the current year's normal cost and the actuarial value of future normal costs; or

(3) By a combination of the two methods.

Under the first method, the difference between the supplemental actuarial value and the value of the plan assets is specifically identified, and is amortized. Under the second method this excess is added to the actuarial value of future normal costs, and therefore increases normal costs prospectively. These actuarial valuation methods explicitly do not have an unfunded supplemental actuarial value, since supplemental actuarial value is defined as being equal to the actuarial value of the assets. This can be demonstrated by continuing with the example first mentioned at ¶ 5.02[6]. Assume the tabular results of the actuarial computations performed as of January 1, 19X4 were:

Supplemental actuarial value	$11,951.02
Actuarial value of projected benefits	$31,016.69
Actuarial value of future normal costs	$19,065.67
Actuarial value of plan assets	$ 8,000.00
Normal costs for 19X4	$ 3,400.88

This valuation indicates an unfunded supplemental value of $3,951.02. Under the first projected benefit method, this would be amortized over a specific time period. The actuary using a valuation method without supplemental cost would perform the following calculations using the tabular data:

Actuarial value of projected benefits	$31,016.69
Supplemental actuarial value (defined as equal to assets)	− 8,000.00
DEFINED VALUE OF FUTURE NORMAL COSTS	$23,016.69
TABULAR VALUE OF FUTURE NORMAL COST	$19,065.67
Tabular normal cost	$ 3,400.88
Ratio of defined normal cost to tabular normal cost	× 1.20723
NORMAL COST, CURRENT YEAR	$ 4,105.65

Unfunded supplemental actuarial value is not recognized under the method. Normal costs are adjusted prospectively at each valuation to spread the effects of changes in the tabular unfunded supplemental actuarial value (prior service costs, experience gains or losses, etc.).

The third method is a hybrid approach combining the first two methods. At the initial actuarial valuation, the supplemental actuarial value arising from past service is determined and is "frozen." The sponsor would amortize this frozen supplemental value over a specific period. The other items affecting the unfunded supplemental value would be recognized pursuant to method (2) above. Only upon the occurrence of certain events would the frozen supplemental value be adjusted for reasons other than amortization. Many actuaries believe that it is appropriate to "unfreeze" this amount to reflect the retrospective effects of amendment(s) to the plan or a change in actuarial assumptions (i.e., actuarial revaluation gains or losses).

Projected methods can be further classified according to the method of computing the plan's normal cost: individual calculation for each participant or by one aggregate calculation using accumulated participant data (e.g., tabular data). Under the aggregate method, individual calculations are performed to arrive at tabular data for relevant salary, projected benefits, and other factors. These tabular results are aggregated for all participants to compute normal cost.

The various combinations of these classification methods give rise to several projected benefit methods that are currently acceptable under APB Opinion No. 8 in the determination of the sponsor's expense, and by the American Academy of Actuaries in the determination of normal costs.

The effect each actuarial valuation method has on the level of the annual pension expense is dependent on the choice of amortization period for the unfunded supplemental actuarial value recognized and the maturity of the work force. Thus, generalities concerning the relationship of one of the projected methods to another are difficult to make. Specific projected benefit methods are discussed in the following paragraphs.

¶ 8.04 ENTRY AGE NORMAL METHOD

The entry age normal method assigns a level normal cost to each year of service for each participant. Normal cost can be computed either as a level amount per year or a level percentage of salary. Entry age into the plan is established for each participant as the earliest time he would have been eligible under the plan had it been in existence. For participants hired after the adoption of the plan, it is the entry age as defined in the plan. Normal cost is computed for the period between the entry date and normal retirement date. For participants eligible at the adoption date of the plan, the initial supplemental actuarial value would equal the actuarial value of the normal cost assigned to years between credited entry date and adoption date of the plan.

The examples presented in Chapter 5 were based on the entry age normal valuation method using a "level dollar benefit," the annual cost being the sum of the normal cost plus supplemental cost—as selected from the available options permitted in Accounting Principles Board (APB) Opinion No. 8.

¶ 8.05 LEVEL PREMIUM METHOD

The level premium method assigns a level normal cost to each year of service subsequent to the adoption of the plan. The normal cost can be either a level amount per year or a level percentage of current salary. Normal cost is computed based on the period between the adoption of the plan and retirement date for each participant at the time of adoption (attained age of each participant). Since normal cost is not assigned to prior periods, initial supplemental actuarial value is not recognized. In effect, the "past service" cost is included with the current service cost as a part of normal cost for each year subsequent to the adoption. For participants hired after the adoption of the plan, the calculation is the same as under the entry age normal method.

Continuing with the example from Chapter 5, the normal cost for the participant age 58 at the adoption of the plan would be:

(1) Calculation of the actuarial value of projected benefits:

Projected benefit at retirement	$ 5,660
Ga (1970) annuity factor with 6% interest $\times$	9.465
AMOUNT NEEDED AT RETIREMENT	$53,572

The amount needed at retirement discounted for interest earnings at 6 percent and for the probability of staying seven years to retirement is:

Amount needed at retirement	$53,572.00
Actuarial discount factor (7 years at 8.12%)	$\times$ .578972
ACTUARIAL VALUE OF PROJECTED BENEFITS	$31,016.69

(2) Calculation of normal cost:

Actuarial value of projected benefits	$31,016.69
Combined annuity due factor (8.12% for 7 years)	$\div$ 5.60610
NORMAL COST	$ 5,532.67

The benefits earned during the period of total active service (ten years) are allocated over the remaining service career of the participant (seven years) by the level premium method. In the initial valuation, the difference between the normal retirement age and age at adoption of plan (attained age) of each participant is used as the period to assign normal cost; the initial supplemental actuarial value is zero because all normal costs are recognized prospectively.

¶ 8.06   COMPARISON OF RESULTS OF ENTRY AGE NORMAL AND LEVEL PREMIUM

The examples presented of the entry age normal and level premium methods can be compared at the initial valuation at the adoption of the plan:

	Entry Age Normal	Level Premium
Actuarial value of projected benefits (age 58)	$31,016.69	$31,016.69
Initial supplemental actuarial value	− 11,951.02	—0—
ACTUARIAL VALUE OF FUTURE NORMAL COSTS	$19,065.67	$31,016.69
NORMAL COST	$ 3,400.88	$ 5,532.67

The level of projected benefits was not affected by the actuarial valuation method selected. Under both methods, the actuarial value of projected benefits at the adoption of the plan was $31,016.69. Under the entry age normal method, normal costs assigned to periods prior to the adoption of the plan (as measured by the initial supplemental actuarial value) result in unfunded supplemental actuarial value. Supplemental cost is determined from factors (i.e., amortization period) unrelated to participants. On the other hand, the level premium method assigns the benefits arising from past periods to the remaining service career as normal cost. Accordingly, the level premium method is not as popular as the entry age normal method because of the "quick" amortization of the past service cost. The entry age normal method permits the sponsor more flexibility in determining the period in which "past service cost" is recognized.

¶ 8.07   ENTRY AGE NORMAL WITH FROZEN INITIAL SUPPLEMENTAL VALUE

The entry age normal method with frozen initial supplemental value is a commonly used variation of the entry age method. The frozen initial method does not explicitly recognize experience gains and losses, and accordingly, they do not affect unfunded supplemental actuarial value. Instead, experience gains and losses are recognized as prospective adjustments to normal costs.

The supplemental actuarial value as determined under the entry age normal method is "frozen" at the adoption of the plan. In subsequent valuations, this "frozen value" is decreased by the sponsor's recognition of supplemental cost. In practice, the initial frozen supplemental value is usually "unfrozen" on the occurrence of:

- Actuarial revaluation gain or loss; or
- Amendments to the plan which result in creating prior service cost.

The calculations required under this valuation method can be demonstrated, by continuing with the example of the participant age 58 at the adoption of the plan and given three years' past service credit.

(1) The frozen initial supplemental value at the adoption of the plan would be:

Actuarial value of projected benefits age 58	$31,016.69
Actuarial value of future normal cost	− 19,065.67
INITIAL SUPPLEMENTAL ACTUARIAL VALUE	$11,951.02
NORMAL COST	$ 3,400.88

The valuation process is identical with that under the entry age normal method at the initial valuation of the plan. The computation of normal cost for the second plan year would rely on the same *tabular data* generated from the entry age normal method. Tabular data is defined as the output from the actuary's calculations performed on an individual basis (usually computerized).

(2) Tabular data generated second valuation:

Actuarial value of projected benefits age 59	$33,535.25
Supplemental actuarial value	− 16,598.47
TABULAR ACTUARIAL VALUE OF FUTURE NORMAL COSTS	$16,936.78
TABULAR NORMAL COST	$ 3,400.88

These methods differ in the use of this tabular data by the actuary, since the individual calculations are the same. For example, assume an experience loss of $500 was recognized in the second valuation. The entry age normal method would recognize the $500 experience loss as an addition to the unfunded supplemental actuarial value, which would change supplemental cost but not affect normal cost. The frozen initial method would recognize the $500 experience loss as an adjustment to future normal costs through a manual adjustment.

(3) Computation of normal costs:

Tabular actuarial value of future normal cost	$16,936.78
Experience loss	+ 500.00
DEFINED ACTUARIAL VALUE OF FUTURE NORMAL COSTS	$17,436.78
Tabular normal cost	$ 3,400.88
Ratio of defined future normal cost to tabular future normal cost	× 1.02952
NORMAL COST	$ 3,501.28

The experience loss is manually added to the tabular actuarial value of future normal costs performed on an aggregate basis.

The use of the frozen initial method can obscure the history of experience gains and losses since they are not separately identified in the actuarial report. In addition, this method can give the sponsor a false sense of security by seeing regular reductions in the unfunded supplemental actuarial value (when amortized over a specific period).

A comparison of the valuation results for the second plan year (participant age 59) between these methods is as follows:

	Entry Age Normal	Frozen Initial	Difference
Actuarial value of projected benefits	$33,535.25	$33,535.25	$ —
Supplemental actuarial value	16,598.47	16,098.47	(500.00)
ACTUARIAL VALUE OF FUTURE NORMAL COST	$16,936.78	$17,436.78	$ 500.00
NORMAL COST	$ 3,400.88	$ 3,501.28	$ 100.40

As demonstrated, the frozen initial variation of the entry age normal method changes the incidence of cost since experience gains and losses adjust future normal costs. The tabular data and calculations are identical for these two methods except for the manual aggregate adjustment made by the actuary. The frozen initial method offers the actuary two advantages over the entry age normal method:

(1) Recognizing experience gains and losses as adjustments to normal costs removes this element from being recognized over an arbitrary amortization method.

(2) Unfunded supplemental actuarial value only decreases, by definition (assuming it is amortized over a fixed period).

¶ 8.08 AGGREGATE METHOD

The aggregate method allocates the actuarial value of projected benefits over the combined future compensation or combined service careers of the active participants. At the adoption of the plan, this method permits a longer recognition period for "past service cost" for those nearing retirement. For example, if a participant was one year from retirement and was given nine years' past service credit, the level premium method would allocate the previous nine years' service credits during the remaining one active service year. The aggregate method would recognize nine years' past service over a longer period based upon the mix of all participants in the plan. Comparison of the aggregate method with the unit credit and entry age normal methods is more difficult, since under these methods nine years' past service credited would result in an unfunded supplemental actuarial value which would be recognized over an arbitrary period as supplemental cost.

[1] Calculation of Normal Cost—Year 1

The actuarial calculations required for normal cost can be demonstrated by expanding the previous example and assuming:

(1) There are two participants in the plan who began employment at age 55 and were given credit for service between age 55 and the adoption date of the plan;

(2) At the adoption of the plan, one participant was 58 (three years' credited service) and the other was 64 (nine years' credited service);

(3) Cost is recognized as a level amount per year;

(4) Normal retirement age is 65; and

(5) The salary at each age and the plan's defined benefit formula are the same as presented in the table at ¶ 5.05.

(1) Tabular calculation of participant data at adoption of plan, year 1:

	Participant Age 58	Participant Age 64	Tabular Data
Amount needed at retirement	$53,572.00	$53,572.00	
Combined discount factor	× .578972	× .924898	
ACTUARIAL VALUE OF PROJECTED BENEFITS	$31,016.69	$49,548.64	$80,565.33
Combined annuity due factor	5.606100	1.000000	6.606100
NORMAL COST, LEVEL PREMIUM METHOD	$ 5,532.67	$49,548.64	$55,081.31

If the level premium method was selected, normal costs at the adoption of the plan would be $55,081.31. This cost is significantly influenced by the participant age 64 being given nine years' past service credit while having only one year of remaining service. Using this tabular data, the actuary will make a manual computation to arrive at the results of the aggregate method.

(2) Manual calculation of normal cost, year 1:

	Aggregate Computation
Actuarial value of projected benefits	$80,565.33
Supplemental actuarial value	—0—
Actuarial value of future normal costs	$80,565.33
Aggregate annuity due factor	÷ 6.606100
NORMAL COST FOR EACH PARTICIPANT	$12,195.60

The actuarial value of projected benefits is combined and allocated over the aggregate service careers of the participants. In this example, normal cost was based upon a level dollar assigned for each year of service. The sponsor's normal cost would be $24,391.20, using the aggregate method, and $55,081.31, using the level premium method.

[2] Calculation of Normal Cost—Year 2

The valuation for the second year would be based upon one active participant, since the other has retired.

(3) Tabular calculation of participant data, year 2:

	Participant Age 59	Participant Age 65	Tabular Data
Amount needed at retirement	$53,572.00	$53,572.00	
Combined discount factor	× .625985	× 1.000000	
ACTUARIAL VALUE OF PROJECTED BENEFITS	$33,535.27	$53,572.00	$87,107.27
NORMAL COST, LEVEL PREMIUM METHOD	$ 5,532.67	—	$ 5,532.67

(4) Manual calculation of normal cost, year 2:

	Aggregate Computation
Actuarial value of projected benefits	$87,107.27
Supplemental actuarial value	− 26,371.74
Actuarial value of future normal costs	60,735.53
Combined annuity due factor	÷ 4.980118
NORMAL COST FOR EACH ACTIVE PARTICIPANT	$12,195.60

Normal cost would be $12,195.60 in the second year compared to $5,532.67 if the level premium method was selected. The difference in normal cost represents the cost of the benefits provided to the retired participant, being recognized over the service career of the active participant. This demonstrates the effect of allocating the "past service costs" (i.e., initial supplemental actuarial value) over the combined service careers of the active participants. The magnitude of the difference between the level premium and aggregate method will depend on the number of participants near retirement in an actual valuation.

¶ 8.09 GENERAL COMPARISION OF METHODS

The three basic actuarial methods are unit credit, entry age normal, and level premium. Other methods presently used by actuaries are the result of modification to these three. For the participant in the example, the supplemental actuarial value *at the end* of each year would be:

	Participant Service	Plan Year	Unit Credit	Entry Age Normal	Level Premium
			Actuarial Valuation Methods		
Prior to	1		$ 2,109.50	$ 3,677.03	—
Plan	2		4,678.15	7,652.64	—
Establishment	3		7,776.08	11,951.06	—
After	4	1	11,494.40	16,598.52	$ 5,981.92
Plan	5	2	15,931.85	21,623.35	12,449.57
Establishment	6	3	21,201.17	27,056.20	19,442.41
	7	4	27,438.35	32,930.20	27,003.05
	8	5	34,791.56	39,281.15	35,177.62
	9	6	43,438.15	46,147.82	44,015.97
Normal Retirement	10	7	53,572.00	53,572.00	53,572.00

At retirement, the supplemental actuarial value under these methods is equal to the amount needed at retirement. Annual pension expense under these three methods can be compared once the amortization pattern for unfunded supplemental value is selected. Since the participant's service was seven years at the adoption of the plan, a seven-year amortization period was selected in this example:

	Unit Credit	Entry Age Normal
Unfunded supplemental value	$ 7,776.08	$11,951.06
Annuity factor— 7 years at 6%	÷ 5.917324	÷ 5.917324
AMORTIZATION	$ 1,314.12	$ 2,019.67

The annual cost is the sum of the normal cost and amortization of the unfunded supplemental actuarial value (supplemental cost):

Plan Year	Unit Credit	Entry Age Normal	Level Premium Method
1	$ 4,169.19	$ 5,420.55	$ 5,532.67
2	4,555.07	5,420.55	5,532.67
3	4,991.19	5,420.55	5,532.67
4	5,490.63	5,420.55	5,532.67
5	6,054.42	5,420.55	5,532.67
6	6,698.43	5,420.55	5,532.67
7	7,424.52	5,420.55	5,532.67
	$39,383.45	$37,943.85	$38,728.69

The slight variations in the total cost are caused by the assumed accounting effects of interest and the probability of staying to retirement. The unit credit method results in a slower accumulation of assets (assuming costs are funded as accrued) which generates less interest earnings by the plan; therefore, sponsor contributions must make up the difference. If the unfunded supplemental actuarial value was amortized at 8.12 percent (equivalent to combined effects of discount for interest and probability of staying to retirement in our example), the results under the entry age normal would be identical to the level premium method in this example.

In actual practice, however, there would be a more significant difference between the entry age normal and level premium methods because the amortization period for the unfunded supplemental actuarial value would ordinarily range from thirty to forty years.

The unit credit method results in less cost being assigned to the early years and more cost being assigned in the later years than does the entry age normal method. If the sponsor has a mature (i.e., average participant age remaining constant over time) work force, there could be little difference in the total annual cost because of the age mix of participants. Therefore, the accountant must use extreme care in forming generalities about these methods in actual practice.

Actuarial valuation methods differ only to the extent of cost assigned to each plan year. The total actual cost of the retirement benefit is the same regardless of the valuation method used, and is a function of the number of retirement payments made. Since the actual cost is not known for fifty or more years for the current group of plan participants, these actuarial valuation methods were designed to estimate the periodic funding requirements in the interim, and have been used to determine pension expense by the accountant.

¶ 8.10   SUMMARY

There are many actuarial valuation methods and even more terms used in describing each method. However, each valuation method, regardless of the term(s) used, has a unique set of characateristics. A valuation method should be viewed considering these characteristics when comparing or understanding the method. These unique characteristics include the following:

☐ *Participant group.* The method is either based upon existing participants in the valuation (closed group) or makes assumptions concerning new entrants to the plan in subsequent years (open group). Most actuarial valuations are performed on the closed-group basis.

☐ *Benefit determinations.* The method is either based upon using accrued benefits without assumptions as to future projected benefits (unprojected benefits—i.e., unit credit method) or projecting the retirement benefits (projected benefits) in valuation determinations.

☐ *Recognition of supplemental cost.* The method could give full, partial (i.e., frozen initial), or no recognition to unfunded supplemental actuarial value. Since the ultimate cost of a plan is not affected by the valuation method selected, the differences in this characteristic affect the annual incidence of normal and supplemental elements of the sponsor's cost.

☐ *Dollar cost.* Normal cost can be determined as a flat amount per participant per year (level dollar benefit method) or as a level percentage of each year's salary (level percentage of pay benefit method).

The examples presented in this section were based upon the level dollar method.

☐ *Age basis.* Normal costs are either computed on the basis of the participant's age at the date of the valuation (attained age basis) or using the participant's age at which he first was included or would have been included if the plan had always been in effect (entry age basis).

☐ *Calculation approach.* The actuarial determinations would be based upon the summation of individual participant calculations (individual approach) or the aggregate tabular data being used to manually calculate results (aggregate approach).

In reviewing an actuarial valuation, the treatment of these factors is more important to the understanding of the approach than the descriptive title. The actuarial valuation methods described in this section could be defined in the following manner:

Characteristic	*Unit Credit*	*Entry Age Normal*	*Frozen Initial*	*Level Premium*	*Aggregate*
(1) Participant group	Closed	Closed	Closed	Closed	Closed
(2) Benefit determination	Unprojected	Projected	Projected	Projected	Projected
(3) Recognition of supplemental cost	Full	Full	Partial	None	None
(4) Dollar cost	Level dollar	Level dollar	Level dollar	Level dollar	Level dollar
(5) Age basis	Entry age	Entry age	Entry age	Attained age	Attained age
(6) Calculation approach	Individual	Individual	Individual	Individual	Aggregate

These six characteristics represent ninety-six possible combinations. Therefore, an understanding of the characteristics of the valuation method selected by the actuary is necessary to understand the valuation results. For example, a valuation method not recognizing supplemental cost will not identify unfunded supplemental actuarial value (regardless of designation as unfunded past service, unfunded prior service, etc.). This method's valuation results would not be comparable to a valuation method giving full recognition to supplemental cost, but which, because of the level of the assets, has no unfunded supplemental actuarial value.

Chapter 9

PLAN EXPERIENCE GAINS AND LOSSES

¶ 9.01 INTRODUCTION

In previous chapters, the experience of the plan was assumed to correspond precisely to the actuarial assumptions. Regardless of the care exercised in this selection, though, assumptions are going to be "wrong." During the current valuation of a pension plan, the degree of variation developed from the prior valuation can be measured in the aggregate and would represent the experience gain or loss. Many actuarial reports do not specifically identify the period's gain or loss; however, this can frequently be developed from the data provided. Since experience gain or loss measures the degree of variance of actual to assumed experience, a long and consistent pattern of significant variances would indicate the assumptions may not be reasonable and realistic in the aggregate.

The difference between the value of the plan's assets and the supplemental actuarial value is the unfunded supplemental value, which provides the basis for determining the experience gain or loss. The procedures to determine the gain or loss would be identical under the unit credit method or the entry age normal method. If the actuary uses a projected method computed on a basis without supplemental value, the measurement of the gain or loss is much more difficult and is beyond the scope of this chapter.

¶ 9.02 MEASURING EXPERIENCE GAIN OR LOSS UNDER THE ENTRY AGE NORMAL METHOD

Assume the results of the valuation dated January 1, 19X3 relating to a participant were:

Normal cost for 19X3	$3,400.88
Supplemental actuarial value at January 1, 19X3	$7,652.63
Value of plan assets at January 1, 19X3	− 6,776.19
UNFUNDED SUPPLEMENTAL ACTUARIAL VALUE	$ 876.44

If the sponsor's contribution for 19X3 consisted of normal cost and amortization of the unfunded supplemental actuarial value (over a ten-year period with 6 percent interest) and was contributed on January 1, 19X3, the contribution would be:

(1) Calculation of supplemental cost:

Unfunded supplemental actuarial value	$ 876.44
Annuity due factor (10 years at 6%)	÷ 7.801692
19X3 SUPPLEMENTAL COST	$ 112.34

(2) Calculation of contribution for 19X3:

Supplemental cost	$ 112.34
Normal cost	+ 3,400.88
19X3 CONTRIBUTION	$3,513.22

Assume the succeeding valuation (dated January 1, 19X4) relating to the participant was:

Normal cost for 19X4	$3,473.57
Supplemental actuarial value at January 1, 19X4	$12,206.50
Value of plan assets at January 1, 19X4	− 11,099.16
UNFUNDED SUPPLEMENTAL ACTUARIAL VALUE	$ 1,107.34

From a comparison of the two valuations, it becomes obvious that a net experience loss occurred during 19X3 because:

(1) Normal cost was computed on the "level dollar" concept (e.g., each year's normal cost remaining constant); however, normal cost increased from $3,400.88 to $3,473.57; and

(2) The unfunded supplemental actuarial value increased from $876.44 to $1,077.34, even though the sponsor was amortizing this over ten years (i.e., balance should have declined).

In an actual valuation covering a large group, a comparison of normal cost (either as a level dollar or level percentage of compensation) would not be the most reliable indicator of the existence of experience gains and losses. The level of normal cost would be affected by the participant mix in addition to experience gains and losses. Accordingly, the key indicator is the unfunded supplemental value which provides the basis for measuring the level of the experience gain or loss. The following reconciliation will measure the level of the experience loss from the data provided:

(1) Anticipated unfunded supplemental actuarial value:

Unfunded supplemental actuarial value January 1, 19X3	$ 876.44
Assumed interest rate used in valuation ×	1.06
Unfunded value assuming no contribution	929.03
Contribution—supplemental cost for 19X3	— 112.34
ANTICIPATED VALUE AT DECEMBER 31, 19X3	$ 816.69

(2) Measurement of experience loss:

Actual unfunded supplemental value, January 1, 19X4	$1,107.34
Anticipated value from step 1	— 816.69
19X3 EXPERIENCE LOSS	$ 290.65

The measurement of experience gain or loss is determined by the relationship of the unfunded supplemental actuarial value at the end of the year to that anticipated. The determination of the underlying *causes* of the experience loss requires more sophisticated analysis than is intended in this presentation; however, the actuary should be able to determine the portion of the gain or loss attributed to investment assumptions and the portion attributed to noninvestment assumptions. The following analysis will measure the level of the experience loss attributed to investment results in this example:

(1) Antcipated investment earnings:

Supplemental actuarial value January 1, 19X3	$ 7,652.63
Normal cost for 19X3	+ 3,400.88
Assumed assets in plan	11,053.51
Interest assumption ×	.06
ASSUMED INTEREST EARNINGS	$ 663.21

(2) Assumed level of assets at December 31, 19X3:

Assets as of January 1, 19X3	$ 6,776.19
Contribution for 19X3	3,513.22
Assumed interest earnings	663.21
Less: Interest elements of sponsors' contribution (unfunded at January 1 times interest assumption)	(52.59)
ASSUMED LEVEL OF ASSETS	$10,900.03

(3) Measurement of investment gain or loss:

Value of assets at December 31, 19X3	$11,099.16
Assumed value of assets at December 31, 19X3	− 10,900.03
INVESTMENT GAIN FOR 19X3	$ 199.13

The plan's experience loss was $290.65; therefore, the portion attributed to noninvestment assumptions was:

19X3 Plan experience	$ 290.65
Investment experience gain	+ 199.13
NONINVESTMENT EXPERIENCE LOSS	$ 489.78

As previously mentioned, analyzing the noninvestment experience loss by assumption (e.g., salary scale and probability of staying to retirement) would require analysis outside the scope of most actuarial valuations; however, the individual reasons for variance are important in evaluating the long-term reasonableness of the assumptions chosen.

¶ 9.03   EFFECT OF EXPERIENCE GAINS OR LOSSES

A deviation between actual and assumed experience will have a direct effect on the actuarial valuation. The effect will result in a change in the level of supplemental cost and/or normal cost depending on the "faulty" assumption(s). In the previous example, the unstated reason for the net experience loss for 19X3 was the salary scale assumption.

The measurement of the experience loss relating to the salary scale assumption is subject to the same degree of complexity as the other noninvestment actuarial assumptions. In the previous example, the participant's salary increased 8 percent on January 1, 19X4, rather than the 5 percent assumed. The higher salary level was used as the basis for applying the 5 percent assumed increase in salary from the current valuation date through retirement. This resulted in the following estimation of the projected benefit:

Age	Plan Year	Assumed Experience	Adjusted Experience
55	19X1	$ 30,000	$ 30,000 actual
56	19X2	31,500	31,500 actual
57	19X3	33,076	33,076 actual
58	19X4	34,728	35,722 actual
59	19X5	36,466	37,508
60	19X6	38,288	39,384
61	19X7	40,202	41,353
62	19X8	42,214	43,421
63	19X9	44,324	45,592
64	19X0	46,540	47,872
Total Salary		377,338	385,428
Benefit Formula		$\times$ .015	$\times$ .015
PROJECTED BENEFIT		$ 5,660	$ 5,781

Not only did the 19X3 deviation of 3 percent increase the annual salary level for 19X4, but also for each succeeding year (5 percent assumption's effect on a higher 19X4 base salary), which increased the projected benefit by $121.

The increase in the projected benefit caused a corresponding increase in the amount needed at retirement and the actuarial value of projected benefits, which resulted in normal cost increasing from $3,400.88 for 19X3 to $3,473.57 for 19X4. The effect of the increase in normal cost as related to prior years caused an experience loss of $290.65. Accordingly, the 19X3 deviation had a prospective (increase in future normal costs) as well as retrospective (increase in future supplemental costs) effect on the valuation.

If the plan's benefit formula gives greater weight to final earnings (e.g., average of highest three years' salary), a deviation in the salary assumption will have a more significant impact than demonstrated by this example. Therefore, the effect on the sponsor's contribution is a function not only of the magnitude of the deviation, but also of the benefit formula defined in the plan.

¶ 9.04   ACTUARIAL REVALUATION GAINS AND LOSSES

Actuarial revaluation gains and losses result from a change in either the actuarial valuation method or actuarial assumption(s). A change in an actuarial assumption would occur when the actuary believes the assumption used no longer is reflective of future experience. The actuary is concerned with the long-term reasonableness of each assumption selected; this requires a historical analysis of the underlying causes of experience gains and losses as well as a prospective analysis of conditions and trends having an effect on future valuations. The latter analysis could require a change in an assumption which had been reasonable based on historical analysis. For example, any of the following conditions could suggest the need for a change in an assumption:

- Different rates of inflation being prospectively anticipated;
- Sponsor's industry on the decline (indicating greater turnover through layoffs, plant closings, etc.);
- Sponsor's decision to increase benefits for retired participants beyond that required by the plan; or
- Trends in earlier retirement by the work force.

This represents a partial listing of conditions which could result in changes in assumptions which were reasonable in the past, but may no longer be reasonable for the future.

If a change in an invalid assumption is not made, the actuarial valuation process is "self-correcting," but only to a limited extent. This self-correction process adjusts only the current year's deviation over a prospective period. For example, a one-year deviation in the salary scale assumption from 5 to 8 percent resulted in an experience loss which would be recognized over a prospective period (as an increase in supplemental cost) and an increase in *future* normal cost. If 8 percent per annum represented the long-term annual increase in this participant's salary (but the assumption remained at 5 percent), each succeeding year the normal cost would increase and an experience loss would occur (as previously demonstrated for 19X3). Changing the salary scale assumption to 8 per percent would have a more immediate effect. For example, assume the assumption was changed in the January 1, 19X4 valuation:

	5% Original Assumption	Continuing With 5% Assumption After an 8% Increase in 19X3	8% Revised Assumption
Total salary projectd	$377,338	$385,428	$413,318
Benefit formula	× .015	× .015	× .015
PROJECTED BENEFITS	$ 5,660	$ 5,872	$ 6,200

Given these levels of the projected benefit, the January 1, 19X4 valuation would result in:

Normal cost	$3,400.88	$3,473.57	$3,725.33
Percentage increase	—	2.1%	9.5%
Unfunded supplemental	$ 816.69	$1,107.34	$1,992.06
Percentage increase	—	35.6%	143.9%

If the one-year deviation (salary increasing 8 percent instead of 5 percent represents a long-range trend, significant distortion of the results of the valuation can occur. Even though the current valuation's "self-correction" increased normal costs by 2.1 percent, normal cost should have increased by 9.5 percent (which is over four times the "self-correction" increase). In addition, if 8 percent was the actual annual salary increase for this participant, normal costs would increase every year if the salary assumption was not changed and an annual experience loss would result. Accordingly, if experience is consistently at variance with an assumption (e.g., the salary scale assumption in this example), a significant under/over statement of the normal cost and unfunded supplemental actuarial value could result. If the assumption was changed, the actuarial revaluation loss would be equal to the difference between the original and revised unfunded supplemental actuarial value.

¶ 9.05 MEASURING EXPERIENCE GAIN OR LOSS UNDER METHODS OTHER THAN UNIT CREDIT OR ENTRY AGE NORMAL

The level premium aggregate cost and frozen initial methods do not explicitly recognize experience gains and losses, but, rather, recognize them implicitly as prospective adjustments to the normal cost. To measure the level of gains and losses, complicated actuarial calculations are required. Because of the added cost of performing these calculations, many actuarial reports, particularly those for plans using these actuarial valuation methods do not routinely disclose experience gains and losses.

¶ 9.06 INQUIRY AS TO GAINS AND LOSSES

As illustrated, it is possible to develop the gross, but not individual, experience gain or loss for a plan using the unit credit or entry age normal method from the data given in the actuarial report—which is not true with respect to many other methods. Since measurement of experience gains and losses is important in assessing the reasonableness of actuarial assumptions, it would not be unreasonable for a plan to request such information from the actuary. When making such a request, however, the plan should be aware of the probable additional calculations necessary and the related additional cost.

Part III

REGULATORY REQUIREMENTS; GENERALLY ACCEPTED ACCOUNTING PRINCIPLES

Chapter 10

REGULATORY REPORTING AND DISCLOSURE REQUIREMENTS

¶ 10.01 INTRODUCTION

The Employee Retirement Income Security Act of 1974 (ERISA) has significantly increased the reporting and disclosure requirements for employee benefit plans. These ERISA requirements include reports to the Department of Labor (DOL), the Internal Revenue Service (IRS), and the Pension Benefit Guaranty Corporation (PBGC), as well as disclosures to plan participants and beneficiaries. Of primary concern to auditors is the joint annual return/report (series 5500 forms) to be filed with the IRS and made available to the DOL, and the summary annual report to be distributed to plan participants and beneficiaries. These reports are primarily of concern to auditors because of the DOL requirements for audited financial statements. In addition, certain types of plans (primarily those involving allocation of employer securities to participants) may also be subject to the registration and annual reporting requirements of the Securities and Exchange Commission (SEC).

This chapter discusses the financial statement and annual reporting requirements of the DOL, IRS, and SEC. Also included is a summary of the various other reporting and disclosure requirements of ERISA.

¶ 10.02   ANNUAL RETURN/REPORT—SERIES 5500 FORMS

The 5500 series of forms are the annual reporting forms prescribed by the IRS and the DOL. For 1977 and subsequent years, the 5500 series is also the PBGC Annual Report. Separate forms have been designed for large and small plans. Plans with 100 or more participants at the beginning of the plan year are required to file on Form 5500, while plans with less than 100 participants may file a simplified Form 5500-C. A further simplified Form 5500-K is provided for Keogh plans with less than 100 participants.

Form 5500 is a six-page form, the specific requirements of which are discussed later in this chapter. The general contents include information identifying the plan, the plan sponsor, and the plan administrator, the type of plan and its operations; participants in the plan and employees of the sponsor; plan amendments, termination, or merger; and, financial, insurance, and actuarial information. Financial information, including assets, liabilities, income, expenses, and other changes in net assets, is included in items 13, 14, and 22 of the form, while the insurance and actuarial information is included in separate Schedules A and B, respectively.

Form 5500-C is a three-page form; however, most of the substantive information required to be filed on Form 5500 is also required on Form 5500-C. Form 5500-K is a two-page form which does not require much of the detailed financial information.

In addition to the financial information included in the forms, Section 2520 of the Department of Labor Rules and Regulations for Reporting and Disclosure under the Employee Retirement Income Security Act of 1974 (DOL Regulations) requires plans with 100 or more participants filing on Form 5500 to attach separate financial statement and schedules, and an accountant's report on the financial statements and schedules. In preparing the regulations, the DOL determined that certain of the statutory reporting requirements provided in ERISA were unnecessarily burdensome. As a result, certain alternative methods for financial reporting were included in the regulations. The regulations provide that financial statements and schedules may be included in compliance with Section 103 of ERISA (statutory method) or, alternatively, in compliance with the requirements of the regulations (alternative method).

The principal difference between the statutory method and the alternative method is that under the statutory method the financial statements are to be prepared in conformity with generally accepted accounting principles, whereas the alternative method allows variances from generally accepted accounting principles. Accordingly, the cash- or modified-accrual basis of accounting is acceptable under the alternative method. The alternative method requires all assets and liabilities to be stated at current value. There are other differences, such as schedule requirements, which are discussed at ¶ 10.04.

[1] Limited Exemption From Financial Requirements

Certain plans *covering 100 or more participants* have been granted a limited exemption from filing financial statements, schedules, and an accountant's report, and from completing the financial information sections of Form 5500. Plans granted this exemption include:

- Unfunded welfare plans;
- Fully insured welfare plans;
- Combination unfunded and fully insured welfare plans;
- Fully insured pension plans.

Definitions of what constitute unfunded and fully insured plans are included in the regulations. A fully insured pension plan is one whose benefits are provided exclusively through insurance contracts or policies, and whose assets are held solely in the general account of the insurance company.

The only asset of some plans is a deposit in the *general account* (as opposed to investments in separate accounts) of an insurance company under a deposit administration contract or an immediate participation guarantee contract. In the past, there has been some confusion as to whether such plans need to engage an auditor and complete the financial sections of the form.

The DOL has been issuing an interpretation letter on request indicating that the criteria for a fully insured plan would not typically be satisfied where plan assets are held in deposit administration or immediate participation guarantee accounts. Final DOL reporting regulations issued on March 10, 1978 state the exemption for unfunded plans "only applies to a pension plan funded entirely with allocated insurance contracts where benefits are fully guaranteed by the insurance company or organization that issued the policy." In addition, the instructions to item 13(f) of the 1977 5500 series forms specify that such deposits be included as plan assets.

The above exclusions do not eliminate the requirements for plans to file an annual report nor do they eliminate the requirements to file Schedule A (insurance information) and Schedule B (actuarial information), if applicable.

[2] Audit Requirements

ERISA required that the financial statements of plans be examined by independent auditors in accordance with generally accepted auditing standards. ERISA also provided that the auditors' examination did not have to extend to statements of assets and liabilities of a common or collective trust maintained by a bank, a separate account maintained by an insurance carrier, or a separate trust maintained by a bank as trustee, if the bank or insurance company is regulated, supervised, and subject to periodic examination by a state or federal agency and certifies to the correctness of the statements.

The statutory language is far from clear and has raised many questions as to the responsibilities of banks and insurance companies and independent auditors. The DOL regulations (Section 2520.103-8) have clarified this confusion by providing that plans may elect to exclude from the scope of the independent auditors' examination assets held by banks or insurance companies and transactions involving those assets. This exclusion applies to assets held under both custodial and discretionary trust agreements if statements or information regarding the assets are prepared and "certified" to by the bank or insurance company. This does *not* eliminate the requirement to engage an independent auditor. The regulations provide that the independent accountant may describe the scope limitation in his report. A special form of report on a limited-scope examination is discussed at ¶ 16.02.

[3] Who Must File

DOL—The requirement to file an annual report applies to all welfare and pension benefit plans except those exempted or excluded by statute or regulations. A summary of those exemptions and exclusions follows:

- Section 4 of ERISA excludes governmental plans, certain church plans, non-U.S. plans primarily for nonresident aliens, workmen's compensation and unemployment compensation plans, and unfunded plans which provide benefits in excess of Internal Revenue Code limitations on contributions and benefits (see ¶ 3.05[2]).
- DOL regulations issued August 15, 1975 exempt welfare benefit plans having fewer than 100 participants from the annual report requirement. The exemption applies only if benefits are paid as needed solely from the general assets of the sponsor (unfunded plans) or are provided exclusively through insurance policies

(fully insured plans), the premiums for which are paid directly by the sponsor from its general assets or partly from its general assets and partly from contributions by its participants.

- The regulations also exclude certain employer-employee benefits not considered to be welfare benefit plans. Examples of such benefits include overtime pay, vacation pay, sick leave, and tuition reimbursement.
- In addition, the regulations exclude certain plans or programs from coverage as a pension plan. Excluded from coverage are severance pay plans, certain bonus programs, gratuitous payments to pre-ERISA retirees, individual retirement accounts, and Keogh plans covering only partners or a sole proprietor.

IRS—The requirement to file an annual return with the IRS is limited to qualified pension benefit plans. This includes qualified plans of governmental units or churches excluded by ERISA from the DOL reporting requirements. Tax-exempt welfare plans should continue to file Form 990.

Both the IRS and DOL filing requirements relate to plans as opposed to employers. Multiple filings are not required for a single plan of a controlled group of corporations, multiemployer, or multiemployer plans. However, separate filings are required for individual plans whose assets are included in a group trust of related corporations.

[4] Where and When to File

For plan years beginning on or after January 1, 1977, the annual return/report is to be filed only with the IRS. The due date is seven months after the plan year-end (e.g., a calendar year 1977 plan report is due July 31, 1978). Previously a copy of the return/report generally had to be filed with both the IRS and the DOL. DOL due dates were based on the plan year-end, while IRS due dates were based on the employer's tax year.

An extension of the due date up to two and a half months may be obtained by filing Form 5558 with the IRS. The extension is not automatic and must be approved by the IRS.

There is a penalty of $10 a day (up to a maximum of $5,000) for filing delinquent returns with the IRS unless reasonable cause for the late filing is shown. There are no specific monetary penalties for late filing with the DOL; however, there are provisions in ERISA for criminal and civil actions for violations of DOL requirements.

¶ 10.03 COMPLETING THE ANUAL RETURN/REPORT

The requirements of Form 5500 and the related instructions are discussed below. The requirements for completing the simplified Forms 5500-C and 5500-K are similar to those for Form 5500.

Most of the information required by Form 5500 is self-explanatory or is covered by the instructions. Items 1 through 6 contain identifying information as to the plan, the plan sponsor, the plan administrator, and the type of plan. Items 11, 12, 15, 16, 17, 18, 19, 20, and 21 require other information relating to the plan and the way it is operated. Item 7 requires information on plan participants, and items 8, 9, and 10 ask a series of questions relating to amendments to the plan or termination or merger of a plan. Item 23 covers matters required to be reported to the PBGC. The financial items on the form are 13, 14, and 22 and are discussed in more detail in the following paragraphs.

[1] Item 13—Plan Assets and Liabilities

This item is a comparative statement of assets and liabilities of the plan at both the beginning and the end of the year. All assets and liabilities are to be included at current value.* The statement may be prepared on the cash basis, accrual basis, or modified accrual basis.** The basis selected should be consistently applied.

For plans maintaining investments in more than one trust or in more than one insurance account, assets and liabilities should be reported on a combined basis. For plans whose assessts are maintained along with those of other plans in a single trust, the instructions require that each plan report its allocable portion of trust assets by line item. This requirement is not applicable for investments in bank-sponsored common or collective trusts (see ¶ 10.10).

Actuarially computed liabilities for future pension payments are specifically *not* to be included as a liability.

The instructions to the form contain comments not included above on certain specific line items.

---

* The instructions define "current value" as "fair market value where available and otherwise the fair value as determined in good faith by a trustee or a named fiduciary pursuant to the terms of the plan, assuming an orderly liquidation at the time of such determination." The current value of liabilities would generally be the face amount of the obligation.

** If the alternative method of compliance is elected, the attached financial statements must be on the same basis.

[2] Item 14—Plan Income, Expenses, and Changes in Net Assets

This item requires a noncomparative statement of income, expenses, and changes in net assets. Detailed instructions are included for specific line items. With the exception of unrealized appreciation or depreciation, amounts may be reported on the cash, accrual, or modified accrual basis.

[3] Item 22—Additional Financial Statements, Schedules, and Accountant's Report

Item 22 covers the schedules and the accountant's report on financial statements required to be filed by certain plans. An explanation of these requirements is contained partly in the instructions to the form and partly in DOL Regulations Sections 2520.103-1 through 2520.103-11. These regulations were initially issued on August 3, 1976 as temporary and proposed regulations. Final regulations were issued on March 10, 1978.

¶ 10.04   FINANCIAL STATEMENT REQUIREMENTS

The form and content of financial statements required to be attached to Form 5500 are specified in DOL Regulations Section 2520.103-1. The regulations provide that financial statements may be included in compliance with Section 103 of ERISA (statutory method) or, alternatively, in compliance with the requirements of the regulations (alternative method). The financial statement requirements are as follows:

	Alternative Method	Statutory Method
Statement of assets and liabilities	X	X
Statement of changes in net assets available for plan benefits, including details of revenues, expenses, and other changes (the alternative method describes this statement as a statement of plan income, expenses, and changes in net assets)	X	X
Statement of changes in financial position (required for welfare benefit plans only)		X

Both this statutory method and the alternative method require that specified notes to the financial statements and schedules be included. The footnote requirements are as follows:

	Alternative Method	*Statutory Method*
A description of the accounting principles and practices and, if applicable, variances from generally accepted accounting principles (GAAP)	X	*
A description of the plan, including any changes in provisions and the effect on benefits	X	X
The funding policy and any changes during the year	X	X
Agreements and transactions with parties known to be parties-in-interest	X	X
Material lease commitments, other commitments, and contingent liabilities	X	X
Priorities on termination of the plan	X	X
The tax status of the plan, including whether a ruling or determination letter has been obtained	X	X
An explanation of the differences, if any, between the information contained in the separate financial statements and the information contained in items 13 and 14 of Form 5500	X	

---

* This footnote would be required by GAAP even though not required by the statute.

	Alternative Method	Statutory Method
Any other material necessary to fully and fairly present the financial statements of the plan	X	X

Financial statements prepared in conformity with the statutory method are to be in conformity with generally accepted accounting principles. The statute contains no further detailed requirements as to accounting principles.

Financial statements intended to meet the requirements of the alternative method must be presented at current value and must include the same amounts included in items 13 and 14 of Form 5500; however, the amounts may be aggregated differently. The requirements for separate statements of assets and liabilities and income, expenses, and changes in plan assets may be complied with by either attaching separate financial statements and schedules and an accountant's report thereon, or attaching required footnotes and an accountant's report on items 13 and 14 and the schedules required by item 22.

¶ 10.05 SCHEDULE REQUIREMENTS

The schedules required to be filed with Form 5500, to the extent they are applicable to the plan, are as follows (again, the requirements are different for a plan filing under the statutory method and the alternative method):

	Alternative Method	Statutory Method
Comparative statement of assets and liabilities at current value		X
Statements of cash receipts and disbursements		X
Assets held for investment	X	X
Transactions involving plan assets and a party known to be a party-in-interest	X	X

	Alternative Method	Statutory Method
Loans or fixed-income obligations in default or classified as uncollectible	X	X
Leases in default or classified as uncollectible	X	X
Transactions or series of transactions in excess of 3% of the current value of plan assets	X	X

¶ 10.06 COMPARISON OF STATUTORY AND ALTERNATIVE METHODS

The purpose of the alternative method of reporting prescribed by the regulations was to simplify the reporting requirements; however, the DOL did not believe it could eliminate the requirements prescribed by ERISA, and, accordingly, both methods are acceptable.

There are several major differences between the requirements of the statutory method and those of the alternative method. The statutory method requires that the financial statements be prepared in conformity with generally accepted accounting principles, whereas the alternative method does not. Financial statements prepared in conformity with the alternative method may be on the cash basis, on the accrual basis, or on a modified accrual basis.

The statutory method does not require the financial statements to be comparative, whereas the alternative method requires a comparative *statement* of assets and liabilities. However, the statutory method does require a comparative *schedule* of assets and liabilities. The alternative method requires all assets and liabilities included in the financial statements to be stated at current value. The comparative schedule of assets and liabilities under the statutory method is required to include assets and liabilities at current value for both years.

The statutory method requires a statement of cash receipts and disbursements to be included as a schedule. This schedule is not required by the alternative method.

As a practical matter, most plans have found that compliance under the alternative method is easier. Plans using the statutory method are generally those not willing to adopt current value as their primary asset valuation method.

¶ 10.07   CONTENT AND FORM OF SCHEDULES

The form and content of the schedules, other than the schedules of assets held for investment and transactions or series of transactions in excess of 3 percent of the current value of plan assets, are governed by the instructions to Form 5500. The requirements for the schedule of assets held for investment are included in DOL Regulations Section 2520.103-11, and the requirements for the schedule of 3 percent transactions are included in DOL Regulations Section 2520.103-6.

[1] Assets Held for Investment

This schedule requires a detailed listing of investment assets held at year-end in a prescribed form. The form is to include the following captions:

- Identity of issue, borrower, lessor, or similar party;
- Description of investment, including maturity date, rate of interest, collateral, and par or maturity value;
- Cost;
- Current value.

In the case of a loan, the description should include details the payment schedule. For example, the description should indicate whether the loan is payable on a self-amortizing basis or whether it includes a balloon payment at the end of its term.

In addition, a schedule is required listing *certain* investment assets which were *both* acquired and disposed of within the plan year. The information required for these investments is as follows:

- Identity of issue, borrower, lessor, or similar party;
- Description of investment, including maturity date, rate of interest, collateral, and par or maturity value;
- Cost of acquisitions;
- Proceeds of dispositions.

Most investment acquisitions and dispositions, however, are excluded from the above reporting requirement. DOL Regulations Section 2520.103-11 provides that the following investment acquisitions and dispositions need not be reported:

- Debt obligations of the United States or any agency of the United States;

- Interests issued by a company registered under the Investment Company Act of 1940;
- Bank certificates of deposit with a maturity of not more than one year;
- Commercial paper with a maturity of not more than nine months if it is ranked in the highest rating category by at least two nationally recognized statistical rating services and is issued by a company required to file reports with the Securities and Exchange Commission under Section 13 of the Securities Exchange Act of 1934;
- Participations in a bank common or collective trust;
- Participations in an insurance company pooled separate account;
- Securities listed on a national securities exchange registered under Section 6 of the Securities Exchange Act of 1934 or quoted on NASDAQ.

Also excluded are any investments acquired and disposed of during the year which are also required to be reported in the following schedules:

- Transactions involving plan assets and a party known to be a party-in-interest;
- Loans or fixed-income obligations in default or classified as uncollectible;
- Leases in default or classified as uncollectible;
- Transactions or series of transactions in excess of 3 percent of the current value of plan assets.

[2] Transactions Involving Plan Assets and a Party Known to Be a Party-in-Interest

The definition of a "party-in-interest" is contained in the instructions to item 13(d) of Form 5500 and at ¶ 2.06 of this manual. The definition is very broad and could potentially cover a large number of transactions. However, the instructions to Form 5500 indicate that only those transactions which are not covered by a statutory or administrative exemption from being a prohibited transaction need be reported. Prohibited transactions and the statutory and administrative exemptions for prohibited transactions are also discussed in this manual at ¶¶ 2.06[1] and 2.06[2]. The effect of these rules is that only prohibited transactions have to be reported.

The information to be filed for any prohibited transactions is as follow:

- Identity of party involved;
- Relationship to plan, employer, or other party-in-interest;
- Description of transactions, including maturity date, rate of interest, collateral, and par or maturity value;
- Purchase price;
- Selling price;
- Lease rental;
- Expenses incurred in connection with transaction;
- Cost of asset;
- Current value of asset;
- Net gain or loss on each transaction.

If an application for an administrative exemption from a prohibited transaction has been filed but not acted on, the transaction should be reported and the pending exemption should be noted.

[3] Loans or Fixed-Income Obligations in Default or Classified as Uncollectible

The following information is required in a prescribed format for loans or fixed-income obligations which were in default at year-end or were classified as uncollectible during the year. The term "classified as uncollectible during the year" includes those loans which were written off or renegotiated during the year.

- Identity and address of obligor;
- Original amount of loan;
- Amount of principal and interest received during the year;
- Unpaid balance at end of year;
- Detailed description of loan, including dates of making and maturity, interest rate, the type and value of collateral, any renegotiation of the loan, including the terms thereof, and other material items;
- Amount of principal and interest overdue.

In addition, a notation should be made for each reported loan or fixed-income obligation as to whether parties involved are known to be parties-in-interest, and a statement should be attached explaining what steps have or will be taken to collect overdue amounts.

[4] Leases in Default or Classified as Uncollectible

The following information is to be reported in a prescribed format for leases which were in default or classified during the year as uncollectible.

- Identity of lessor/lessee;
- Relationship to plan, employer, employee organization, or other party-in-interest;
- Terms and description (type of property, location, and date purchased, terms regarding rent, taxes, insurance, repairs, expenses, renewal options, and date property was leased);
- Original cost;
- Current value at time of lease;
- Gross rental receipts during the year;
- Expenses paid during the year;
- Net receipts;
- Amount in arrears.

In addition, a statement should be included as to what steps have been taken to collect amounts due or otherwise remedy the default.

[5] Transaction or Series of Transactions in Excess of 3 Percent of the Current Value of Plan Assets

This schedule is the most complex and potentially the most burdensome of the required schedules. A separate section of the DOL regulations (Section 2520.103-6) defines what transactions are reportable and prescribes the information to be reported.

The regulations include the following definitions of terms used to describe the categories of reportable transactions:

☐ *Current value.* The current value of plan assets is the fair market value of assets at the beginning of the plan year. For investments acquired or disposed of during the year, current value is measured as of the date of acquisition or disposition.

☐ *Transaction with respect to securities.* A transaction with respect to securities is any purchase, sale, or exchange of securities. It occurs on either the trade date or settlement date, provided that either the trade date or settlement date is used consistently during the plan year. The term "security" includes a unit of participation in a common or commingled trust or a pooled separate account.

☐ *Transaction with or in conjunction with a person.* A transaction is "with or in conjunction with" a person if that person benefits from, executes, facilitates, participates in, promotes, or solicits a transaction or part of a transaction involving plan assets. The term "person" means an individual, partnership, joint venture, corporation, mutual company, joint-stock company, trust, estate, unincorporated organization, association, or employee organization.

☐ *Security.* The term "security" is defined in Section 3(20) of ERISA as having the same meaning as in the Securities Act of 1933, which reads as follows:

> "The term 'security' means any note, stock, treasury stock, bond, debenture, evidence of indebtedness, certificate of interest or participation in any profit-sharing agreement, collateral-trust certificate, preorganization certificate or subscription, transferable share, investment contract, voting trust certificate, certificate of deposit for a security, fractional undivided interest in oil, gas or other mineral rights, or, in general, any interest or instrument commonly known as a 'security,' or any certificate of interest or participation in, temporary or interim certificate for, receipt for, guarantee of, or warrant or right to subscribe to or purchase, any of the foregoing."

The DOL regulations also provide certain exemptions from these definitions for purposes of reporting specified categories of transactions. These exemptions are discussed under the affected category.

A transaction is a reportable transaction if it falls within any of the following four categories. Each category is illustrated by an example contained in the regulations.

[a] Individual Transactions in Excess of 3 Percent of Plan Assets

This category requires reporting of any individual transaction involving plan investments during the year which is in excess of 3 percent of the current value of plan assets. Essentially, a transaction is a reportable transaction under this category if, at the time of acquisition or disposition of a plan asset, its current value is in excess of 3 percent of the current value of the plan assets at the beginning of the year.

> *Example*: At the beginning of the plan year, *XYZ* Plan has 10 percent of the current value of its plan assets invested in *ABC* Company common stock. Halfway through the plan year, *XYZ* purchases *ABC* Company common stock in a single transaction in an amount equal to 5 percent of the current value of plan assets. At about this time, *XYZ* Plan also purchases a commercial development property in an amount equal to 4 percent of the current value of plan assets. Under this category, the stock transaction is a reportable transaction for the plan year because it exceeds 3 percent of the current value of plan assets. The land transaction is also reportable because it exceeds 3 percent of current value of plan assets.

[b] Series of Transactions Other Than Securities Transactions

Under this category, where a series of transactions, other than securities transactions, with or in conjunction with a person, when aggregated, regardless of gain or loss, involves an amount in excess of 3 percent of the current value of the plan assets, that series of transactions is a reportable transaction.

> *Example*: During the plan year, *AAA* Plan purchases a commercial lot from *ZZZ* Corporation at a cost equal to 2 percent of the current value of plan assets. Two months later, *AAA* Plan loans *ZZZ* Corporation an amount of money equal to 1.5 percent of the current value of plan assets. Under the provisions for this category, the plan has engaged in a reportable series of transactions with or in conjunction with the same person which, when aggregated, involves 3.5 percent of plan assets.

[c] Series of Securities Transactions

The requirements of the third category of reportable transactions are satisfied when a series of transactions involving securities of the *same issue, when aggregated, regardless of gain or loss*, involves an amount in excess of 3 percent of the current value of the plan assets. Once a series of transactions of the same issue is reportable under this category, *all transactions* in that issue during the same plan year are also reportable.

The term "issue" relates to the class of security involved in the transaction (e.g., common stock or preferred stock).

As previously noted, securities include units of participation in common or collective trusts and pooled separate accounts, and they include short-term money-market investments such as Treasury bills and commercial paper.

There are special provisions for reporting information with respect to series of securities transactions. These provisions generally allow aggregate reporting of such transactions and are discussed at ¶ 10.07[5][e].

Example: At the beginning of the plan year, *ABC* Plan has 10 percent of the current value of plan assets invested equally in a combination of the common and preferred stock of *XYZ* Corporation. One month into the plan year, *ABC* Plan sells *XYZ* Corporation common stock in an amount equal to 2 percent of the current value of plan assets.

(i) Six weeks later, the *ABC* Plan sells *XYZ* Corporation preferred stock in an amount equal to 2 percent of the current value of plan assets. A reportable series of transactions has not occurred because only transactions involving securities of the same issue are to be aggregated under this category.

(ii) Two weeks later, when the *ABC* Plan purchases *XYZ* Corporation common stock in an amount equal to 2.5 percent of the current value of plan assets, a reportable series of transactions under this category has occurred. The sale of *XYZ* Corporation common stock worth 2 percent of plan assets and the purchase of *XYZ* Corporation common stock worth 2.5 percent of plan assets aggregate to exceed 3 percent of the total value of plan assets. Purchases and sales should be aggregated; a net calculation should not be made. Both the purchase and sale of *XYZ* Corporation common stock are part of the reportable series under this category.

[d] Other Transactions

The fourth category of reportable transactions includes transactions with a person or with respect to a security if any prior or subsequent single transaction within the plan year with such person with respect to securities exceeds 3 percent of the current value of plan assets. In essence, where a transaction with respect to securities is reportable under category 1, all transactions with the same person with respect to securities are reportable transactions under this category.

However, to eliminate much of the burden of this reporting category, the definitions of "a transaction with or in conjunction with a person" and "securities" have been modified for purposes of this reporting category in accordance with DOL Regulations Section 2520.103-6.

A transaction is not considered to be "with or in conjunction with a person" if:

- That person is a broker-dealer registered under the Securities Exchange Act of 1934;
- The transaction involves the purchase or sale of securities listed on a national securities exchange registered under Section 6 of the Securities Exchange Act of 1934 or quoted on NASDAQ; and
- The broker-dealer does not purchase or sell securities involved in the transaction for its own account or the account of an affiliated person.

The transaction is not considered to involve a security if it is a transaction involving a bank or insurance company regulated by a federal or state agency, an investment company registered under the Investment Company Act of 1940, or a broker-dealer registered under the Securities Exchange Act of 1934 in the following types of investments:

- Debt obligations of the United States or any United States agency with a maturity of not more than one year;
- Debt obligations of the United States or any United States agency with a maturity of more than one year if purchased or sold under a repurchase agreement having a term of less than ninety-one days;
- Interests issued by a company registered under the Investment Company Act of 1940;
- Bank certificates of deposit with a maturity of not more than one year;
- Commercial paper with a maturity of not more than nine months if it is ranked in the highest rating category by at least two nationally recognized statistical rating services and is issued by a company required to file reports under Section 13 of the Securities Exchange Act of 1934;

- Participations in a bank common or collective trust;
- Participations in an insurance company pooled separate account.

Examples: At the beginning of the plan year, Plan X purchases through broker-dealer Y common stock of Able Industries in an amount equal to 4 percent of plan assets. The common stock of Able Industries is not listed on any national securities exchange or quoted on NASDAQ. This purchase is a reportable transaction under category 1. Three months later, Plan X purchases short-term debt obligations of Charley Company through broker-dealer Y in the amount of 0.2 percent of plan assets. This purchase is also a reportable transaction under the provisions of category 4.

At the beginning of the plan year, Plan X purchases from Bank B certificates of deposit having a 180-day maturity in an amount equal to 5 percent of plan assets. Bank B is a national bank regulated by the Comptroller of the Currency. This purchase is a reportable transaction under category 1. Three months later, Plan X purchases through Bank B ninety-one-day Treasury bills in the amount of 0.2 percent of plan assets. This purchase is not a reportable transaction under category 4 of this section because of the modified definition of "securities."

At the beginning of the plan year, Plan X purchases through broker-dealer Y common stock of Able Industries, a New York Stock Exchange-listed security, in an amount equal to 4 percent of plan assets. This purchase is a reportable transaction under category 1. Three months later, Plan X purchases through broker-dealer Y, acting as agent, common stock of Baker Corporation, also a New York Stock Exchange-listed security, in an amount equal to 0.2 percent of plan assets. This latter purchase is not a reportable transaction under category 4 of this section because it is not a transaction "with or in conjunction with a person" pursuant to the exemption for this category.

[e] Information to Be Reported

The regulations require the following information in a prescribed format for each reportable transaction:

- The name of each party, except that in the case of a transaction or series of transactions involving a purchase or sale of a security on the market, the schedule need not include the person from whom it was purchased or to whom it was sold. A purchase or sale on the market is a purchase or sale of a security through a registered broker-dealer acting as a broker under the Securities Exchange Act of 1934.

- A brief description of each asset.
- The purchase or selling price in the case of a purchase or sale, the rental in the case of a lease, and the amount of principal, interest rate, payment schedule (e.g., fully amortized, partly amortized with balloon), and maturity date in the case of a loan.
- Expenses incurred, including, but not limited to, any fees or commissions.
- The cost of any asset.
- The current value of any asset acquired or disposed of at the time of acquisition or disposition.
- The net gain or loss.

For transactions in the same issue of a security, the following information may be substituted for that listed above:

- The total number of purchases of such securities made by the plan within the plan year.
- The total number of sales of such securities made by the plan within the plan year.
- The total dollar value of such purchases.
- The total dollar value of such sales.
- The net gain or loss as a result of these transactions.

¶ 10.08   OTHER REPORTING SCHEDULES

In addition to the basic forms, financial statements, and financial schedules, certain plans are required to file Schedule A, Schedule B, and Schedule SSA. The requirements for these schedules are discussed in the following paragraphs.

[1] Schedule A—Insurance Information

Schedule A is to be completed and attached to Forms 5500, 5500-C, and 5500-K by plans where any benefits are provided by an insurance company, insurance service, or other similar organization.

This requirement is applicable to both pension and welfare benefit plans.

The schedule is comprised of three parts. Part I contains identifying information as to the plan, the insurance carrier, and soliciting agents and brokers, and is to be completed by both pension and welfare benefit plans. Part II is applicable to pension benefit plans and calls for information as to premium rates, premiums paid, and deposits under unallocated contracts. Part III is applicable to welfare benefit plans and requires information on premiums, benefits, retention and dividends for experience-rated contracts, and premiums paid under non-experience-rated contracts.

[2] Schedule B—Actuarial Information

Item 21 of Form 5500, item 20 of Form 5500-C, and item 19 of Form 5500-K require information as to the amount of required employer contributions to the plan, the amount of contributions made to the plan during the year, and any resulting funding deficiency for plans which were subject to the minimum funding standards for the plan year. All defined benefit plans and certain defined contribution plans (i.e., money-purchase and target benefit plans) are subject to the minimum funding standards. In addition to completing item 21, covered plans are required to file a separate Schedule B.

In addition to the identifying information as to the plan, Schedule B requires information as to compliance with the funding standards and the actuarial methods, assumptions, and liabilities of the plan, and a statement by an enrolled actuary as follows: "To the best of my knowledge, the information supplied in this schedule and on the accompanying statement, if any, is complete and accurate, and in my opinion the assumptions used in the aggregate (a) are reasonably related to the experience of the plan and to reasonable expectations, and (b) represent my best estimate of anticipated experience under the plan."

[3] Schedule SSA—Annual Registration Statement Identifying Separated Participants With Deferred Vested Benefits

Section 6057(e) of the Internal Revenue Code imposes a requirement on plan administrators to report participants who have separated with deferred vested benefits. This information is then forwarded to the Social Security Administration where it is maintained. When an individual applies for Social Security benefits, he or she is then informed of deferred vested benefit entitlements from past employment. Information to be reported for each participant terminated with a vested benefit during the year includes: (1) Social Security number, (2) name of participant, (3) nature and form of benefit, and (4) amount of vested benefit.

¶ 10.09   INFORMATION TO BE SUPPLIED BY BANKS AND INSURANCE COMPANIES

DOL Regulations Section 2520.103-5 provides that banks and insurance companies must provide plan administrators with "such information as is needed by the plan administrator to comply with the requirements of Title I of the Act." This information must be "certified" by the bank or insurance company and must be transmitted to the plan within 120 days after the close of the plan year.

There is no limitation on the information to be supplied except that it includes only that information contained "within the ordinary business records" of the institution. As a result, some institutions may be in a position to provide information relating to party-in-interest transactions or 3 percent reportable transactions, while other institutions may not.

The form of the bank or insurance company "certification" is flexible. Suggested language is included in the regulations; however, "any other signed statement which assures the accuracy and completeness of the facts transmitted may be used." The example given in the regulations is as follows:

> "The XYZ Bank (Insurance Carrier) hereby certifies that the foregoing statement furnished pursuant to 29 C.F.R. § 2520.103-5(c) is complete and accurate."

As previously discussed at ¶ 10.02[2], information so certified may be excluded from the scope of the auditors' examination.

¶ 10.10   SPECIAL RULES FOR COLLECTIVE TRUSTS AND POOLED SEPARATE ACCOUNTS

Many employee benefit plans have investments in commingled funds sponsored by banks (common or collective trusts) and insurance companies (pooled separate accounts). The regulations provide that transactions of the trust or account are not transactions of the plan for DOL reporting purposes (this is also true under GAAP). Plans with investments in such trusts or accounts should include the following information relating to those assets in the annual report:

- The value of the plan's units of participation in the trust or account;
- Transactions involving the acquisition or disposition of units of participation in the trust or account.

Section 103 of ERISA requires that each plan with an investment in a common or collective trust or separate account attach the most recent annual statement of assets and liabilities of that trust or account; however, the regulations provide that plans can be relieved of the requirement if the bank or insurance company files a statement of assets and liabilities of the trust or account on behalf of all plans with the DOL. The bank or insurance company must also file a list of participating plans and their employer identification numbers.

Banks and insurance companies are required to provide the plan with a copy of the statement of assets and liabilities and the employer identification number of the trust or account. The plan should include in its annual report the employer identification number of the trust in which it participates, along with a statement that it has received a copy of the statement of assets and liabilities.

¶ 10.11   REPORTING ON CONTROLLED GROUP TRUSTS

A number of companies have established group trusts which hold the assets of the separate plans of the company and its subsidiaries. DOL Regulations Section 2520.103-3 states that a controlled group of corporations as defined in Section 1563(a) of the Internal Revenue Code shall be considered a single participant in a common or collective trust. As a result, a common or collective trust consisting solely of the assets of a plan or plans of a controlled group of corporations *would not* qualify for the exemption from reporting of transactions of the trust and for filing of the statement of assets and liabilities of the trust.

The regulations do not give any guidance on how plans whose assets are held in such a trust should comply with the reporting requirements. However, the instructions to Form 5500 state that "if the assets of two or more plans are maintained in one trust, such as where an employer has two plans which are funded through a single trust, items 13 and 14 should be completed by entering the plan's allocable portion of each line item."

Since plans investing in controlled group trusts basically have an undivided interest in the assets of the trust, this form of reporting would appear to be appropriate only for completing the form and not for separate financial statements prepared in conformity with GAAP. The financial statements, notes, and schedules to be covered by the accountant's report and attached to Form 5500 should be prepared on the basis that the plan has an investment in units of participation in a group trust. A footnote should summarize the financial position and changes in net assets of the trust.

¶ 10.12   SPECIAL RULES FOR GROUP INSURANCE AR-RANGEMENTS

DOL Regulations Section 2520.103-2 provides that "plans participating in a group insurance arrangement may be exempted from filing an Annual Report provided that the trust, trade association, or other entity which owns the insurance contracts and acts as a conduit for the insurance premiums files an Annual Report for the entire arrangement." A "group insurance arrangement" is defined in part as a welfare benefit plan which provides benefits to the employees of *two or more unaffiliated employers.*

¶ 10.13   SUMMARY ANNUAL REPORT

Generally, plans which are required to file annual reports in accordance with DOL regulations are also required to distribute summary annual reports to participants and beneficiaries within nine months of the plan year-end in accordance with DOL Regulations Section 2520.104b-10. The summary annual report does not have to be filed with the DOL.

Plans electing the alternative method provided by DOL regulations and filing form 5500 should include in the summary annual report:

- Identifying information as to the plan, the sponsor, and the administrator;

- Statements of assets and liabilities and income, expenses and changes in assets, and the accompanying footnotes;
- A notice to participants, in a format prescribed in the regulations, that a complete annual report is available on request for a reasonable charge;
- For insured plans, specified information from Schedule A, "Insurance Information."

The summary annual report of plans electing the alternative method and filing Form 5500-C or 5500-K should include a copy of the form and a notice to participants that a complete annual report is available on request for a reasonable charge.

For plans not electing the alternative method of compliance, the summary annual report should include the items prescribed by Section 104(b)(3) of ERISA:

- A comparative schedule of assets and liabilities at current value;
- A schedule of receipts and disbursements; and
- Any other material necessary to summarize the annual report.

¶ 10.14   OTHER REPORTS AND DISCLOSURE REQUIREMENTS

[1] Department of Labor

The principal document required to be filed with the DOL is the Plan Description Form EBS-1. This form is to be filed within 120 days after adoption of a new plan. The form requires identifying information as to the plan and plan sponsor, information as to the type of plan, number of participants and beneficiaries, persons providing services to the plan, sources and methods of determining contributions, how assets are accumulated and benefits disbursed, and claims procedures. For pension plans, information is required as to participation, vesting, and benefit provisions. For welfare plans, an indication of the type of benefit is required.

[2] Internal Revenue Service

Generally, the reporting requirements to the IRS are satisfied by filing one of the 5500 series forms. However, reports of merger, consolidation, or transfer of assets are required to be made at least thirty days prior to such action.

[3] Pension Benefit Guaranty Corporation

Effective for plan years beginning in 1977, the requirement of Section 4065 of ERISA to file an annual report with the PBGC will be satisfied by the filing of Form 5500, 5500-C, or 5500-K. This replaces the PBGC annual report filing on Form PBGC-1. However, Form PBGC-1 is still required to be filed to pay premiums prescribed by Section 4007 of ERISA. In addition, specified events are reportable to the PBGC within thirty days of their occurrence. Notice is also required if a plan is to be terminated. Reportable events include the following:

(1) Plan amendments that would decrease a benefit of any participant;

(2) Failure to meet minimum funding requirements or to pay current benefits;

(3) Disqualification of the plan by the IRS or a determination that the plan is not in accordance with the regulatory provisions of ERISA;

(4) Certain specified decreases in the number of plan participants;

(5) Mergers and consolidation of plans or transfers of plan assets;

(6) Certain other events which might indicate a need for plan termination.

[4] Disclosures to Participants

The administrator of every employee benefit plan must furnish a summary plan description and a summary annual report to participants and beneficiaries of the plan. The summary plan description is to be written in a manner "calculated to be understood by the average plan participant."

Administrators are required to make copies of the plan description, latest annual report, trust agreements, and all other plan documents available for examination by plan participants and beneficiaries. Upon written request, the administrator must provide copies of the above documents to participants and beneficiaries for a reasonable charge to cover the cost of reproduction.

The administrator of an employee pension benefit plan must furnish once a year, upon written request, a statement indicating a participant's or beneficiary's benefit status. The statement is to include the total benefits accrued and the nonforfeitable pension benefits, if any, which have accrued, or the earliest date on which benefits will become nonforfeitable. Further, a statement must be furnished to participants who terminate employment indicating their right to any deferred vested benefit.

¶ 10.15   SEC REPORTING REQUIREMENTS

The Securities Act of 1933 and the Securities Exchange Act of 1934 established federal regulation of the purchase and sale of securities. They provide for registration of securities and disclosure of information concerning securities offered for sale, and for periodic reporting of financial information. Securities laws and related regulations and their applicability to employee benefit plans are highly complex and require consultation with legal counsel. The primary question which needs to be answered is whether the plan involves an offer to sell securities or whether interests in the plan themselves are securities.

The material which follows is intended to summarize in general terms the application of securities laws to employee benefit plans.

[1] Plans Involving an Offer to Sell Securities

Plans which may involve an offer to sell securities and, therefore, subject the secruities to registration requirements, include "any purchase, savings, options, bonus, appreciation, profit sharing, thrift, incentive, pension or similar plan."

The employer securities involved in such plans are subject to registration unless otherwise exempted or unless the plan provisions do not constitute an offer to sell. Typically, there is not an offer to sell where the plan is noncontributory or where the participant has no elective rights under the plan.

Under these guidelines, securities offered under a typical stock option plan are usually registered. On the other hand, it has generally been held that a typical employee stock ownership plan does not require registration because the plan is noncontributory and there is no offer to sell.

[2] Interests Which Constitute Securities

The 1933 Act defines a security as:

"Any note, stock, treasury stock, bond, debenture, evidence of indebtedness, certificate of interest or participation in any profit-sharing agreement, collateral-trust certificate, preorganization certificate or subscription, transferable share, investment contract, voting-trust certificate, certificate of deposit for a security, fractional undivided interest in oil, gas, or mineral rights, or, in general, any interest or instrument commonly known as a 'security,' or any certificate of interest or participation in, temporary or interim certificate of, receipt for, guarantee of, or warrant or right to subcribe to or purchase, any of the foregoing."

A broad interpretation of this definition would seem to include employee interests in at least some kinds of employee benefit plans. However, the securities law provides exemptions for certain types of plans, including:

"Any interest or participation in a single or collective trust fund maintained by a bank or in a separate account maintained by an insurance company which interest or participation is issued in connection with (A) a stock bonus, pension, or profit-sharing plan which meets the requirements for qualification under section 401 of the Internal Revenue Code of 1954, or (B) an annuity plan which meets the requirements for the deduction of the employer's contribution under section 404(a)(2) of such Code, other than any plan described in clause (A) or (B) of this paragraph (i) the contributions under which are held in a single trust fund maintained by a bank or in a separate account maintained by an insurance company for a single employer and under which an amount in excess of the employer's contribution is allocated to the purchase of securities (other than interests or participations in the trust or separate account itself) issued by the employer, or by any company directly or indirectly controlling, controlled by or under common control with the employer or (ii) which covers employees some or all of whom are employees within the meaning of section 401(c)(1) of such Code."

This exemption has traditionally been construed to include interests in typical defined benefit plans and in defined contribution plans not involving the purchase of employer securities with employee contributions. Not included under this exemption are typical stock purchase, savings, and similar plans where employee contributions are used to purchase employer securities.

However, in a recent case, *Daniel v. International Brotherhood of*

Teamsters, Chauffeurs, Warehouseman & Helpers of America, the U.S. Court of Appeals for the Seventh Circuit has upheld a lower court decision that a participant's interest in a collectively bargained, noncontributory pension plan is an "investment contract" and, therefore, a security. The court also held that participation in the plan constitutes a "sale" of the security for services rendered. It is expected that the decision will be further appealed to the U.S. Supreme Court.

The SEC has indicated that even if the decision is upheld, most plans would still not be subject to the registration and reporting requirements, but only to the antifraud provisions of the securities laws. The antifraud provisions basically prohibit fraudulent or deceptive conduct, including the making of fake or misleading representations.

[3] Registration and Reporting Requirements

The basic form for registering securities or interest in plans is Form S-8. Like other registration forms, it is comprised of two parts: the information included in the prospectus given to offerees (participants in the case of employee benefit plan) and that included in the registration statement but not required in the prospectus. As with all SEC registration statements, financial statements included in the filing are required to be audited. The required contents of Form S-8 are summarized below:

Item 1.   General information regarding the plan.

Item 2.   Securities to be offered to employees who may participate in the plan.

Item 3.   Purchase of securities pursuant to the plan.

Item 4.   Payment for securities offered.

Item 5.   Contributions under the plan.

Item 6.   Withdrawal from the plan—Assignment of interest.

Item 7.   Defaults under the plan.

Item 8.   Administration of the plan.

Item 9.   Investment of funds.

Item 10. Charges and deductions and liens therefore.

Item 11. Financial statements of the plan.

Item 12. Capital stock to be registered.

Item 13. Other securities to be registered.

Item 14. Summary of operations of the issuer.

Item 15. Market prices of the issuer's securities and dividend policy.

Item 16. Description of certain significant developments in the last three years.

Item 17. Financial statements of the issuer.

Item 18. The issuer's business and management.

Item 19. Parents of registrant.

For plans in which interests constituting securities have been registered (e.g., stock purchase, savings, and similar plans), an annual report on Form 11-K is also required to be filed with the SEC. Form 11-K includes the following:

Item 1. Changes in the plan.

Item 2. Changes in investment policy.

Item 3. Participating employees.

Item 4. Administration of the plan.

Item 5. Custodian of investments.

Item 6. Reports to participating employees.

Item 7. Financial statements and exhibits.

¶ 10.16 SUMMARY OF DOL/IRS REQUIRED FINANCIAL, INSURANCE, AND ACTUARIAL CONTENTS OF ANNUAL RETURN/REPORT

Form 5500—Statutory Method of Compliance

- Item 13—Assets and liabilities.
- Item 14—Income, expenses, and changes in net assets.
- Item 22—Financial statements and schedules.
- Accountant's report.
- Statement of assets and liabilities.
- Statement of changes in net assets available for plan benefits.
- Footnotes to financial statements.
- Schedules:

  —Comparative statement of assets and liabilities at current value;

  —Statement of cash receipts and disbursements;

—Assets held for investment;

—Transactions involving plan assets and a party known to be a party-in-interest*;

—Loans or fixed-income obligations in default or classified as uncollectible*;

—Leases in default or classified as uncollectible*;

—Transactions or series of transactions in excess of 3 percent of the current value of plan assets.*

- Schedule A—Insurance information.*
- Schedule B—Actuarial information.*
- Schedule SSA—Annual registration statement.*

Form 5500—Alternative Method of Compliance

- Item 13—Assets and liabilities.
- Item 14—Income, expenses, and changes in net assets.
- Item 21—Financial statements and schedules.
- Accountant's report.
- Statement of assets and liabilities—Comparative and at current value.
- Statement of plan income, expense, and changes in net assets.
- Footnotes to financial statements.
- Schedules:

—Assets held for investment;

—Transactions involving plan assets and a party known to be a party-in-interest*;

—Loans or fixed-income obligations in default or classified as uncollectible*;

—Leases in default or classfied as uncollectible*;

—Transactions or series of transactions in excess of 3 percent of the current value of plan assets.*

- Schedule A—Insurance information.*
- Schedule B—Actuarial information.*
- Schedule SSA—Annual registration statement.*

---

* These schedules need to be filed only to the extent they are applicable to a particular plan.

Form 5500-C

- Item 13—Assets and liabilities.
- Item 14—Income, expenses, and changes in net assets.
- Item 21—Schedules of transactions involving plan assets and a party known to be a party-in-interest, and loans or fixed-income obligations and leases in default or classified as uncollectible.*
- Schedule A—Insurance information.*
- Schedule B—Actuarial information.*
- Schedule SSA—Annual registration statement.*

Form 5500-K

- Item 13—Summarized financial information.
- Item 17—Schedules of transactions involving plan assets and a party known to be a party-in-interest, and loans or fixed-income obligations and leases in default or classified as uncollectible.*
- Schedule A—Insurance information.*
- Schedule B—Actuarial information.*
- Schedule SSA—Annual registration statement.*

¶ 10.17   ILLUSTRATIVE FORM 5500

Following is a completed illustrative Form 5500 and the financial statements, schedules, and accountant's report required to be attached in accordance with Item 22 of the form and DOL regulations:

SUMMARY COMMENTS

The Plan

The plan is a single-employer-defined benefit pension plan administered by the company pension board. Benefits under the plan are determined based on a percentage of the employee's average highest five years' compensation per year of service. The plan is not integrated with Social Security.

---

*These schedules need to be filed only to the extent they are applicable to a particular plan.

Funding of the Plan

The plan is funded based on actuarial calculations, and Schedule B (actuarial information) has been included.

Plan Investments

The plan assets are held in a custodial trust by City Midway Bank. Investment decisions are made by the pension board, and the pension board maintains the primary accounting records of the plan.

Plan Financial Statements

The plan has elected the alternative method of compliance with the annual reporting requirements as prescribed by DOL regulations. In accordance with those regulations, plan assets and liabilities have been stated at current value.

The financial statements have been prepared on the accrual basis and are in conformity with generally accepted accounting principles in all material respects.

Audit Scope

The plan has not elected to exclude assets held by City Midway Bank from the scope of the independent accountant's examination, and such examination was made in accordance with generally accepted auditing standards. Had the plan elected to exclude such assets, the independent accountant's report would have included a disclaimer of opinion on the financial statements.

Schedules

The plan has included the following required schedules:

- Assets Held for Investment.
- Loans and Fixed-Income Obligations in Default or Classified as Uncollectible.
- Transactions or Series of Transactions in Excess of 3 Percent of the Current Value of Plan Assets.

A schedule of leases in default has not been included since the plan owns no leased property. A schedule of transactions with parties-in-interest has not been included since all such transactions were covered by statutory or administrative exemptions.

Form **5500** Department of the Treasury Internal Revenue Service Department of Labor Pension and Welfare Benefit Programs Pension Benefit Guaranty Corporation	**Annual Return/Report of Employee Benefit Plan** **(With 100 or more participants)** This form is required to be filed under sections 104 and 4065 of the Employee Retirement Income Security Act of 1974 and sections 6057(b) and 6058(a) of the Internal Revenue Code, referred to as the Code.	**1977** **This Form is Open to Public Inspection**

For the calendar plan year 1977 or fiscal plan year beginning _____ , 1977 and ending _____ 19_____

File original of this form, including schedules and attachments, completed in ink or type.

▶ Keogh (H.R. 10) plans with fewer than 100 participants and with at least one owner-employee participant **do not file this form.** File Form 5500—K instead.
▶ Other pension benefit plans and certain welfare benefit plans with fewer than 100 participants **do not file this form.** File Form 5500—C instead.
▶ Welfare benefit plans with 100 or more participants complete only items 1 through 16 and item 22.
▶ Pension benefit plans, unless otherwise excepted, complete all items. Annuity arrangements of certain exempt organizations and individual retirement account trusts of employers complete only items 1 through 6, 9 and 10.
▶ Government plans and church plans (not electing coverage under section 410(d) of the Code) complete only items 1 through 7, 9, 10(a), (b), (c), (d), 11 and 17.
▶ Plan number—Your 3 digit plan number must be entered in item 5(c); see instruction 5(c) for explanation of "plan number."
▶ If any item does not apply, enter "N/A."

1 **(a)** Name of plan sponsor (employer if for a single employer plan)	1 **(b)** Employer identification number
Employer Company	24-6810120
Address (number and street)	1 **(c)** Telephone number of sponsor
7000 Easy Road	(404) 365-8000
City or town, State and ZIP code	1 **(d)** Employer taxable year ends
City, State 12345	Month 12 Day 31 Year 1977
2 **(a)** Name of plan administrator (if other than plan sponsor)	1 **(e)** Business code number
Pension Board of the Employer Company Pension Plan	3580
Address (number and street)	2 **(b)** Administrator's employer identification no.
7000 Easy Road	36 ⁞ 9121518
City or town, State and ZIP code	2 **(c)** Telephone number of administrator
City, State 12345	(404) 365-8000

3   Name, address and identification number of ☐ plan sponsor and/or ☐ plan administrator as they appeared on the last return/report filed for this plan if not the same as in 1 or 2 above ▶ .... N/A ....

4   Check appropriate box to indicate the type of plan entity (check only one box):
    (a) ☒ Single-employer plan   **(c)** ☐ Multiemployer plan   **(e)** ☐ Multiple-employer plan (other)
    (b) ☐ Plan of controlled group of corporations   **(d)** ☐ Multiple-employer-collec-   **(f)** ☐ Group insurance arrangement (of
        or common control employers   tively-bargained plan   welfare plans)

5 **(a)** *(i)* Name of plan	5 **(b)** Effective date of plan
Employer Company Pension Plan	January 1, 1968
	5 **(c)** Enter three digit
(ii) ☐ Check if changed since last return/report	plan number ▶ 0 0 1

6   Check at least one item in (a) or (b) and applicable items in (c). Item (d) on page 2 must be completed:
    (a) Welfare benefit plan: *(i)* ☐ Health insurance   *(ii)* ☐ Life insurance   *(iii)* ☐ Supplemental unemployment
         (iv) ☐ Other (specify) ▶ .....N/A...
    (b) Pension benefit plan:
        (i)   Defined benefit plan—(Indicate type of defined benefit plan below):
           (A) ☐ Fixed benefit   **(B)** ☒ Unit benefit   **(C)** ☐ Flat benefit   **(D)** ☐ Other (specify) ▶ ....
        (ii)   Defined contribution plan—(indicate type of defined contribution plan below):
           (A) ☐ Profit-sharing   **(B)** ☐ Stock bonus   **(C)** ☐ Target benefit   **(D)** ☐ Other money purchase
           (E) ☐ Other (specify) ▶
        (iii) ☐ Defined benefit plan with benefits based partly on balance of separate account of participant (section 414(k) of the Code)
        (iv) ☐ Annuity arrangement of a certain exempt organization (section 403(b)(1) of the Code)
        (v) ☐ Custodial account for regulated investment company stock (section 403(b)(7) of the Code)
        (vi) ☐ Trust treated as an individual retirement account (section 408(c) of the Code)
        (vii) ☐ Employee stock ownership plan not part of a qualified plan (section 301(d) of the Tax Reduction Act of 1975)
        (viii) ☐ Other (specify) ▶

Under penalties of perjury and other penalties set forth in the instructions, I declare that I have examined this report, including accompanying schedules and statements, and to the best of my knowledge and belief, it is true, correct, and complete.

Date ▶ March 15, 1978   Signature of employer/plan sponsor ▶   Employer Company

Date ▶ March 15, 1978   Signature of plan administrator ▶ Pension Board of the Employer Company Pension Plan

Form 5500 (1977)   Page **2**

(c) Other plan features: N/A   *(i)* ☐ Thrift-savings   *(ii)* ☐ Keogh (H.R. 10) plan

     (iii) ☐ Employee stock ownership as part of a qualified plan (check only if you checked a box in (b)(ii) above)

(d) Is this a defined benefit plan covered under the Pension Benefit Guaranty Corporation

     termination insurance program? . . . . ☐ Yes ☐ No ☐ Not determined

7 Number of participants as of the end of the plan year (welfare plans complete only (a)(iv), (b), (c) and (d)):

     (a) Active participants (employed or carried as active) *(i)* Number fully vested . .   217

                                    (ii) Number partially vested .   2,316

                                    (iii) Number nonvested. . .   941

                                    (iv) Total 3,474

     (b) Retired or separated participants receiving benefits 378

     (c) Retired or separated participants entitled to future benefits 122

     (d) Subtotal, sum of (a), (b) and (c) 3,974

     (e) Deceased participants whose beneficiaries are receiving or are entitled to receive benefits . . . 94

     (f) Total, (d) plus (e) 4,068

	Yes	No
(g) During the plan year, was any participant(s) separated from service with a deferred vested benefit? . . . . If "Yes," see instructions.	X	

8 Plan amendment information (welfare plans complete only (a), (b)(i) and (c)):

		Yes	No
(a) Was any amendment to this plan adopted in this plan year?			X
(b) If "Yes," *(i)* And if a material modification, has a summary description of this modification—			
	(A) Been sent to plan participants?	N/A	
	(B) Been filed with DOL?	N/A	
	(ii) Does any such amendment result in the reduction of the accrued benefit of any participant under the plan? . .	N/A	
	(iii) Will amendment result in a reduction of current or future benefits?	N/A	
	(iv) Has a determination letter been requested from IRS with respect to such amendment? . .		
(c) Enter the date the most recent amendment was adopted . . ▶ Month 9 Day 4 Year 76			

9 Plan termination information (welfare plans complete only (a), (b), (c) and (f)):

		Yes	No
(a) Was this plan terminated during this plan year or any prior plan year?			X
(b) If "Yes," were all trust assets distributed to participants or beneficiaries or transferred to another plan? . .	N/A	
(c) Was a resolution to terminate this plan adopted during this plan year or any prior plan year?			X
(d) If (a) or (c) is "Yes," have you received a favorable determination letter from IRS with respect to such termination?	N/A	
(e) If (d) is "No," has a determination letter been requested from IRS?	N/A	
(f) If (a) or (c) is "Yes," have participants and beneficiaries been notified of the termination or the proposed termination?	N/A	

10 (a) In this plan year, was this plan merged or consolidated into another plan or were assets or liabilities transferred to another plan? . .   X

If "Yes," identify other plan(s):   **(c)** Employer identification number(s)   **(d)** Plan number(s)

(b) Name of plan(s) ▶ .... N/A ....

(e) Has Form 5310 been filed with IRS? . . . . ☐ Yes ☐ No

11 Indicate funding arrangement:

     (a) ☐ Trust (benefits provided in whole from trust funds)

     (b) ☐ Trust or arrangement providing benefits partially through insurance and/or annuity contracts

     (c) ☐ Trust or arrangement providing benefits exclusively through insurance and/or annuity contracts

     (d) ☐ Custodial account described in section 401(f) of the Code and not included in (c) above

     (e) ☐ Other (specify) ▶ ....

     (f) If (b) or (c) is checked, enter the number of Schedule A's (Form 5500) which are attached . . . . . . ▶ N/A

12 Did any person who rendered services to the plan receive, directly or indirectly, compensation **from the plan** in the plan year? . . ☐ Yes ☐ No

If "Yes," furnish the following information:

a. Name	b. Official plan position	c. Relationship to employer, employee organization or person known to be a party-in-interest	d. Gross salary or allowances paid by plan	e. Fees and commissions paid by plan	f. Nature of service code (see Instructions)
City Midway Bank	Trustee	None		72,500	26
John R. Good	Administrator	None	35,000		13
Stock & Bonds	Invest. Agent	None		7,500	20
Jones & Knight	Accountants	None		6,000	10
Smith & Finagel	Legal Counsel	None		36,731	22
W. E. Calculate	Actuary	None		20,000	11
I. R. Swift	Ass't Admin.	None	18,400		24

Form 5500 (1977)   Page **3**

13 Plan assets and liabilities at the beginning and the end of the plan year (list all assets and liabilities at current value). If plan is funded entirely by allocated insurance contracts for which no trust is involved, check box and do not complete this item . . ☐

Note: *Include all plan assets and liabilities of a trust or separately maintained fund. (If more than one trust/fund, report on a combined basis.) Include unallocated, but not allocated, insurance contracts. Round off amounts to nearest dollar.*

Assets	a. Beginning of year	b. End of year
(a) Cash: *(i)* On hand		
(ii) In bank: (A) Certificates of deposit	1,000,450	
(B) Other interest bearing		
(C) Noninterest bearing	95,813	187,439
(iii) Total cash	1,096,263	187,439
(b) Receivables: *(i)* Employer contributions	238,695	263,305
(ii) Employee contributions		
(iii) Other . . Accrued income.	199,663	229,386
(iv) Reserve for doubtful accounts		
(v) Net receivables, sum of (i), (ii) and (iii) minus (iv)	438,358	492,691
(c) General investments other than party-in-interest investments:		
(i) U.S. Government securities:		
(A) Long term	606,214	3,183,922
(B) Short term		510,818
(ii) State and municipal securities		
(iii) Corporate debt instruments:		
(A) Long term	8,458,329	7,800,875
(B) Short term		
(iv) Corporate stocks: (A) Preferred		
(B) Common	15,608,171	20,600,494
(v) Shares of a registered investment company		
(vi) Real estate		
(vii) Mortgages		
(viii) Loans other than mortgages		
(ix) Value of interest in pooled fund(s)		
(x) Other investments		
(xi) Total general investments, sum of (i) through (x)		
(d) Party-in-interest investments:		
(i) Corporate debt instruments	24,672,714	32,096,109
(ii) Corporate stocks: (A) Preferred		
(B) Common	1,498,000	1,725,000
(iii) Real estate		
(iv) Mortgages		
(v) Loans other than mortgages		
(vi) Other investments		
(vii) Total party-in-interest investments, sum of (i) through (vi)	1,498,000	1,725,000
(e) Buildings and other depreciable property		
(f) Value of unallocated insurance contracts:		
(i) Separate accounts		
(ii) Other		
(iii) Total, (i) plus (ii)		
(g) Other assets . .Prepaid insurance premium.	11,632	6,816
(h) Total assets, sum of (a)(iii), (b)(v), (c)(xi), (d)(vii), (e), (f)(iii) and (g)	27,716,967	34,508,055
Liabilities		
(i) Payables: *(i)* Plan claims	78,000	160,000
(ii) Other payables	29,968	39,145
(iii) Total payables, (i) plus (ii)	107,968	199,145
(j) Acquisition indebtedness		
(k) Other liabilities		
(l) Total liabilities, sum of (i)(iii), (j) and (k)	107,968	199,145
(m) Net assets, (h) less (l)	27,609,999	34,308,910
(n) During the plan year what were the:		
(i) Total cost of acquisitions for common stock?		5,091,364
(ii) Total proceeds from dispositions of common stock?		867,749

Form 5500 (1977)   Page 4

14 Plan income, expenses and changes in net assets for the plan year:

Note: *Include all income and expenses of a trust(s) or separately maintained fund(s). Round off amounts to nearest dollar.*

Income	a. Amount	b. Total
(a) Contributions received or receivable in cash from—		
(i) Employer(s) (including contributions on behalf of self-employed individuals)	3,509,855	
(ii) Employees		
(iii) Others		3,509,855
(b) Noncash contributions (specify nature and by whom made) ▶		
(c) Total contributions, sum of (a) and (b)		3,509,855
(d) Earnings from investments—		
(i) Interest	855,481	
(ii) Dividends	701,631	
(iii) Rents		
(iv) Royalties		1,557,112
(e) Net realized gain (loss) on sale or exchange of assets—		
(i) Aggregate proceeds	27,239,015	
(ii) Aggregate costs	27,270,706	(31,691)
(f) Other income (specify) ▶		
(g) Total income, sum of (c) through (f)		5,035,276

Expenses	a. Amount	b. Total
(h) Distribution of benefits and payments to provide benefits—		
(i) Directly to participants or their beneficiaries	1,395,821	
(ii) To insurance carrier or similar organization for provision of benefits		
(iii) To other organizations or individuals providing welfare benefits		1,395,821
(i) Interest expense		
(j) Administrative expenses—		
(i) Salaries and allowances	53,400	
(ii) Fees and commissions	142,731	
(iii) Insurance premiums for Pension Benefit Guaranty Corporation	8,327	
(iv) Insurance premiums for fiduciary insurance other than bonding	4,791	
(v) Other administrative expenses	6,723	215,972
(k) Other expenses (specify) ▶		
(l) Total expenses, sum of (h) through (k)		1,611,793
(m) Net income (expenses), (g) minus (l)		3,423,483

(n) Change in net assets—	a. Amount	b. Total
(i) Unrealized appreciation (depreciation) of assets	3,276,428	
(ii) Other changes (specify) ▶		3,276,428
(o) Net increase (decrease) in net assets for the year, (m) plus (n)		6,699,911
(p) Net assets at beginning of year, line 13(m), column a		27,608,999
(q) Net assets at end of year, (o) plus (p) (equals line 13(m), column b)		34,308,910

15 Has there been any change since the last report in the appointment of any trustee, accountant, insurance carrier, enrolled actuary, administrator, investment manager or custodian?   Yes ☐   No ☒

If "Yes," explain and include the name, position, address and telephone number of the individual who left or was removed by the plan ▶

Form 5500 (1977)   Page **5**

	Yes	No
16 Bonding:		
(a) Was the plan insured by a fidelity bond against losses through fraud or dishonesty?	X	
(b) If "Yes," enter the maximum amount of loss recoverable ▶ 500,000		
(c) Enter the name of the surety company ▶ Insurance Company, Inc.		
(d) Does the plan, or a known party-in-interest with respect to the plan, have any control or significant financial interest, direct or indirect, in the surety company or its agents or brokers?		X
(e) If the plan is not insured by a fidelity bond, explain why not ▶		
(f) In the current plan year was any loss to the plan caused by the fraud or dishonesty of any plan official or employee of the plan or of other person handling funds of the plan? . . . . If "Yes," see specific instructions.		X

17 Information about employees of employer at end of the plan year (Plans not purporting to satisfy the percentage tests of section 410(b)(1)(A) of the Code complete only (a) below and see specific instructions):

(a) Total number of employees	3,652
(b) Number of employees excluded under the plan—	
(i) Minimum age or years of service	178
(ii) Employees on whose behalf retirement benefits were the subject of collective bargaining . . .	
(iii) Nonresident aliens who receive no earned income from United States sources	
(iv) Total excluded, sum of (i), (ii) and (iii)	178
(c) Total number of employees not excluded, (a) less (b)(iv)	3,474
(d) Employees ineligible (specify reason) ▶	
(e) Employees eligible to participate, (c) less (d)	
(f) Employees eligible but not participating	
(g) Employees participating, (e) less (f)	

	Yes	No
18 Is this plan an adoption of a:		
(a) ☐ Master/prototype, (b) ☐ Field prototype, (c) ☐ Pattern or (d) ☐ Model plan? . . .		X
If "Yes," enter the four or eight digit IRS serial number (see instructions) ▶		
19 (a) Is it intended that this plan qualify under section 401(a) or 405 of the Code?	X	
(b) Have you requested or received a determination letter from the IRS for this plan?	X	
20 If plan is integrated, check appropriate box:		
(a) ☐ Social security (b) ☐ Railroad retirement (c) ☐ Other N/A		
21 (a) Is this a defined benefit plan subject to the minimum funding standards for this plan year?	X	
If "Yes," attach Schedule B (Form 5500).		
(b) Is this a defined contribution plan, i.e., money purchase or target benefit, subject to the minimum funding standards? (If a waiver was granted, see instructions.)		X
If "Yes," complete (i), (ii) and (iii) below:		
(i) Amount of employer contribution required for the plan year under section 412 of the Code . .		
(ii) Amount of contribution paid by the employer for the plan year . . . . Enter date of last payment by employer . . . . . ▶ Month .... Day .... Year		
(iii) Funding deficiency, excess, if any, of (i) over (ii)		

	Yes	No
22 The following questions relate to the plan year. If (a)(i), (ii), (iii), (iv) or (v) is checked "Yes," schedules of such items in the format set forth in the instructions are required to be attached to this form.		
(a) (i) Did the plan have assets held for investment?	X	
(ii) Did any non-exempt transaction involving plan assets involve a party known to be a party-in-interest? . .		X
(iii) Were any loans by the plan or fixed income obligations due the plan in default as of the close of the plan year or classified during the year as uncollectable?	X	
(iv) Were any leases to which the plan was a party in default or classified during the year as uncollectable? . .		X
(v) Were any plan transactions or series of transactions in excess of 3% of the current value of plan assets? . .	X	
(b) The accountant's opinion is ☐ not required or ☒ required, attached to this form, and is—		
(i) ☒ Unqualified		
(ii) ☐ Qualified		
(iii) ☐ Adverse		
(iv) ☐ Other (explain)		

Form 5500 (1977)   Page **6**

		Yes	No
23	Complete this item only if you answered "Yes," to Item 6(d)		
	Did one or more of the reportable events or other events requiring notice to the Pension Benefit Guaranty Corporation occur during this plan year?		X
	If "Yes," complete (a) through (h) below.		
(a)	Notification by the Internal Revenue Service that the plan has ceased to be a plan as described in Section 4021(a)(2) of ERISA or a determination by the Secretary of Labor of non-compliance with Title I of ERISA . .	N/A	
(b)	A decrease in active participants to the extent specified in the instructions	N/A	
(c)	A determination by the Internal Revenue Service that there has been a termination or partial termination of the plan within the meaning of Section 411(d)(3) of the Code	N/A	
(d)	An inability to pay benefits when due	N/A	
(e)	A distribution to a Substantial Owner to the extent specified in the instructions	N/A	
(f)	An alternative method of compliance has been prescribed for this plan by the Secretary of Labor under Section 110 of ERISA	N/A	
(g)	A cessation of operations at a facility to the extent specified in the instructions	N/A	
(h)	A withdrawal of a substantial employer	N/A	

If additional space is required for any item, attach additional sheets the same size as this form.

☆ U.S. GOVERNMENT PRINTING OFFICE : 1977—O-235-186   23-0916750

SCHEDULE B (Form 5500) Department of the Treasury Internal Revenue Service Department of Labor Pension and Welfare Benefit Programs Pension Benefit Guaranty Corporation	**Actuarial Information** This schedule is required to be filed under section 104 of the Employee Retirement Income Security Act of 1974, referred to as ERISA, and section 6059(a) of the Internal Revenue Code, referred to as the Code. ▶ **Attach to Forms 5500, 5500–C and 5500–K if applicable.**	**1977** This Form is Open to Public Inspection

For plan year beginning _____ , 1977 and ending _____ 19

▶ Please complete every applicable item on this form. If an item does not apply, enter "N/A."
▶ Round off amounts to nearest dollar.

Name of plan sponsor as shown on line 1(a) of Form 5500, 5500–C or 5500–K **Employer Company**	Employer identification number 24 : 6810120		

Name of plan **Employer Company Pension Plan**	Enter three digit plan number ▶ 0:0 1		Yes	No

			Yes	No
1 Has a waiver of a funding deficiency for the current plan year been approved by the IRS?				X
If "Yes," attach a copy of the IRS approval letter.				
2 Is a waived funding deficiency of a prior plan year being amortized in the current year?				X
3 Have any of the periods of amortization for charges described in section 412(b)(2)(B) of the Code been extended by DOL?				X
If "Yes," attach a copy of the DOL approval of extension letter.				
4 (a) Has the shortfall funding method been used?				X
(b) *(i)* If (a) is "Yes," has the deferral of the amortization of the shortfall gain (loss), beyond the plan year following the year in which the shortfall gain (loss) arose, been elected?				N/A
(ii) If (a) is "Yes," has the deferral of the amortization of the actuarial gain (loss), beyond the first plan year after valuation, been elected?				N/A

5 Actuarial method and operational information: **(a)** Enter most recent actuarial valuation date ▶ **June 30, 1977**

(b) Enter date(s) and amount of contributions received this plan year for prior plan years and not previously reported:
Date(s) ▶ _____ , Amount ▶ **None**

(c) Accumulated funding deficiency at end of plan year (amount of contribution certified by the actuary as necessary to reduce the funding deficiency to zero), from 7(m) or 8(g) . . . . **None**

(d) *(i)* Accrued liabilities as of (enter date) ▶ **June 30, 1977**		43,250,271
(ii) Value of assets as determined for funding standard account		31,000,000
(iii) Unfunded accrued liability		12,250,271
(e) Value of vested benefits (if calculated)		29,750,835
(f) Current value of the assets accumulated in the plan as of (enter date) ▶ **June 30, 1977**		31,000,000
(g) Number of persons covered (included in the most recent actuarial valuation): *(i)* Active participants . .		3,215
(ii) Terminated participants with vested benefits		120
(iii) Retired participants and beneficiaries of deceased participants		375
(h) *(i)* Actuarial gains or (losses) for period ending ▶ **June 30, 1977**		124,000
(ii) Shortfall gains or (losses) for period ending ▶ **N/A**		

(i) Attach a statement of actuarial assumptions and methods used to determine *(i)* the normal cost and liabilities shown on lines 7(b) or 8(b) and 5(d)*(i)*, and *(ii)* the value of assets shown on line 5(d)*(ii)*. The statement is to include a summary of the principal eligibility and benefit provisions upon which the valuation was based, an identification of benefits not included in the calculation, and other facts, such as, any change in actuarial assumptions or cost methods and justifications for any such change. Include also such other information, if any, needed to fully and fairly disclose the actuarial position of the plan.

6 Contributions made to the plan for the plan year by employer(s) and employees:

(a) Month Year	(b) Amount paid by employer	(c) Amount paid by employees	(a) Month Year	(b) Amount paid by employer	(c) Amount paid by employees
12/15/77	3,509,855	None			
			Total . . .	3,509,855	None

Statement by enrolled actuary (see instructions before signing):
To the best of my knowledge, the information supplied in this schedule and on the accompanying statement, if any, is complete and accurate, and in my opinion the assumptions used in the aggregate (a) are reasonably related to the experience of the plan and to reasonable expectations, and (b) represent my best estimate of anticipated experience under the plan.

W.E. Calculate	March 15, 1978
Signature of actuary	Date
W.E. Calculate	001
Print or type name of actuary	Enrollment number
17 Morerless St., City, State 12345	(404) 911-0000
Address	Telephone number (including area code)

Schedule B (Form 5500) 1977   Page **2**

7 Funding standard account statement for plan year ending ▶   June 30, 1977

Charges to funding standard account:	
(a) Prior year funding deficiency, if any	None
(b) Employer's normal cost for plan year	2,520,201
(c) Amortization charges (outstanding balance at beginning of plan year ▶ $ 10,150,312)	507,515
(d) Interest on (a), (b) and (c)	482,139
(e) Total charge, sum of (a) through (d)	3,509,855
Credits to funding standard account:	
(f) Prior year credit balance, if any	None
(g) (i) Employer contributions (total from column (b) of item 6)	3,509,855
(ii) Employer contributions received this plan year for prior plan years and not previously reported . .	-0-
(h) Amortization credits (outstanding balance at beginning of plan year ▶ $ ....)	-0-
(i) Interest on (f), (g) and (h)	-0-
(j) Other (specify) ▶	-0-
(k) Total credits, sum of (f) through (j)	3,509,855
Balance:	
(l) Credit balance, excess, if any, of (k) over (e)	None
(m) Funding deficiency, excess, if any, of (e) over (k)	None

8 Alternative minimum funding standard account (omit if not used):

(a) Was the entry age normal cost method used to determine entries in item 7 above?	☐ Yes ☐ No
If "No," omit (b) through (g) below.	
(b) Normal cost . . . . N/A	
(c) Excess, if any, of value of accrued benefits over market value of assets	
(d) Interest on (b) and (c)	
(e) Employer contributions (total from column (b) of item 6)	
(f) Interest on (e)	
(g) Funding deficiency, excess, if any, of the sum of (b) through (d) over the sum of (e) and (f)	

Instructions

Who Must File.—The employer or plan administrator of a defined benefit plan that is subject to the minimum funding standards of section 412 of the Code and Part 3 of Title I of ERISA) must file this schedule as an attachment to the annual return/report filed for plan years beginning on or after January 1, 1976. Plans maintained on January 1, 1974, pursuant to one or more collective bargaining agreements entered into before September 2, 1974, are not subject to the minimum funding standards for plan years beginning before the earlier of the termination of the collective bargaining agreement(s) or January 1, 1981.

For split funded plans, the costs and contributions reported on Schedule B should include those relating to both trust funds and insurance carriers.

Specific Instructions

(References are to line items on the form.)

4(a) A collectively bargained plan only may elect the shortfall funding method (see regulations under section 412 of the Code). Advance approval from the IRS of the election of the shortfall method of funding is NOT required if it is first adopted on or before the later of (i) the first plan year to which section 412 of the Code applies or (ii) the last plan year commencing before December 31, 1980. However, advance approval from IRS is required, if adopted at a later time or if discontinued.

4(b) Advance approval for the amortization of the shortfall gain (loss) and/or the amortization of the actuarial gain (loss) is required for a plan year, subsequent to the first plan year to which the shortfall method applies. Advance approval from IRS is required for discontinuance.

5(a) The valuation for a plan year may be as of any date in the year, including the first and last. Valuations must be performed within the period specified by section 103(d) of ERISA and section 6059(a) of the Code.

5(b) Not applicable to the first plan year to which the minimum funding standards apply.

5(c) Insert amount from item 7(m). However, if the alternative method is elected, and item 8(g) is smaller than item 7(m), enter the amount from item 8(g). File Form 5330 with the Internal Revenue Service to pay the 5% excise tax on the funding deficiency.

5(d) Amounts in 5(d) should all be as of the same date which should be the date of the end of the plan year or date as of which the most recent actuarial valuation was made. If amounts are not as of the date of the most recent actuarial valuation, indicate in the statement of actuarial assumptions and methods as required by 5(i)) how the amounts in 5(d) were determined. Liabilities fully funded by annuity and insurance contracts other than any contract funds not allocated to individuals may be omitted from both items 5(d)(i) and 5(d)(ii).

5(d)(i) If the aggregate cost or frozen initial liability method is used, enter "N/A."

5(d)(ii) Determine the value of assets in accordance with section 412(c)(2) of the Code or 302(c)(2) of ERISA.

5(d)(iii) If the aggregate cost or frozen initial liability method is used, enter "N/A."

5(f) This should be as of the same date as 5(d) or, if not, the method of adjustment between the two dates should be indicated in 5(i).

5(h)(i) If the aggregate cost or frozen initial liability method is used, enter "N/A."

5(h)(ii) For the methods to be used to determine the shortfall gain (loss) see the regulations under section 412 of the Code.

5(i) A summary of one page or less of plan provisions will ordinarily be adequate. For the first year for which Schedule B is required to be filed, no change in the actuarial method or assumptions needs to the noted or justified. In subsequent years, a change in actuarial method or plan year requires IRS approval. Actuarial methods should be described in accordance with section 3(31) of ERISA as accrued benefit cost (or unit credit), entry age normal cost, individual level premium, aggregate cost, attained age normal cost or frozen initial liability, where those terms are applicable. If the shortfall method of funding is used, all pertinent facts relating to funding peculiar to this method should be included in the statement.

6 Show all employer and employee contributions for the plan year, and employer contributions made not later than 2½ months (or such later date allowed under section 412(c)(10) of the Code and section 302(c)(10) of ERISA) after the end of the plan year.

Statement by enrolled actuary.—In lieu of signing the statement, an enrolled actuary may attach a signed statement containing the name, address, enrollment number, telephone number and the actuary's opinion that the assumptions used in preparing Schedule B are in the aggregate reasonably related to the experience of the plan and to reasonable expectations, and represent his or her best estimate of anticipated experience under the plan and to the best of his or her knowledge the report is complete and accurate. In addition, the actuary may offer any other comments related to the information contained in Schedule B.

7 Under the shortfall method of funding, the Normal Cost in the funding standard account, is the charge per unit of production (or per unit of service) multiplied by the actual number of units of production (or units of service) which occurred during the plan year. Each amortization installment in the funding standard account is similarly calculated. For a plan maintained by more than one employer, the amortization of the shortfall gain (loss) and the actuarial gain (loss) may be deferred. See regulations under section 412 of the Code.

7(b) If no valuation was made for the current year, enter the normal cost calculated in the most recent actuarial valuation, or the estimated cost for the current year based on such valuation. If amounts are not as of the date of the most recent actuarial valuation, indicate in the statement of actuarial assumptions and methods (as required by 5(i)) how the amounts shown were determined.

8(a) If the entry age normal cost method was not used to determine the entries in item 7, the alternative minimum funding standard account may not be used.

8(c) The value of accrued benefits should exclude benefits accrued for the current plan year. The market value of assets should be reduced by the amount of any contributions for the current plan year.

☆ U.S. GOVERNMENT PRINTING OFFICE : 1977—O-235-189   K I # 430814328

EMPLOYER COMPANY PENSION PLAN

Employer Company
I.D. NO. 24-6810120

Attachment to Schedule B (Form 5500)

Statement of Actuarial Valuation Method and Assumptions:

Actuarial valuation method	Entry age normal
Assumed rate of return on investments	5%
Mortality basis	1951 group annuity tables set back 1 year
Employee turnover	a moderate scale (6% per year) consistent with the Company's prior exeperience
Salary increases	a 5% annual rate of salary increase
Retirement	at normal retirement age (65)

Actuarial Asset Valuation Method:

Asset valuation	current value

Summary of Principal Eligibility and Benefit Provisions:

Eligibility	employee age 21 and older
Credited service	all service with company
Normal retirement benefit	1½% average monthly compensation times credited service not exceeding 25 years
Average monthly compensation	average of highest 5 years
Vesting provisions	25% after 5 years, 5% for each of next 5 years, and 10% for each year thereafter

SCHEDULE SSA (Form 5500) Department of the Treasury Internal Revenue Service	Annual Registration Statement Identifying Separated Participants With Deferred Vested Benefits Under Section 6057(a) of the Internal Revenue Code ▶ File as an attachment to Form 5500, 5500–C or 5500–K.	19**77** This Form is NOT Open to Public Inspection Page of

For the calendar year 1977 or fiscal plan year beginning _____ , 1977 and ending _____ , 19

▶ This form must be filed for each plan year in which one or more participants with deferred vested benefit rights separated from the service covered by the plan. See instructions on when to report a separated employee.

1 (a) Name of sponsor (employer if for a single employer plan) Employer Company	1 (b) Employer identification number 24 6810120
Address (number and street) 7000 Easy Road	1 (c) Is this a plan to which more than one employer contributes? . . . . ☐ Yes ☒ No
City or town, State and ZIP code City, State 12345	
2 (a) Name of plan administrator (if other than sponsor) · Pension Board of the Employer Company Pension Plan	2 (b) Administrator's employer identification no. 36 9121518
Address (number and street) 7000 Easy Road	
City or town, State and ZIP code City, State 12345	

3 (a) Name of plan Employer Company Pension Plan	3 (b) Plan number ▶ 0 0 1

4 Does the plan provide a death benefit payable prior to the normal retirement age for separated participants? . . ☐ Yes ☒ No

5 Enter the normal retirement age under the plan ▶ 65

6 Have you notified each separated participant of his/her deferred benefit? . . . . ☒ Yes ☐ No

7 Separated participants with deferred vested benefits:

(a) Social Security Number	(b) Name of participant	Nature and form of benefit code		Amount of vested benefit		
		(c) Type of annuity	(d) Payment frequency	(e) Defined benefit plan—periodic payment	Defined contribution plan	
					(f) Units or shares	(g) Total value of account
000-00-001	William Milstone	G	E	162.50		
000-00-002	Charles Buckeye	G	E	87.00		
000-00-003	James Employee	G	E	150.00		
000-00-004	Sally Secretary	D	E	127.05		

8 Under penalties of perjury, I declare that I have examined this report and to the best of my knowledge and belief it is true, correct and complete.

March 15, 1978   Pension Board of the Employer Company Pension Plan

--------   --
Date   Signature of plan administrator

ACCOUNTANTS' REPORT

Jones & Knight
1 Dupont Avenue
City, State

Pension Board of the Employer Company Pension Plan
City, State

We have examined the statements of assets and liabilities of Employer Company Pension Plan as of December 31, 1977 and 1976, the related statements of changes in net assets available for plan benefits for the years then ended, and the schedules of assets held for investment, transactions or series of transactions in excess of 3% of the current value of plan assets, and loans and fixed-income obligations in default or classified as uncollectible. Our examinations were made in accordance with generally accepted auditing standards and, accordingly, included such tests of the accounting records and such other auditing procedures as we considered necessary in the circumstances.

In our opinion, the financial statements referred to above present fairly the financial position of Employer Company Pension Plan at December 31, 1977 and 1976, and the changes in net assets available for plan benefits for the years then ended, in conformity with generally accepted accounting principles applied on a consistent basis. Further, it is our opinion that the schedules referred to above present fairly the information set forth therein in compliance with the applicable rules and regulations for reporting and disclosure of the Department of Labor.

Jones & Knight

City, State
March 10, 1978

Statement of Assets and Liabilities
Employer Company Pension Plan

	December 31	
	1977	1976
ASSETS		
Cash	$ 187,439	$ 95,813
Certificates of deposit		1,000,450
Marketable securities—Notes A and D:		
United States Government securities	3,694,740	606,214
Corporate bonds and notes	7,800,875	8,458,329
Common stocks	20,600,494	15,608,171
Common stock of Employer Company	1,725,000	1,498,000
	33,821,109	26,170,714
Accrued income	229,386	199,663
Contribution receivable from Employer Company	263,305	238,695
Prepaid insurance premium	6,816	11,632
	$34,508,055	$27,716,967

LIABILITIES AND NET ASSETS AVAILABLE
FOR PLAN BENEFITS

Benefits payable to participants	$ 160,000	$ 78,000
Accounts payable and accrued expenses	39,145	29,968
	199,145	107,968
Net assets available for plan benefits—Note C	34,308,910	27,608,999
Contingency—Note G		
	$34,508,055	$27,716,967

See Notes to Financial Statements.

Statement of Changes in Net Assets
Available for Plan Benefits
Employer Company Pension Plan

	Year Ended December 31	
Additions:	1977	1976
Contribution from Employer		
Company	$ 3,509,855	$ 4,044,264
Interest and dividend income	1,505,112	1,350,007
Dividends from Employer Company	52,000	47,000
	5,066,967	5,441,271
Deductions:		
Benefit payments:		
Retirement	928,298	777,150
Disability	246,987	189,308
Death	76,383	61,535
Termination	144,153	94,474
	1,395,821	1,122,467
Administrative expenses:		
Salaries and allowances	53,400	78,200
Fees and commissions	142,731	76,781
Insurance premiums—Pension Benefit		
Guaranty Corporation	8,327	5,551
Insurance premiums—fiduciary insur-		
ance other than bonding	4,791	3,795
Other administrative expenses	6,723	10,231
	215,972	174,558
Net loss on sale of securities	31,691	330,111
	1,643,484	1,627,136
	3,423,483	3,814,135
Unrealized appreciation (depreciation)		
in aggregate current value of		
securities	3,276,428	(1,033,252)
NET ADDITIONS	6,699,911	2,780,883
Net assets available for plan benefits		
at beginning of year	27,608,999	24,828,116
NET ASSETS AVAILABLE FOR PLAN BENEFITS AT END OF YEAR	$34,308,910	$27,608,999

See Notes to Financial Statements.

Notes to Financial Statements
Employer Company Pension Plan
(December 31, 1977)

Note A—Significant Accounting Policies

The accounting records of the Plan are maintained on the accrual basis.

Marketable securities are stated at aggregate current value. Securities which are traded on a national securities exchange are valued at the last reported sales price on the last business day of the year; investments traded in the over-the-counter market and listed securities for which no sale was reported on that date are valued at the average of the last reported bid and ask prices. For investments in restricted and other securities which do not have an established market, the administrative committee has established a current value for such securities. (See Note D.)

The change in the difference between current value and the cost of investments is reflected in the statement of changes in net assets available for plan benefits as unrealized appreciation (depreciation) in the aggregate current value of securities.

The realized gain or loss on investments is the difference between the proceeds received and the average cost of investments sold.

Note B—Description of the Plan

The pension plan of the Employer Company is a defined benefit plan which covers substantially all employees and which provides for pension and disability benefits. The Company has agreed to voluntarily contribute such amounts as are necessary to provide assets sufficient to meet the benefits to be paid to Plan members. The Company has the right under the Plan to discontinue such contributions at any time and terminate the Plan. In the event of a termination of the Plan, the net assets of the Plan are to be set aside first for the payment of vested benefits and second to the remaining participants on a pro rata basis. However, the Pension Benefit Guaranty Corporation guarantees the payment of all nonforfeitable basic benefits subject to certain limitations prescribed by the Employee Retirement Income Security Act of 1974.

The contributions of the Company are made in amounts sufficient to find the Plan's current service cost on a current basis and to fund the initial past service costs plus interest thereon over a period of 30 years.

There were no significant changes in the Plan or in the method of funding the Plan during 1977 or 1976.

Note C—Benefits

| | June 30 | |
	1977	*1976*
Present value of vested benefits:		
For retired and terminated employees receiving benefits	$ 4,960,414	$ 4,108,207
For active and terminated employees not presently receiving benefits	24,790,421	20,542,036
	$29,750,835	$24,650,243
ESTIMATED ACTUARIALLY DETERMINED UNFUNDED PRIOR SERVICE COSTS	$12,250,271	$10,150,312

The calculations of the present value of vested benefits under the Plan, and of the actuarially determined unfunded prior service cost were made by consulting actuaries as of June 30, 1977 and 1976. The actuaries do not expect that there would be any material change in such amounts to December 31, 1977 and 1976. The actuarial valuation as of June 30, 1977 estimated that the current rate of employer contributions to the Plan should be sufficient to meet current service cost and to fund the initial past service costs plus interest thereon over a period of 30 years.

The more significant assumptions underlying the actuarial computations are as follows:

Actuarial cost method	Entry age normal
Assumed rate of return on investments	5%
Mortality basis	1951 group annuity table, set back 1 year
Employee turnover	a moderate scale (6% per year) consistent with the Company's prior experience
Salary increases	a 5% annual rate of salary increase
Retirement	at normal retirement age (65)

Note D—Marketable Securities

The cost of marketable securities as of December 31, 1977 and 1976 was as follows:

| | *December 31* | |
	1977	*1976*
United States Government securities	$ 3,648,412	$ 645,694
Corporate bonds and notes	8,260,216	9,381,887
Common stocks	19,670,103	17,172,183
	$31,578,731	$27,204,164

The aggregate current value of securities which do not have an established market amounted to approximately $5,016,000 at December 31, 1977 and $3,873,000 at December 31, 1976.

The Plan is authorized to invest up to 10% of the fair value of its total assets in the common stock of the Company. Such investment totaled approximately 5% at December 31, 1977 and 1976.

Note E—Transactions With Parties-in-Interest

During the year ended December 31, 1977, the Plan purchased 2,675 shares of the common stock of the Company for $227,250 and received $52,000 in dividends.

Fees paid during the year for legal, accounting, and other services rendered by parties-in-interest were based on customary and reasonable rates for such services.

Note F—Income Tax Status

The Internal Revenue Service has ruled that the Plan qualifies under Section 401(a) of the Internal Revenue Code and is, therefore, not subject to tax under present income tax laws.

Note G—Litigation

The Plan and the Company are defendants in a class action suit wherein the plaintiffs seek minor actual damages, plus punitive damages aggregating $3,000,000. The suit involves the question as to whether the Plan has in the past been discriminatory in favor of highly compensated personnel. In the opinion of counsel and the Board of Trustees, the claims for damages are without merit.

Assets Held for Investment
Employer Company Pension Plan
(December 31, 1977)

Identity of Issue, Borrower, Lessor, or Similar Party	Description of Investment Including Maturity Date, Rate of Interest, Par, or Maturity Value	Cost	Current Value
United States Government Securities:			
Treasury Bills	$515,000 principal amount, 4.78%, due July 1, 1976	$ 510,773	$ 510,818
Treasury Bills	Series A, $250,000 principal amount, 8%, due May 15, 1982	250,000	256,640
Treasury Note	Series B, $750,000 principal amount, 8¼%, due August 15, 1982	749,449	774,375
Treasury Note	Series F, $500,000 principal amount, 8½%, due September 30, 1979	499,200	521,720
Treasury Note	Series A, $200,000 principal amount, 8%, due February 15, 1983	201,188	205,312
Federal Home Loan Bank	Bank Series 1979-D, $800,000 principal amount, 9.45% due February 26, 1979	825,094	848,000

Federal Land Bank	Bank Series 1985-B, $300,000 principal amount, 8¾%, due October 21, 1985	311,906	317,625
		3,648,412	3,694,740
Corporate Bonds and Trust Demand Notes:			
Finance:			
Bankamerica Corporation	$150,000 principal amount, 6.625% note, due February 1, 1980	$ 148,507	$ 143,250
General Motors Acceptance Corporation	$150,000 principal amount, 7.125% debentures, due December 1, 1990	148,875	133,500
General Electric Company	$120,000 principal amount, 5.75% note, due November 1, 1991	120,000	105,883
		$ 7,350,953	$ 7,096,072
Public Utility:			
Southern Bell Telephone & Telegraph Company	$200,000 principal amount, 7.625% debentures, due March 15, 2003	175,000	168,312
Northwestern Bell Telephone Company	$150,000 principal amount, 6.25% debentures, due January 1, 2007	150,000	117,365
		908,895	704,803
		$ 8,260,216	$ 7,800,875

Assets Held for Investment
Employer Company Pension Plan
(December 31, 1977)
(continued)

Identity of Issue, Borrower, Lessor, or Similar Party	Description of Investment Including Maturity Date, Rate of Interest, Par, or Maturity Value	Cost	Current Value
Common Stocks:			
Banking:			
First Bank System, Inc.	7,100 shares common stock	$ 326,154	$ 330,150
Drugs:			
Sterling Drug, Inc.	14,800 shares common stock	420,983	253,450
Food and Allied:			
Small Company, Inc.	3,000 shares common stock	6,000	6,000[1]
General Foods Corporation	18,700 shares common stock	482,807	532,950
Employer Company*	43,000 shares common stock	1,725,250	1,725,000
		19,670,103	22,325,494
		$31,578,731	$33,821,109

* Indicates party-in-interest to the plan.
[1] Current value as determined by the Administrative Committee (See Note A to financial statements.)

Investment assets acquired and disposed during 1977

Identity of Issue, Borrower, Lessor, or Similar Party	Description of Investment Including Maturity Date, Rate of Interest, Par, or Maturity Value	Cost of Acquisition	Proceeds of Dispositions
Corporate Note: Smith & Company	$100,000 principal amount, 9.5% note, due December 15, 1977	$ 100,025	$ 100,000

**Transactions or Series of Transactions in Excess
of 3 Percent of Current Value of Plan Assets
Employer Company Pension Plan
(Year ended December 31, 1977)**

Category (i)—A single transaction in excess of 3% of plan assets

Identity of Party Involved	Description of Assets	Purchase Price	Selling Price	Lease Rental	Expenses Incurred With Transaction	Cost of Asset	Current Value of Asset on Transaction Date	Net Gain (Loss)
*	American Telephone and Telegraph Co.—25,000 shares of common stock		$1,250,000		$ 3,125	$1,500,000	$1,250,000	$ 253,125
*	Southern Bell Telephone & Telegraph Co. — $1,500,000 principal amount, 8.8% debentures, due May 15, 2005		$1,417,500		$ 1,540	$1,500,000	$1,417,500	$ 84,040
XYZ Broker	United States Government — $1,200,000 principal amount, 4.25% Treasury bonds, due May 15, 1985	$1,140,000				$1,140,000	$1,140,000	

There were no category (ii), (iii), or (iv) reportable transactions during 1977.

*The instructions for this schedule indicate that in the case of a purchase or sale of a security on the market, it is not necessary to identify the person from whom purchased or to whom sold.

Loans and Fixed-Income Obligations in Default or Classified as Uncollectible
Employer Comany Pension Plan
(December 31, 1977)

Identity of Party Involved	Original Amount of Loan	Amount Received During Year		Unpaid Balance	Description of Loan	Amount Overdue	
		Principal	Interest			Principal	Interest
A.B. Investment Corp.	$100,000	$ -0-	$ 3,000	$100,000	6% subordinated debenture, due June 1, 1984—(A)	$ -0-	$ 3,000
Ajx Manufacturing, Inc.	50,000	5,164	2,261	37,622	8% first mortage loan on warehouse in Pittsburgh Pa., due in monthly principal and interest payments of $825—(B)	1,900	575
Roadside Motels	350,000	12,500	15,000	175,000	9% first mortgage loan on motel buildings in Springfield, Illinois, due in monthly installments of $2,917—(C)	2,600	4,904

Note A—A.B. Investment Corp is in receivership. The receiver has not yet determined creditor priorities.

Note B—In February 1978, the overdue principal and interest amounts were collected.

Note C—The Trustees of the Plan have filed suit in federal district court in an attempt to collect the amounts due.

¶ 10.18 ILLUSTRATIVE SUMMARY ANNUAL REPORT

Following is an illustrative summary annual report for the plan whose annual report is illustrated at ¶ 10.17. The summary annual report is intended to meet the minimum requirements of DOL Regulations Section 2520.104 b-10.

In addition to the required information, some plans have used the summary annual report as a vehicle for communicating with employees and have added additional explanatory material. DOL regulations allow inclusion of such material as long as it is readily understood, not inaccurate or misleading, and does not obscure the required material. Additional explanatory material which plans may want to consider include:

(1) A message from the CEO similar to the president's letter in an annual report.

(2) Highlight information:
   (a) Total assets;
   (b) Net increase in assets;
   (c) Company contribution;
   (d) Benefits paid.

(3) Description of benefit improvements and other plan changes.

SUMMARY ANNUAL REPORT
EMPLOYER COMPANY PENSION PLAN
December 31, 1977

Plan Sponsor

Employer Company
7000 Easy Road
City, State 12345

Plan Administrator

Pension Board of the Employer
Company Pension Plan
7000 Easy Road
City, State 12345
(404) 365-8000

EMPLOYER COMPANY PENSION PLAN
7000 EASY ROAD
CITY, STATE 12345

To Plan Participants and Beneficiaries:

The attached financial statements of Employer Company Pension Plan for the years ended December 31, 1977 are provided to you in order to keep you fully informed of the financial condition of your Plan.

Plan participants and beneficiaries may obtain copies of the following more detailed annual report information for a reasonable charge, or inspect it without charge: The latest full annual report, or any parts of the report including a list of any assets held for investment; a list of certain party-in-interest transactions; a list of any loans or obligations in default; a list of any leases in default; and a list of transactions involving more than 3% of plan assets. To obtain a copy of any documents listed, please direct your requests to the Pension Board of the Employer Company Pension Plan. The charge for specific documents will be furnished on request, so that you may determine the cost before ordering. All documents listed may be examined between the hours of nine and five at the corporate office of Employer Company, Suite 3000, 7000 Easy Road, City, State 12345.

Very truly yours,

John R. Good
Administrator

ACCOUNTANTS' REPORT

Jones & Knight
1 Dupont Avenue
City, State

Pension Board of the Employer Company Pension Plan
City, State

We have examined the statements of assets and liabilities of Employer Company Pension Plan as of December 31, 1977 and 1976, and the related statements of changes in net assets available for plan benefits for the years then ended. Our examinations were made in accordance with generally accepted auditing standards and, accordingly, included such tests of the accounting records and such other auditing procedures as we considered necessary in the circumstances.

In our opinion, the financial statements referred to above present fairly the financial position of Employer Company Pension Plan at December 31, 1977, and 1976, and the changes in net assets available for plan benefits for the year then ended, in conformity with generally accepted accounting principles applied on a consistent basis.

Jones & Knight

City, State
March, 10, 1978

Note: DOL regulations do not require the summary annual report to include an accountant's report on the financial statements; however, they do *not preclude* including such a report.

Statement of Assets and Liabilities
Employer Company Pension Plan

	December 31	
	1977	*1976*
ASSETS		
Cash	$ 187,439	$ 95,813
Certificates of deposit		1,000,450
Marketable securities—Notes A and D:		
United States Government securities	3,694,740	606,214
Corporate bonds and notes	7,800,875	8,458,329
Common stocks	20,600,494	15,608,171
Common stock of Employer Company	1,725,000	1,498,000
	33,821,109	26,170,714
Accrued income	229,386	199,663
Contribution receivable from Employer		
Company	263,305	238,695
Prepaid insurance premium	6,816	11,632
	$34,508,055	$27,716,967
LIABILITIES AND NET ASSETS		
AVAILABLE FOR PLAN BENEFITS		
Benefits payable to participants	$ 160,000	$ 78,000
Accounts payable and accrued expenses	39,145	29,968
	199,145	107,968
Net assets available for plan		
benefits—Note C	34,308,910	27,608,999
Contingency—Note G		
	$34,508,055	$27,716,967

See Notes to Financial Statements.

Statement of Changes in Net Assets
Available for Plan Benefits
Employer Company Pension Plan

	Year Ending December 31	
	1977	*1976*
Additions:		
Contributon from Employer Company	$ 3,509,855	$ 4,044,264
Interest and dividend income	1,505,112	1,350,007
Dividends from Employer Company	52,000	47,000
	5,066,967	5,441,271
Deductions:		
Benefit payments:		
Retirement	928,298	777,150
Disability	246,987	189,308
Death	76,383	61,535
Termination	144,153	94,474
	1,395,821	1,122,467
Administrative expenses:		
Salaries and allowances	53,400	78,200
Fees and commissions	142,731	76,781
Insurance premiums—Pension Benefit		
Guaranty Corporation	8,327	5,551
Insurance premiums—fiduciary insurance		
other than bonding	4,791	3,795
Other administrative expenses	6,723	10,231
	215,972	174,558
Net loss on sale of securities	31,691	330,111
	1,643,484	1,627,136
	3,423,483	3,814,135
Unrealized appreciation (depreciation)		
in aggregate current value of securities	3,276,428	(1,033,252)
NET ADDITIONS	6,669,911	2,780,883
Net assets available for plan benefits		
at beginnng of year	27,608,999	24,828,116
NET ASSETS AVAILABLE FOR PLAN BENEFITS AT END OF YEAR	$34,308,910	$27,608,999

See Notes to Financial Statements.

Notes to Financial Statements
Employer Company Pension Plan

(December 31, 1977)

Note A—Significant Accounting Policies

The accounting records of the Plan are maintained on the accrual basis.

Marketable securities are stated at aggregate current value. Securities which are traded on a national securities exchange are valued at the last reported sales price on the last business day of the year; investments traded in the over-the-counter market and listed securities for which no sale was reported on that date are valued at the average of the last reported bid and ask prices. For investments in restricted and other securities which do not have an established market, the administrative committee has established a current value for such securities. (See Note **D**.)

The change in the difference between current value and the cost of investments is reflected in the statement of changes in net assets available for plan benefits as unrealized appreciation (depreciation) in the aggregate current value of securities.

The realized gain or loss on investments is the difference between the proceeds received and the average cost of investments sold.

Note B—Description of the Plan

The pension plan of the Employer Company is a defined benefit plan which covers substantially all employees and which provides for pension and disability benefits. The Company has agreed to voluntarily contribute such amounts as are necessary to provide assets sufficient to meet the benefits to be paid to Plan members. The Company has the right under the Plan to discontinue such contributions at any time and terminate the Plan. In the event of a termination of the Plan, the net assets of the Plan are to be set aside first for the payment of vested benefits and second to the remaining participants on a pro rata basis. However, the Pension Benefit Guaranty Corporation guarantees the payment of all nonforfeitable basic benefits subject to certain limitations prescribed by the Employee Retirement Income Security Act of 1974.

The contributions of the Company are made in amounts sufficient to fund the Plan's current service cost on a current basis and to fund the initial past service costs plus interest thereon over a period of 30 years.

There were no significant changes in the Plan or in the method of funding the Plan during 1977 or 1976.

Note C—Benefits

	June 30	
	1977	*1976*
Present value of vested benefits:		
For retired and terminated employees receiving benefits	$ 4,960,414	$ 4,108,207
For active and terminated employees not presently receiving benefits	24,790,421	20,542,036
	$29,750,835	$24,650,243
ESTIMATED ACTUARIALLY DETERMINED UNFUNDED PRIOR SERVICE COSTS	$12,250,271	$10,150,312

The calculations of the present value of vested benefits under the Plan, and of the actuarially determined unfunded prior service cost were made by consulting actuaries as of June 30, 1977 and 1976. The actuaries do not expect that there would be any material change in such amounts to December 31, 1977 and 1976. The actuarial valuation as of June 30, 1977 estimated that the current rate of employer contributions to the Plan should be sufficient to meet current service cost and to fund the initial past service costs plus interest thereon over a period of 30 years.

The more significant assumptions underlying the actuarial computations are as follows:

Actuarial cost method	Entry age normal
Assumed rate of return on investments	5%
Mortality basis	1951 group annuity table, set back 1 year

Employee turnover	a moderate scale (6% per year) consistent with the Company's prior experience
Salary increases	a 5% annual rate of salary increase
Retirement	at normal retirement age (65)

Note D—Marketable Securities

The cost of marketable securities as of December 31, 1977 and 1976 was as follows:

| | *December 31* | |
	1977	*1976*
United States Government securities	$ 3,648,412	$ 645,694
Corporate bonds and note	8,260,216	9,381,887
Common stocks	19,670,103	17,172,183
	$31,578,731	$27,204,164

The aggregate current value of securities which do not have an established market amounted to approximately $5,016,000 at December 31, 1977 and $3,873,000 at December 31, 1976.

The Plan is authorized to invest up to 10% of the fair value of its total assets in the common stock of the Company. Such investment totaled approximately 5% at December 31, 1977 and 1976.

Note E—Transactions With Parties-in-Interest

During the year ended December 31, 1977, the Plan purchased 2,675 shares of the common stock of the Company for $227,250 and received $52,000 in dividends.

Fees paid during the year for legal, accounting, and other services rendered by parties-in-interest were based on customary and reasonable rates for such services.

Note F—Income Tax Status

The Internal Revenue Service has ruled that the Plan qualifies under Section 401(a) of the Internal Revenue Code and is, therefore, not subject to tax under present income tax laws.

Note G—Litigation

The Plan and the Company are defendants in a class action suit wherein the plaintiffs seek minor actual damages, plus punitive damages aggregating $3,000,000. The suit involves the question as to whether the Plan has in the past been discriminatory in favor of highly compensated personnel. In the opinion of counsel and the Board of Trustees, the claims for damages are without merit.

Chapter 11

CURRENT STATUS OF FASB, AICPA, AND SEC GUIDELINES FOR PLAN ACCOUNTING

¶ 11.01   INTRODUCTION

Prior to the Employee Retirement Income Security Act of 1974 (ERISA), statutory and regulatory requirements for public financial reporting on employee benefit plans were limited to the Taft-Hartley Act requirements for audited financial statements of multiemployer plans, and the Securities and Exchange Commission (SEC) registration and reporting requirements for plans involving an offer to sell securities. The form and content of financial statements of employee stock purchase, savings, and similar plans required to be filed with the SEC are governed by Article 6C of Regulation S-X. In

1972, the American Institute of Certified Public Accountants (AICPA) issued an industry audit guide, "Audits of Employee Health and Welfare Benefit Funds," which includes a discussion of generally accepted accounting principles (GAAP) for welfare benefit plans.

In March 1973, the AICPA also issued an exposure draft of an industry audit guide for pension plans; however, that guide was never issued in final form. As a result, there was little guidance for implementing ERISA's requirements for financial statements prepared in conformity with GAAP. Accordingly, the Financial Accounting Standards Board (FASB) placed the entire subject of accounting and reporting for employee benefit plans on its technical agenda after ERISA was passed. A Discussion Memorandum was issued in October 1975, public hearings were held in January 1976, and an exposure draft of a proposed Statement was issued in April 1977.

The proposed effective date of a Statement on "Accounting and Reporting for Defined Benefit Pension Plans" was for plan years beginning after December 15, 1977, and it was anticipated that the final Statement would be issued prior to December 31, 1977. However, the FASB received over 700 comment letters and decided to defer issuance of a Statement until the comments could be analyzed.

The purpose of this chapter is to summarize the existing literature on the subject of accounting for employee benefit plans. A summary of the FASB Exposure Draft is incuded even though it has not been finalized. The purpose of including this material is to give the reader an idea of the Board's direction. In this regard, it should be noted that a large number of commentators to the Exposure Draft objected to the requirements for statements of accumulated benefits and changes in accumulated benefits.

Chapter 12, which follows, provides guidance for coordinating the existing and proposed authoritative literature with the regulatory accounting and reporting requirements discussed in Chapter 10.

¶ 11.02 SUMMARY OF FASB EXPOSURE DRAFT

[1] Applicability of Proposed Statement

The proposed Statement would apply to all defined benefit pension plans under which there is a promise to pay participants a determinable benefit, usually based on factors such as age, years of service, and salary, including such plans not presently subject to the provisions of

ERISA (e.g., governmental and church plans). Defined contribution plans (e.g., profit-sharing and thrift plans), government-sponsored Social Security plans, welfare benefit plans, terminated plans, and plans for which a decision to terminate has been made are excluded from the scope of the proposed Statement.

[2] Objectives of Financial Accounting and Reporting for Pension Plans

In order to reach a conclusion on the objectives of financial accounting and reporting for pension plans, the Board determined that it must first identify the primary users of plan financial statements. The Board considered participants, employers, governmental authorities, and others having a relationship with the employer (e.g., creditors). It was concluded that plan financial statements should be primarily directed to participants because other interested parties have access to necessary information through other sources (e.g., Form 5500 for the Department of Labor (DOL) and the Internal Revenue Service (IRS), Form 11-K for the SEC, and internal reports for management).

Having identified the plan participants as the primary users of plan financial statements, the Board concluded that the objective of the financial statements "should be to provide information, within the limits of financial accounting, that is useful to plan participants in assessing the security with respect to the receipt of their accumulated benefits."

[3] Plan Financial Statements

To meet the objective described above, the Statement calls for four basic financial statements:

(1) Statement of Net Assets Available for Benefits (see ¶ 11.02[12][a];

(2) Statement of Accumulated Benefits (see ¶ 11.02[12][b]);

(3) Statement of Changes in Net Assets Available for Benefits (see ¶ 11.02[12][c]);

(4) Statement of Changes in Accumulated Benefits (see ¶ 11.02 [12][d]).

The proposed statements represent a significant break from traditional presentation in that the statements of net assets available for benefits and changes in net assets available for benefits would be independent of the statements of accumulated benefits and changes in accumulated benefits, and no surplus or deficiency of assets would be shown.

[4] Reporting Entity

The Discussion Memorandum suggested the fund and the plan as two alternatives for the reporting entity. The concept of the fund as the reporting entity would generally limit the scope of accounting and reporting to plan investments. Since the Board concluded that financial information concerning both the assets and the promise to pay benefits was essential, the plan was determined to be the appropriate reporting entity.

[5] Basis of Accounting

The proposed Statement prescribes the accrual basis of accounting, which is the only basis that provides participants with complete financial information relating to transactions and events occurring during the period. It would generally require that purchases and sales of securities be recorded on a trade-date basis and would include accrual of dividends and interest, and accrual of employer and employee contributions to the extent they are legally or contractually required to be paid.

The requirement that purchases and sales of securities be recorded on a trade-date basis could impose an administrative burden on those plans presently on a settlement-date basis. However, the use of the settlement date is permissible to the extent that the effect on the financial statements would not be material. Thus, where the settlement date is subsequent to the plan's year-end *and* (1) the current value of those securities purchased or sold just before year-end does not change significantly from the trade-date to the date of the financial statements, *and* (2) the purchases or sales do not significantly affect the composition of the plan's assets available for benefits, accounting on a settlement-date basis for such sales and purchases is acceptable.

[6] Symmetry Between Plan and Sponsor Accounting

Neither the Discussion Memorandum nor the Exposure Draft covers the question of accounting for pension cost by the sponsoring employer since that subject is being considered by the FASB as a separate project. However, the Discussion Memorandum commented on the relationship of employer accounting to plan accounting as follows:

"A consideration that is outside the scope of this project is whether, or to what extent, the financial accounting for the plan should be consistent with the financial reporting of the employer or other sponsoring organizations. The issue, which is sometimes referred to as the questions of employer/plan symmetry, will be specifically considered in the FASB project, 'Accounting for the Cost of Pension Plans.' However, the possible implication of solutions to plan accounting problems on the accounting by the employer or other sponsoring organization should not be overlooked by respondents to this Discussion Memorandum."

The Board considered and rejected the view that symmetrical reporting should be a necessary factor in determining the accounting for employer contributions receivable or in selecting the method of accounting for and measuring accumulated benefits for purposes of financial reporting by the plan.

[7] Statement of Net Assets Available for Benefits

An example of the statement of net assets available for benefits included in the Exposure Draft is reproduced at ¶ 11.02[12][a]. The following paragraphs contain comments on the more significant aspects of the statement.

[a] Contributions Receivable

Contributions receivable should include all amounts legally or contractually required to be paid to the plan by either the employer(s) or participants as of the date of the financial statements. The mere promise or intent of the employer(s) to contribute does not constitute a recordable economic resource of the plan. The terms "legally" or "contractually" required to be paid as used in connection with the accrual of contributions are not defined.

An employer would be contractually required to contribute to a pension plan if such requirement, for example, was included in the provisions of a labor contract. ERISA imposes a legal obligation to fund a minimum amount annually unless a waiver is obtained from the Secretary of the Treasury. The funding requirements of ERISA are discussed at ¶ 2.05.

Contributions due from the employer(s) should be identified separately from those due from participants. An adequate allowance should be provided for estimated uncollectible amounts.

[b] Investments

All plan investments would be presented at their current value at the date of the financial statements. "Current value" is defined as the amount that the plan could reasonably expect to receive for the investment in a current sale. This measurement basis was selected as the most appropriate measure of plan investments because in the Board's opinion "that basis provides the most relevant information about the economic resources of a plan consistent with the objective of the financial statements."

Current value should be measured by quoted market prices, if they exist. If no active market exists, the Exposure Draft suggests the use of selling prices of similar investments (without regard to normal costs of sale), the use of forecasts of expected cash flows discounted at a rate commensurate with the risk involved, or the use of independent experts who are qualified to estimate current value.

For unquoted bonds, for example, current value would be determined by computing the present value of the yield using a discount rate similar to the rates on comparable bonds. Forecasts of expected cash flows, discounted at a rate commensurate with the risk involved, might be used in determining the current value of mortgage loans. For leased real estate and other similar assets, current value generally would be estimated on a discounted cash-flow basis or by using independent appraisers.

The Board concluded that insurance company contracts requiring the insurance company to provide certain specified benefit payments (e.g., deferred group annuity contracts) are not plan assets, since in assessing the security of those benefits, participants should look to the financial statements of the insurance company rather than those of the plan. Insurance company contracts such as deposit administration and immediate participation guarantee contracts, for which no benefits are required to be provided by the insurance company, are plan assets since they provide for participation by the plan in the investment performance of the insurance company.

The proposed Statement would require that plan investments be presented in sufficient detail to permit identification of their nature (e.g., marketable securities, employer securities, and real estate in which the plan and the sponsor are jointly involved). The cost of investments would have to be disclosed either parenthetically or by footnote for each significant category.

[8] Statement of Accumulated Benefits

An example of a statement of accumulated benefits included in the Exposure Draft is reproduced at ¶ 11.02[12][b]. The following paragraphs contain comments on the more significant aspects of the statement.

[a] Obligation for Pension Benefits

The Board's decision to require presentation of some measure of the obligation for pension benefits is a logical extension of its conclusion on the objective of the plan financial statements. It concluded that "in order for participants to be in a position to assess the benefit security that is provided by plan assets, it is essential to present a measure of benefits. The financial status of a plan cannot be properly evaluated, analyzed, or understood in the absence of such information."

How to present the obligation for plan benefits gave the Board a separate problem. No conclusion was reached on whether the obligation represented a liability of the plan (or of the sponsoring employer) or an equity interest because the Board concluded that resolution of that issue was not necessary for plan participants to assess the security of their benefits. The Board determined, however, that information on accumulated benefits is too important to be relegated to a footnote, and presentation in a separate statement is appropriate.

[b] Definition of "Accumulated Benefits"

Accumulated benefits are defined as those benefits that are attributable under the provisions of a pension plan to employees' service rendered to the date of the financial statements. In effect, these are the benefits "earned" to date by participants regardless of whether they are vested. Examples are pension benefits, death benefits including survivor annuities and refunds of participants' contributions, and expected disability benefits payable under the plan to participants who are presently entitled to receive those benefits.

[c] Measure of Accumulated Benefits

The measure of benefits to be included in the statement of accumulated benefits would be the aggregate of employees' accumulated benefits as determined by the plan's "benefit accrual provision" using employee data as of the date of the financial statements. No recognition would be given to benefits which employees could accumulate only through further advancement in age or service or to cost-of-living or other benefit increases which become effective after the date of the financial statements.

The plan's benefit-accrual provision is usually contained in the plan as a formula or schedule that specifies the rate at which employees' benefits are accumulated. For example, some plans specify that employees accumulate a fixed dollar (e.g., $20 a month) benefit to be paid at age 65 for each year of service. Other plans determine benefits based on both service and salary. One example of this type of benefit-accrual provision would be one which provides for a benefit of 1½ percent of final (or average) annual compensation per year of service.

The Board feels that the use of the benefit-accrual provision method results in a measure of benefits that approximates that amount that would be required to purchase annuities payable on retirement for benefits participants have accumulated to the date of the financial statements on the basis of the plan's provision. It believes that measure is objective and verifiable and best meets the needs of participants for financial accounting information about the plan.

To illustrate this concept, assume an employee has ten years of service under a plan providing an annual benefit of 1½ percent of final salary per year of service. Since future salary increases are not considered, his salary, in this example, $30,000, for the latest year would be used to determine his accumulated benefit. The employee's annual benefit earned to date would be $4,500 (10 years × 1½ per year × $30,000). That benefit for the estimated number of years it would be received by the employee (e.g., until his death), discounted to its present value, and combined with the current value of accumulated benefits of other employees, would be the plan's total accumulated benefits. Again, it should be noted that total accumulated benefits are not reduced for anticipated employee turnover.

[d] Current Value of Accumulated Benefits

To measure their current value, accumulated benefits should be adjusted for mortality and discounted to the date of the financial statements. Plans covered by Title IV of ERISA, which at the date of the financial statements are insufficient plans (e.g., a plan with an excess of guaranteed benefits over assets), would be required to use the interest and mortality rates used by the Pension Benefit Guaranty Corporation (PBGC) to value accrued benefits upon plan termination.

The use of PBGC rates also would be required for all other plans unless it could be demonstrated that other rates for those plans were clearly preferable. The Exposure Draft cites factors such as sufficient plan mortality experience and anticipated rates of return on plan investments, which are significantly different from corresponding factors reflected in the PBGC rates, as indications that other rates are clearly preferable.

[e] Changes in Assumptions

Changes in the interest rate(s) made to reflect changes in the anticipated rate(s) of return on investments, and changes in the mortality rates made to reflect changes in the life expectancy of participants should be viewed as changes in estimates and accounted for in the year of change with no restatement of financial statements of prior years. Changes in these assumptions and their effects on measuring the current value of accumulated benefits should, if practicable, be disclosed in the final statements in the year of change.

[f] Presentation

The statement of accumulated benefits should present separately the current value as of the date of the financial statements of each of the following:

(1) Vested benefits of retired participants;

(2) Other vested benefits;

(3) Nonvested benefits.

Further segregation of the above categories would be required if such segregation would provide information that is particularly useful to a significant number of participants in assessing their benefit security. Examples of situations which would require further segregation are (1) the existence of specific assets to provide benefits to specified participants within the above categories, and (2) the extent to which benefits are covered by the PBGC.

[9] Statements of Changes in Net Assets Available for Benefits and Changes in Accumulated Benefits

The Board concluded that plan financial statements should provide information about changes in investment performance, level of contributions, services rendered, improvements of benefits, and changes in accounting estimates to assist participants in properly understanding any change in their benefit security during the period, and to assist them in their assessment of future benefit security. To accomplish that, plan financial statements should include a statement of changes in net assets available for benefits and a statement of changes in accumulated benefits. These statements should be presented in sufficient detail and arranged in a manner that the nature and effects of all significant changes can be identified.

[a] Statement of Changes in Net Assets Available for Benefits

The following categories should be presented at a minimum:

(1)   The net change in current value of investments held at year-end;

(2)   The net change in current value (from the beginning of the year to date of sale) of investments sold during the year;

(3)   Investment income (exclusive of (1) and (2) above).

(4)   Contributions from the employer(s) (nonmonetary contributions from the employer(s) should be recorded at their current value);

(5)   Contributions from participants, including those transmitted by the sponsor;

(6)   Benefits paid;

(7)   Other distributions;

(8)   Administrative expenses.

The net gain or loss realized (based on historical cost) during the year on sales of investments would have to be disclosed either parenthetically or in a footnote.

An example of this statement included in the Exposure Draft is at ¶ 11.02[12][c].

[b] Statement of Changes in Accumulated Benefits

The statement of changes in accumulated benefits would have to disclose all significant changes in accumulated benefits during the year, including, but not necessarily limited to, the following:

(1)   Plan amendments;

(2)   Changes in mortality and interest rates;

(3)   Benefits accumulated;

(4) Benefits paid (not including any benefit payments made by an insurance company under a contract that requires the insurance company to provide these benefits);

(5) Payments to an insurance company for contracts that require the insurance company to provide certain benefits;

(6) Forfeitures;

(7) The increase in the current value of accumulated benefits due to the passage of time.

An example of this statement included in the Exposure Draft is at ¶ 11.02[12][d].

[10] Other Financial Statement Disclosures

Sample footnotes are included in the Exposure Draft and are reproduced at ¶ 11.02[12][e]. Parenthetical references included in the following discussions of the disclosure requirements are to the sample footnotes.

All disclosures required by generally accepted accounting principles for other entities should be made, if applicable to the plan, including a description of all significant accounting policies. The disclosure of accounting policies for a plan should include:

(1) A description of the method(s) and principal assumptions used to determine the current value of investments (Note B);

(2) A description of the method and principal assumptions used to determine the current value of accumulated benefits (Note B).

The following disclosures which are unique to defined benefit plans are also required:

☐ A brief, general description of the plan agreement, including, but not limited to, contributory characteristics, vesting and benefit provisions, any plan amendments scheduled to become effective after the date of financial statements (and not reflected therein), and the priority order of participants' claims to the assets of the plan (Note A).

☐ A description of significant changes made in the plan agreement during the year (not applicable in sample).

☐ A description of significant changes in methods or assumptions used to measure the net assets available for benefits or the accumulated benefits (Note F).

☐ The extent to which the plan holds investments in securities or has made loans to the sponsor; disclosure of real estate or other transactions in which the plan and the sponsor may be jointly involved (Note D).

☐ The aggregate amount of annual benefits, if any, to be paid by insurance companies under annuity contracts together with a description of the participants whose benefits will be so provided (not applicable in sample).

☐ The funding policy of the sponsor, and any changes in such policy during the year (Note C).

☐ The tax status of the plan if the plan has not received a letter of determination from the Internal Revenue Service or if such letter has been revoked (not applicable in sample).

☐ The nature of any subsequent events (e.g., significant plan amendments, large and unusual terminations of employees who have nonvested benefits, and a change in the tax status of the plan) that in the aggregate significantly affect the relationship between net assets available for the plan benefits. If reasonably determinable, the effects of such events or transactions should be quantified (not applicable in sample).

☐ A brief, general description of benefits guaranteed by the PBGC (Note A).

[11] Effective Date and Transition

The Statement as originally proposed would have been effective for plan years beginning on or after December 15, 1977, and would require retroactive restatement of prior years' financial statements. Disclosure of the nature of the restatement would be required in the year the Statement is first applied. The delay in issuance of the Statement will probably result in a delay in the effective date.

[12] Illustration of Financial Statements

Appendix D of the Exposure Draft contains illustrative financial statements, which are reproduced on the following pages. The FASB introduction to these statements states:

"This Appendix illustrates one way of meeting the requirements of this Statement that are applicable for a hypothetical plan, the C&H Company Pension Plan. The illustration does not encompass other requirements of this Statement that would be applicable in other circumstances."

The financial statements illustrated are for a contributory defined benefit pension plan having investments in mortgages, real estate, and a deposit with an insurance company in addition to security investments. In this way, the FASB was able to illustrate the presentation and disclosures (see Notes B and D) of these types of investments. In general, the illustrative financial statements provide excellent guidance for applying the provisions of the Exposure Draft. In addition, the presentation and disclosures relating to investments, accounting policies, and matters other than "accumulated benefits" can in many cases be adapted to current DOL and GAAP reporting requirements.

[a] **FASB Exposure Draft Example of the Statement of Net Assets Available for Benefits**

EXPOSURE DRAFT

C&H Company Pension Plan
Statement of Net Assets Available for Benefits

	December 31	
	1978	*1977*
Assets		
Investments, at current value (Notes B(1) and D)		
United States Government securities	$ 450,000	$ 370,000
Corporate bonds	3,400,000	3,570,000
Common stock		
C&H Company	690,000	880,000
Other	2,250,000	1,860,000
Mortgages	480,000	460,000
Real estate	270,000	240,000
Account with insurance company	1,000,000	890,000
	8,540,000	8,270,000
Receivables		
Employees' contributions	40,000	35,000
Securities sold	310,000	175,000
Accrued interest and dividends	77,000	76,000
	427,000	286,000
Cash	200,000	90,000
Total assets	9,167,000	8,646,000

The accompanying notes are an integral part of the financial statements.

	December 31	
	1978	*1977*
Liabilities		
Accounts payable		
Securities purchased	—	400,000
Other	70,000	60,000
	70,000	460,000
Accrued expenses	85,000	40,000
Total liabilities	155,000	500,000
Net assets available for benefits	$9,012,000	$8,146,000

[b] FASB Exposure Draft Example of the Statement of Accumulated Benefits

Statement of Accumulated Benefits

	December 31	
	1978	*1977*
Current value of accumulated benefits (Notes A(5), B(2), and E)		
Vested benefits		
Retired participants	$ 3,040,000	$ 2,950,000
Other participants	8,120,000	6,530,000
	11,160,000	9,480,000
Nonvested benefits	3,000,000	2,400,000
Total current value of accumulated benefits	$14,160,000	$11,880,000

The accompanying notes are an integral part of the financial statements.

[c] FASB Exposure Draft Example of the Statement of Changes in Net Assets Available for Benefits

Statement of Changes in Net Assets Available for Benefits

	Year Ended December 31	
	1978	1977
Investment income (Notes B(3) and D)		
Increase (decrease) in current value of:		
Investment sold during the year	$ 50,000	$ (39,000)
Investments held at year-end	157,000	(33,000)
	207,000	(72,000)
Interest	345,000	320,000
Dividends	130,000	110,000
Rents	55,000	43,000
	737,000	401,000
Less investment expenses	39,000	35,000
	698,000	366,000
Contributions		
Employer (Note C)	780,000	710,000
Employees (Note A(4))	450,000	430,000
	1,230,000	1,140,000
Total additions	1,928,000	1,506,000
Benefits paid	997,000	746,000
Administrative expenses	65,000	58,000
Total deductions	1,062,000	804,000
Net additions	866,000	702,000
Net assets available for benefits		
Beginning of year	8,146,000	7,444,000
End of year	$9,012,000	$8,146,000

The accompanying notes are an integral part of the financial statements.

[d] FASB Exposure Draft Example of the Statement of Changes in Accumulated Benefits

Statement of Changes in Accumulated Benefits

| | *Year Ended December 31* | |
	1978	*1977*
Current value of accumulated benefits at beginning of year	$11,880,000	$11,543,700
Increase (decrease) during the year attributable to:		
Change in interest rates (Note E)	(101,450)	—
Benefits accumulated by employees of Company L (Note E)	2,235,950	—
Benefits accumulated by employees of C&H Company	575,000	582,300
Nonvested benefits forfeited due to employee terminations (Note A(2))	(52,500)	(50,000)
Benefits paid (Note E)	(997,000)	(746,000)
Passage of time (Note B(2))	620,000	550,000
Net increase	2,280,000	336,300
Current value of accumulated benefits at end of year	$14,160,000	$11,880,000

The accompanying notes are an integral part of the financial statements.

[e] **FASB Exposure Draft Example of Notes to Financial Statements**

Notes to Financial Statements

A. **Description of Plan**

1. *General.* The C&H Company Pension Plan (*Plan*) is a defined benefit pension plan covering substantially all employees of C&H Company (*Company*). Established in 1964, the Plan provides for pension, death, and disability benefits. It is subject to the provisions of the Employee Retirement Income Security Act of 1974 (*ERISA*).

2. *Pension Benefits.* Under the Plan, employees with 10 or more years of service are entitled to annual pension benefits beginning at normal retirement age (65) equal to 1½ percent of their final annual compensation for each year of service. Participants may elect to receive their pension benefits in the form of a joint and survivor annuity. If employees terminate before rendering 10 years of service, they forfeit the right to receive the benefits they have accumulated. Employees may elect to receive the current value of their accumulated benefits as a lump-sum distribution upon retirement or early termination, or they may elect to receive their benefits as a life annuity payable monthly from retirement. For employees electing a life annuity, payments will not be less than the greater of (a) accumulated employee contributions plus interest, or (b) an annuity for 5 years.

3. *Death and Disability Benefits.* When an active employee dies at age 55 or older, a death benefit, equal to the current value of the employee's accumulated pension benefits, is paid to the employee's beneficiary. Active employees who become totally disabled receive annual disability benefits that are equal to the normal retirement benefits they have accumulated as of the time they become disabled. Disability benefits are paid until normal retirement age at which time disabled participants begin receiving normal retirement benefits computed as though they had been employed to normal retirement age with their annual compensation remaining the same as at the time they became disabled.

4. *Contributions.* As a condition of participation, employees are required to contribute three percent of their salary to the Plan. The Company intends to contribute such additional amounts as are necessary to provide assets sufficient to meet benefit payments (Note C). While it has not expressed any intention to do so, the Company has the right under the Plan to discontinue such contributions at any time and to terminate the Plan subject to the provisions set forth in ERISA.

5. *Plan Termination.* In the event the Plan terminates, the net assets of the Plan will be allocated, as prescribed by ERISA and regulations issued pursuant thereto, generally to provide the following benefits in the order indicated:

(a) Benefits attributable to employee contributions, taking into account those paid out before termination.

(b) Benefits participants have been receiving, or would have been receiving if they had retired at normal retirement age, for at least three years. The priority attaches only to the lowest benefit level under the Plan during the five years prior to retirement. For those actually retired for three or more years the priority applies only to the lowest benefit level in effect during the most recent three-year period.

(c) Other vested benefits insured by the Pension Benefit Guaranty Corporation *(PBGC)* (a U.S. governmental agency) up to the applicable limitations (see following paragraph).

(d) All other vested benefits (that is, vested benefits not insured by the PBGC).

(e) All nonvested benefits.

Certain benefits under the Plan are insured by the PBGC if the Plan terminates. Generally, the PBGC guarantees most vested normal age retirement benefits, early retirement benefits, and certain disability and survivor's pensions. However, the PBGC does not guarantee all types of benefits under the Plan, and the amount of benefit protection is subject to certain limitations.

The PBGC guarantees vested benefits under the Plan at the level in effect on the date of the Plan's termination. However, if benefits have been increased within the five years before the Plan's termination, the whole amount of vested benefits, or the benefit increase may not be guaranteed. In addition, there is a statutory ceiling on the amount of an individual's monthly benefit that the PBGC guarantees. As of December 31, 1978 and December 31, 1977, that ceiling which is adjusted periodically was $XXX and $937.50 per month, respectively.

As indicated by the preceding paragraphs, whether all participants receive their accumulated benefits should the Plan terminate at some time in the future will depend on the sufficiency, at that time, of the Plan's net assets to provide those benefits. If assets must be allocated to participants at that time, the allocation will be made on the priority basis generally described above so that some benefits under the Plan may be provided for in full by existing plan assets and the PBGC guaranty, while other benefits, primarily nonvested benefits but possibly including some vested benefits as well, may not be provided for at all by existing assets or by the guaranty. At December 31, 1978, approximately $1,900,000 of the current value of non-retired participants' vested benefits represents the current value of former Company L employees' vested benefits (Note E). Had the Plan terminated at December 31, 1978, none of the Plan's net assets (nor any PBGC guaranty) would have been available to provide those participants with their benefits.

B. Summary of Accounting Policies

The following are the significant accounting polcies followed by the Plan:

1. *Valuation of Investments.* Investments in securities traded on a national securities exchange are valued at the last reported sales price on the last business day of the year; securities traded in the over-the-counter market and listed securities for which no sale was reported on that date are valued at the mean between the last reported bid and asked prices.

Certain securities have no quoted market value. The amounts shown in Note D for such securities represent current value as determined by the Plan's administrator. Many factors are considered in arriving at that current value. In general, however, corporate bonds are valued based on yields currently available on comparable securities of other issuers with similar credit ratings. Investments in certain restricted common stocks are valued at the quoted market price of the issuer's unrestricted common stock less a discount of 10-20 percent. Where a quoted market price for unrestricted common stock of the issurer is not available, restricted common stocks are valued at a multiple of current earnings less a discount of 10-20 percent. The multiple chosen is consistent with multiples of other similar companies based upon current market prices.

Mortgages have been valued on the basis of their future principal and interest payments discounted at prevailing interest rates for similar instruments. The current value of real estate investments, principally rental property subject to long-term net leases, has been estimated on the basis of future rental receipts and estimated residual values discounted at interest rates commensurate with the risks involved. The Plan's separate account with an insurance company is invested in real estate. The current value of that account was determined by the insurance company on a basis consistent with that used to measure the Plan's other real estate investments.

2. *Accumulated Benefits.* Accumulated benefits are those annual pension benefits that individual participants have accumulated under the Plan's benefit accrual provision based on their current salary and service to date. The current value of those accumulated benefits presented in the financial statements is the aggregate of participants' accumulated benefits adjusted to reflect the life expectancy of participants and discounted for the time value of money (that is, interest). An appropriate adjustment in the interest rate is made to reflect the anticipated administrative expenses associated with providing benefits. The mortality and adjusted interest rates used in the foregoing computations are the same as those the PBGC would have used at the date of the financial statements to measure participants' accumulated benefits for purposes of determining the

sufficiency of the plan's assets to meet pension benefits. The adjusted interest rates used by the PBGC decline at stated time intervals during the period that payment of benefits is deferred. Applying those rates resulted in a weighted average interest rate of 5.2 percent and 5.1 percent in 1978 and 1977, respectively. The current value of prior years' accumulated benefits increases each year to reflect a decrease of one year in the period that payment of benefits is deferred.

In addition to pension benefits, the current value of accumulated benefits reflects, using the same mortality rates indicated above and a 5 percent interest rate, those death benefits expected to be paid to participants' beneficiaries.

3. *Other.* Purchases and sales of securities are recorded on the date the transaction order is executed. Dividend income is recorded on the ex-dividend date. Income from other investments is recorded as earned.

C. Funding Policy

The Company's funding policy is to make annual contributions to the Plan in amounts that are a constant percentage of employees compensation each year (approximately 5 percent for both 1978 and 1977), such that, when combined with employees contributions (Note A(4)), all employees' pension benefits will be fully provided for by the time they retire. Beginning in 1979, the Company's contribution is expected to increase to approximately 6 percent to provide for the benefits that are attributable to the service of former Company L employees prior to the time they joined the Company (Note E).

D. Investments

Except for an insurance company account, the investment assets of the Plan are held by a bank-administered trust fund.

During the year ended December 31, 1977, the Plan purchased 100,000 shares of the Company's common stock for $800,000. At December 31, 1978, the current value of that investment aggregated approximately 8 percent of the current value of the Plan's assets. The Plan received $40,000 in dividends from the Company in both 1978 and 1977.

During the years ended December 31, 1978 and December 31, 1977, the aggregate proceeds from sales of investments exceeded the aggregate cost of investments sold by $107,000 and $259,000, respectively. The following table presents the aggregate current value and cost, respectively, for each of the plan's significant investment categories:

| | December 31 | | | |
| | 1978 | | 1977 | |
	Current Value	Cost	Current Value	Cost
Investments Readily Marketable				
U.S. Government securities	$ 450,000	$ 500,000	$ 370,000	$ 400,000
Corporate bonds	3,1600,000	3,540,000	3,260,000	3,370,000
Common stocks				
C&H Company	690,000	800,000	880,000	800,000
Other	1,780,000	1,265,000	1,400,000	1,365,000
	6,080,000	6,105,000	5,910,000	5,935,000
Investments Not Readily Marketable				
Corporate bonds	240,000	250,000	310,000	300,000
Common stocks	470,000	305,000	460,000	355,000
Mortgage	480,000	400,000	460,000	400,000
Real estate	270,000	230,000	240,000	230,000
Account with insur-ance company	1,000,000	900,000	890,000	800,000
	2,460,000	2,085,000	2,360,000	2,085,000
	$8,540,000	$8,190,000	$8,270,000	$8,020,000

E. Accumulated Benefits

During 1978 the interest rates used to measure the current value of accumulated benefits were changed to reflect changes in the interest rates used by the PBGC.

Late in 1978 the Company acquired Company L. Company L did not have a pension plan. As part of the purchase agreement, the Company agreed to include Company L's employees in the Company's pension plan and to recognize their service to Company L for purposes of measuring their pension benefits.

Pension benefits paid during 1978 include a lump-sum distribution of $114,000. There were no such distributions in 1977. During 1977 and 1978, there were no participants receiving disability benefits under the Plan.

F. Accounting Changes

In 1978 the Plan changed its method of accounting and reporting to comply with the provisions of a Statement of Financial Accounting Standards issued by the Financial Accounting Standards Board. The financial statements for 1977 have been restated to present them on a comparable basis.

¶ 11.03   REQUIREMENT OF ARTICLE 6C OF REGULATION S-X

As previously noted, the form and content of financial statements of employee stock purchase, savings, and similar plans required to be filed with the SEC are governed by Article 6C of Regulation S-X. The specific requirements of Article 6C are in addition to the general requirements of Articles 1, 2, 3, and 4; however, the specific rules take precedence over the general rules if there are conflicts.

[1] Financial Statements

The financial statements prescribed by Article 6C are statements of financial condition, and income and changes in plan equity.

[a] Statement of Financial Condition

The statement of financial condition should include separate sections for each class of securities of participating employers, investments in securities or unaffiliated issuers, U.S. Government bonds and other direct obligations of the U.S. Government, other securities, investments other than securities, dividends and interest receivable, cash, and other assets.

Each major class of investment other than securities should be separately stated, and other securities should be segregated between marketable and other securities. Other assets should state separately amounts due from participating employers or their director, officers, and principal holders of equity securities, amounts due from trustees or managers of the plan, and any other significant amounts.

Liabilities and plan equity should be broken down by amounts payable to participating employers, amounts payable to participating employees, reserves and other credits, other significant liabilities, and plan equity. Reserves and other credits should be appropriately described, either in the caption or in a footnote.

[b] Statements of Income and Changes in Plan Equity

Net investment income should be broken down by source—cash dividends, interest, and other. Separate aggregation should be made of income from securities of participating employers. Any significant expenses should be stated separately.

Realized gains and losses on investment transactions should be stated separately for investments in securities of participating employers, other security investments, and other investments. Footnote disclosure should be made of how the cost of securities sold was determined (e.g., first in-first out, average cost). Also, the aggregate cost, proceeds, and gain or loss from transactions in each separate category of investments should be given.

Unrealized appreciation or depreciation of investments should be disclosed at the beginning and end of the period. The increase or decrease during the period should be stated separately if investments are accounted for at fair value, or disclosed if investments are accounted for at cost.

Contributions and deposits to the fund should be segregated between employers and employees. Footnote disclosure should be made of employer and employee contributions by participating employer if more than one employer participates in the plan. Withdrawals, lapses, and forfeitures of employees' accounts should be separately stated as well as amounts disbursed in settlement of such accounts and the disposition of balances remaining after settlement.

[2] Other Accounting and Disclosure Requirements

Article 6C provides that all assets may be valued at either cost or market, provided cost or market, whichever is not used for the primary valuation, is shown parenthetically. For plans providing investment options to participants, footnote disclosure of the various investment programs and the number of employees in each program is required. For plans which measure participant's equity in terms of units, the number of units and net asset value per unit should be disclosed.

Income taxes should be provided if the plan is not exempt from federal income taxes, including appropriate taxes on recognized unrealized appreciation on investments. If the plan is not subject to federal income taxes, a brief statement as to why should be included. In addition, the federal income tax status of the employee with respect to the plan should be disclosed.

[3] Schedule Requirements

A detailed schedule of investments is required for each statement of condition. Information to be included in the schedule is as follows: (1) name of issuer and title of issue, (2) balance held at close of period-number of shares, principal amount of bonds and notes, (3) cost of each item, and (4) value of each item at close of period.

For plans providing separate investment programs with separate funds, a schedule allocating all assets and plan income and changes in plan equity to the applicable funds should be filed unless this information is shown in the basic financial statements.

[4] Illustrative Financial Statements

Illustrative financial statements complying with the requirements of Article 6C are included on the following pages. These financial statements are also intended to meet the DOL financial statement requirements.

[a] Statement of Financial Condition

In addition to complying with the SEC and DOL requirements, this statement would generally meet the requirements of the FASB Exposure Draft. Of particular note with respect to this statement is the segregation of the investment funds A, B, and C. This was done to meet the SEC requirement for a schedule allocating all assets and plan income and changes in plan equity to the applicable funds unless this information is shown in the basic financial statements.

[b] Statement of Income and Changes in Plan Equity

This statement would also meet most of the proposed requirements of the FASB Exposure Draft. The principal exception is the accounting for and reporting of realized gain on sale of investments and unrealized appreciation on investments. The FASB Exposure Draft would require reporting of only the increase (decrease) in the current value of investments in the basic financial statements with footnote disclose of amounts realized.

[c] Notes to Financial Statements and Other Matters

The most significant difference between the financial statements complying with Article 6C and those of the FASB Exposure Draft is that the Article 6C financial statements do not include statements of accumulated benefits and changes in accumulated benefits and related disclosures.

STATEMENT OF FINANCIAL CONDITION
EMPLOYEE SAVINGS PLAN OF EMPLOYER COMPANY

	December 31, 1977			December 31, 1976		
	Fund A	Fund B	Fund C	Fund A	Fund B	Fund C
ASSETS						
Cash	$ 509,395	$ 20,320	$ 2,511,951	$ 39,628		$ 36,489
Contributions receivable	735,690	646,291	740,090	519,843	$ 866,796	3,319,045
Accrued income		545,058		619,848	420,198	670,949
Investments, at current value (cost: 1977—$264,532,644; 1976—$267,895,322) Schedule I:						
Temporary investments	32,201,766			7,400,000		
Governmental obligations	12,858,202		2,660,000	23,795,730	3,360,000	2,650,000
Corporate bonds—Note C				11,899,237		
Common stock:						
Employer Company						
Other		98,283,126	151,296,113		100,128,061	104,125,990
	45,059,968	98,283,126	153,956,113	43,094,967	103,488,061	106,775,990
	$46,305,053	$99,494,795	$157,208,154	$44,274,286	$104,775,055	$110,802,473
LIABILITIES						
Cash overdraft	$ 34,538		$ 239,895	$ 1,160,405	$ 98,415	
Withdrawals due members	933,241	$ 1,994,055	1,772,796	17,158	2,627,558	$ 1,723,244
Accrued trustee fees					43,371	20,387
Plan equity	45,337,274	97,500,740	155,195,463	43,096,723	102,005,711	109,058,842
	$46,305,053	$99,494,795	$157,208,154	$44,274,286	$104,775,055	$110,802,473

See Notes to Financial Statements.

STATEMENT OF INCOME AND CHANGES IN PLAN EQUITY
EMPLOYEE SAVINGS PLAN OF EMPLOYER COMPANY

	Year Ended December 31, 1977			Year Ended December 31, 1976		
	Fund A	Fund B	Fund C	Fund A	Fund B	Fund C
Plan Equity at Beginning of Year	$43,096,723	$102,005,711	$109,058,842	$38,244,789	$ 78,491,036	$ 58,423,028
Contributions:						
Member	6,037,942	8,933,283	12,596,464	5,049,434	9,393,474	14,906,268
Employer Company	(76,201)	(226,216)	20,361,281	3,532,552	10,617,612	7,273,407
Net Investment Income:						
Interest	3,065,608	38,703	95,899	3,257,140	623,886	65,139
Dividends:						
Employer Company			2,956,102			2,607,195
Other		2,449,924			2,034,466	
Realized Gain (Loss) on Investments:						
Proceeds	91,778,337	52,710,768	34,676,251	32,280,293	35,037,084	16,217,177
Less Cost	91,788,982	48,608,492	33,572,037	32,495,468	40,650,786	22,460,181
	(10,645)	4,102,276	1,104,214	(215,175)	(5,613,702)	(6,243,004)
Unrealized Appreciation (Depreciation) of Investments:						
Ending balance	1,569,659	10,002,556	21,194,348	(735,393)	8,946,907	(22,747,818)
Less beginning balance	(735,393)	8,946,907	(22,747,818)	(1,201,123)	(11,644,255)	(72,178,099)
Change During Year	2,305,052	1,055,649	43,942,166	465,730	20,591,162	49,430,281
Withdrawals	(9,047,295)	(20,776,030)	(34,857,458)	(7,206,414)	(14,069,219)	(17,334,847)
Administration Expense	(33,910)	(82,560)	(62,047)	(31,333)	(63,277)	(68,625)
PLAN EQUITY AT END OF YEAR	$45,337,274	$ 97,500,740	$155,195,463	$43,096,723	$102,005,711	$109,058,842
Net Assets Value Per Unit:						
December 31, 1977	$2.2721	$1.6414	$2.6193			
December 31, 1976				$2.0140	$1.5347	$1.8232

See Notes to Financial Statements.

Notes to Financial Statements

Employee Savings Plan of Employer Company

(December 31, 1977)

Note A—Significant Accounting Policies

The financial statements of the Plan are reported on the accrual basis.

The investments are stated at current published market prices, except for private placement securities, for which the current values are determined by the Trustee.

The difference between the current value and the cost of investments is reflected in the statement of income and changes in plan equity as unrealized appreciation (depreciation) of investments.

The realized gain (loss) on investments is the excess (deficiency) of the proceeds over (under) the average cost of investments. Proceeds for Fund C represent the market value of Employer Company shares distributed to withdrawing Members.

Note B—Description of the Plan

The Plan is a contributory defined contribution plan of Employer Company. Each employee who elects to become a Member of the Plan authorizes a deduction from every paycheck of either 2%, 4%, 6%, or 8% of his base salary for contribution to his account in the Plan. He elects one of six methods of investing in Fund A (a fixed-income fund), Fund B (an equity fund), and/or Fund C (Employer Common Stock). The approximate number of Members electing each alternative at December 31, 1977 was as follows:

100% in Fund A	3,048
100% in Fund B	3,352
100% in Fund C	7,553
50% in Fund A, 50% in Fund B	2,324
50% in Fund A, 50% in Fund C	1,005
50% in Fund B, 50% in Fund C	2,005
	19,287

Employer contributions may be made in either cash or Common Stock of Employer Company and are deposited in Fund C.

Amounts contributed by Members and employers during the years ended December 31, 1977 and 1976 were as follows:

| | 1976 | | 1975 | |
Company	Members	Employer	Members	Employer
Employer Company	$27,497,348	$20,006,108	$29,260,558	$21,356,904
Subsidiary 1	5,902	4,427	18,643	13,982
Subsidiary 2			659	494
Subsidiary 3	64,439	48,329	69,589	52,191
	$27,567,689	$20,058,864	$29,349,449	$21,423,571

A terminating Member of the Plan is paid the current value of his contributions to the Plan but, unless terminating by reason of normal retirement or other specified circumstances, will forfeit a portion of the current value of the employer's contributions to his account. Such forfeitures were applied to reduce contributions required of the Employer Company.

Withdrawals from Members' accounts during the year ended December 31, 1977 amounted to $65,296,442, of which $64,680,783 was distributed to the Members, and $615,659 reduced the contributions of Employer Company. Comparable amounts for the year ended December 31, 1976 were $39,198,994, $38,610,480, and $588,514, respectively.

Plan assets are managed by XYZ Trust Company, Trustee. The Trustee, at its discretion, invests and reinvests plan assets. Investments are monitored by the Investment Review Committee.

In the event of the termination of the Plan, Members affected by the termination will receive the value of their accounts in Funds A, B, and C.

Note C—Investment in Private Placement Securities

The Plan's investment in certain fixed income investments having a current value at December 31, 1977, as determined by the Trustee, of $1,636,327 (cost $1,623,949) are not actively traded securities.

Note D—Compliance With ERISA

The Employee Retirement Income Security Act of 1974 (ERISA) required that several new standards be incorporated into certain employee benefit plans. The required modifications were made to the Plan effective January 1, 1976.

The Trustee, from time to time, purchases Employer Company Common Stock in the open market. Fees paid for administrative services were based on customary rates for such services.

Note E—Federal Income Taxes

Since its inception, the Plan has been qualified under Section 401 and the Trust has been exempt from federal income tax under Section 501 of the Internal Revenue Code of 1954, as amended. The Plan as amended effective January 1, 1976, and Trust thereunder, have been resubmitted to the Internal Revenue Service for a determination of continued qualification and exemption, respectively. Such determination has been received.

Assets Held for Investment
Employee Savings Plan of Employer Company

(December 31, 1977)

Col. A *Name of Issuer and Title of Issue*	Col. B *Balance Held at Close of Period. Number of Shares— Principal Amount of Bonds and Notes*	Col. C *Cost of Each Item*	Col. D *Value of Each Item at Close of Period*
FUND A			
Governmental Obligations:			
United States Treasury Notes			
7.000%, February 1979	$30,600,000	$30,872,926	$32,201,766
Corporate Bonds:			
Industrial Obligations:			
Cities Service Company, Note,			
7%, January 1978	400,000	369,684	365,625
Merck & Company, Inc., Note,			
7.85%, June 1985	4,530,000	4,638,398	4,717,125
Banking and Finance Obligations:			
General Motors Acceptance			
Corporation, Senior Subordinated			
Note, 8.15%, August 1986	3,000,000	3,013,125	3,108,750
Other Obligations:			
Compagnie Des Bauxites De Guinee,			
Certificates of Beneficial			
Interest, 6.50% March 1987	1,219,031	1,219,031	1,225,469
Equicap Corporation, Secured			
Installment Note, 7.25%,			
July 1972	3,378,395	3,377,145	3,441,233
TOTAL CORPORATE BONDS	12,527,426	12,617,383	12,858,202
TOTAL INVESTMENTS— FUND A	$43,127,426	$43,490,309	$45,059,968

Assets Held for Investment—Continued

Col. A Name of Issuer and Title of Issue	Col. B Balance Held at Close of Period. Number of Shares— Principal Amount of Bonds and Notes	Col. C Cost of Each Item	Col. D Value of Each Item at Close of Period
FUND B			
Common Stock:			
Air Transport UAL, Inc.	$ 65,000	$ 2,265,960	$ 2,492,500
Autos and Accessories:			
Ford Motor Company	5,000	287,350	273,125
General Motors Corporation	25,000	1,319,420	1,784,375
Banks:			
First Bank System, Inc.	64,000	2,080,739	1,845,500
Beverage:			
PepsiCo, Inc.	14,000	853,994	1,137,500
The Seven-Up Company	13,000	174,128	406,250
Building:			
Dover International	101,000	2,750,420	3,947,250
Chemicals:			
Air Shamrock Corporation	215,700	7,139,290	8,112,625
Coal:			
Eastern Gas & Fuel Associates	30,000	685,838	798,750
Mapco, Inc.	27,000	752,884	1,140,750
Pittston Company	36,756	562,416	1,240,515
Cosmetics:			
Revlon, Inc.	14,000	463,719	619,500
Drugs:			
Abbott Squibb Corp.	61,500	2,031,628	2,068,500
Electrical and Electronics:			
Texaco Company	135,000	8,651,628	8,468,875
Donald's Corporation	130,000	3,499,878	3,359,047
Medical Supply and Service:			
Dickinson & Company	143,000	5,373,328	5,068,625
Metals:			
United States Corporation	97,000	4,076,963	4,371,062
Office and Business Equipment:			
Honey, Inc.	80,000	3,627,412	3,461,875
International Business Machines Corporation	30,000	6,582,680	8,130,000
Sperry Rand Corporation	27,000	1,010,957	1,184,625
Oil:			
Atlantic Richfield Company	12,000	504,113	705,000
Continental Oil Company	30,000	911,140	1,095,000
Exxon Corporation	54,000	2,477,432	2,760,750
Getty Oil Company	4,000	571,482	739,000
Gulf Oil Corporation	10,000	273,055	272,500
Halliburton Company	30,000	1,412,299	1,961,250

Assets Held for Investment—Continued

Col. A *Name of Issuer and Title of Issue*	Col. B *Balance Held at Close of Period. Number of Shares— Principal Amount of Bonds and Notes*	Col. C *Cost of Each Item*	Col. D *Value of Each Item at Close of Period*
Hughes Tool Company	23,000	1,075,607	914,250
Marathon Oil Company	20,000	1,182,099	1,087,500
J. Ray McDermott & Company	10,000	529,584	468,750
Mobil Corporation	21,000	1,366,951	1,257,375
Royal Dutch Petroleum Company	15,000	718,558	741,375
Schlumberger, Ltd.	15,000	1,196,620	1,445,625
Shell Oil Company	20,000	1,525,195	1,537,500
East Company	38,568	2,391,439	2,560,422
Ganold Company, Inc.	108,329	4,660,327	4,986,857
Retail Trade:			
Dayton-Hudson Corporation			
Jack Eckered Corporation			696,000
S. S. Kresge Company			1,040,625
Lowe's Companies			945,009
Mercantile Stores, Inc.			480,000
Penn Company	115,000	4,060,372	3,521,625
Miscellaneous:			
Soo Morris, Inc.	118,000	4,187,786	5,477,132
Bendix Corporation	33,333	1,478,330	1,404,153
Western Industries, Inc.	37,500	3,567,549	2,274,188
TOTAL COMMON STOCKS		88,280,570	98,283,126
TOTAL INVESTMENTS—FUND B	$ 88,280,570	$ 98,283,126	

FUND C

Temporary Investment:			
General Employee Benefit Trust of Bankers Trust Company—Iterim Investment Fund	$ 2,660,000	$ 2,660,000	$ 2,660,000
Common Stock:			
Employer Company	$ 6,687,121	130,101,765	151,296,113
TOTAL INVESTMENTS—FUND C	$132,761,765	$153,956,113	
TOTAL INVESTMENTS	$264,532,644	$297,299,207	

¶ 11.04 GUIDANCE ON PREPARING STATEMENTS FOR WELFARE BENEFIT PLANS

The primary subject of this manual is qualified retirement benefit plans because these plans are primarily the ones subject to reporting and audit requirements. However, a limited number of welfare benefit plans, particularly multiemployer plans, are also subject to the requirements. Since the FASB has tentatively excluded welfare benefit plans from its proposed Statement, the American Institute of Certified Public Accounts (AICPA) audit guide, "Audits of Employer Health and Welfare Benefit Funds," continues to represent the most authoritative* literature on accounting for these plans.

The accounting principles included in the guide are summarized in the following paragraphs.

[1] Basis and Form of Financial Statements

The guide concludes that the accrual basis is the most appropriate. Changes to adopt the accrual basis should be made retroactively in accordance with paragraphs 27 and 28 of Accounting Principles Board (APB) Opinion No. 20.

The illustrative financial statements presented in the guide include a balance sheet, a statement of operations and fund balance, and a statement of changes in financial position.

[2] Investments

Investments of welfare benefit plans are generally short term in nature; accordingly, the audit guide concluded that cost is the appropriate basis for carrying all investments. However, market is also probably now acceptable because of ERISA's requirements and the generally insignificant difference for short-term investments.

---

* The audit guides contain the following notice to readers: "This audit guide is published for the guidance of members of the Institute in examining and reporting on financial statements of employee health and welfare benefit funds. It represents the considered opinion of the Committee on Health, Welfare, and Pension Funds and as such contains the best thought of the profession as to the best practices in the industry. Members should be aware that they may be called upon to justify departures from the Committee's recommendation."

[3] Contributions Receivable

Contributions are generally paid on a self-assessment basis and are received by the plan the month after they accrue. Such contributions should be accrued by the plan.

[4] Premium Deposits

Premium deposits should be reported as assets of the plan until applied against future premiums.

[5] Accrued Experience Rating Adjustments

Any excess of premiums paid over claims paid, reserves required by the insurance company, and the insurance company's retention (fee) should be accrued. These experience rating refunds may have to be estimated. Experience rating deficits for which the plan has a liability should also be accrued.

[6] Property and Equipment

Buildings, equipment, furniture and fixtures, and leasehold improvements used in operations should be carried at cost and depreciated or amortized over their estimated useful lives.

[7] Claims Reported But Not Paid and Claims Incurred But Not Reported

Benefit claims in fully insured plans are liabilities of the insurance company and not the plan. Self-insured funds should accrue estimated liabilities for claims reported but not paid and claims incurred but not reported. In addition, the financial statements of a self-insured plan which provides death benefits should reflect an estimated liability for such benefits based upon determinations by the funds' insurance consultants or actuaries.

[8] Insurance Premiums Payable

Insurance premiums due but not paid as well as any estimated contingent premiums (usually based on excess loss ratios) should be accrued.

[9] Liability for Accumulated Eligibility Credits

Some welfare benefit plans provide for continued eligibility for benefits during periods of unemployment based on accumulated eligibility credits or hours. The guide requires that a liability for such future benefits based on past service be provided in the financial statements.

[10] Fund Balance

The fund balance is represented by the excess of assets over liabilities. Consideration should be given to segregating amounts applicable to specific plans if the fund consists of more than one plan.

[11] Other Financial Statement Disclosures

The guide lists the following three items as recommended disclosures:

- The nature of the plan's activities and any changes in the plan;
- The tax status of the fund;
- Any other matters necessary to fairly present the financial statements of a particular fund. Examples given are lease commitments and transactions which may involve conflicts of interest.

[12] Illustrative Financial Statements

The audit guide includes illustrative examples of financial statements for three types of employee welfare benefit plans. These financial statements are reproduced on the following pages. In using these statements, it should be noted that they have not been modified to meet the specific disclosure requirements of ERISA.

[a] Financial Statements of an Insured Fund

Below is an example of financial statements of an insured fund from "Audits of Employee Health and Welfare Benefit Funds."

The PAM Employee Health and Welfare Fund is an insured plan providing primarily accident, hospital medical, surgical, and disability benefits. Under this type of arrangement, insurance premiums are generally adjusted based on experience, but the plan has no direct liability for the payment of claims.

PAM Employee Health and Welfare Benefit Fund Balance Sheet
(April 30, 19X2 and 19X1)

Assets	April 30 19X2	April 30 19X1
Cash	$ 322,400	$ 69,000
Receivables:		
Estimated employers' contributions (less allowance for doubtful accounts of $8,000 in 19X2 and 19X1)	700,000	645,000
Accrued interest and dividends	3,000	4,500
Total	703,000	649,500
Investments—at Cost:		
United States Government bonds and notes (approximate quoted market value $921,000 in 19X2 and $570,000 in 19X1)	949,000	567,000
Corporate bonds and notes (approximate quoted market value $485,000 in 19X2 and $652,000 in 19X1)	487,000	653,000
Common stocks (approximate quoted market value $109,000 in 19X2 and $112,000 in 19X1)	83,000	102,000
Total	1,519,000	1,322,000
Equipment—at Cost: (Less accumulated depreciation of $121,000 in 19X2 and $110,000 in 19X1)	328,300	324,600
Other Assets:		
Prepaid expenses	3,000	4,000
Advance deposit with insurance carrier	22,000	22,000
Miscellaneous	5,000	20,000
Total	30,000	46,000
Total Assets	$2,902,700	$2,411,100

Liabilities and Fund Balance	April 30 19X2	April 30 19X1
Liabilities:		
Accounts payable and accrued expenses	$ 38,000	$ 31,000
Group insurance premium payable	863,000	800,000
Estimated liability for future group insurance premiums based on participants' accumulated eligibility, arising from hours accumulated	430,000	275,000
Estimated liability for retired participants' benefits	385,000	300,000
Estimated liability for future death benefits	615,000	500,000
Total	2,331,000	1,906,000
Fund Balance	571,700	505,100
Total Liabilities and Fund Balance	$2,902,700	$2,411,100

See Notes to Financial Statements.

PAM Employee Health and Welfare Benefit Fund
Statement of Operations and Fund Balance

(For the Years Ended April 30, 19X2 and 19X1)

| | Year Ended April 30 | |
	19X2	19X1
Revenues:		
Contributions:		
Employers	$ 9,700,000	$ 9,850,000
Employees	600,000	400,000
Interest and dividends	110,000	81,000
Gain on the sale of investments—net	42,600	1,000
Total Revenues	10,452,600	10,332,000
Expenses:		
Group insurance premiums	9,932,800	9,974,000
Retired participants' benefits	162,200	53,000
Death benefits	190,000	136,000
Administrative expenses	101,000	113,900
Total Expenses	10,386,000	10,276,900
Excess of Revenues Over Expenses	66,600	55,100
Fund Balance:		
Beginning of year	505,100	450,000
End of year	$ 571,700	$ 505,100

See Notes to Financial Statements.

PAM Employee Health and Welfare Benefit Fund
Statement of Changes in Financial Position

(For the Years Ended April 30, 19X2 and 19X1)

	Year Ended April 30	
	19X2	19X1
Increases in Cash Resulted From:		
Excess of revenues over expenses	$ 66,600	$ 55,100
Add expenses not requiring outlay of operating funds:		
Provision for future group insurance premiums, retired participants' benefits, and death benefits	587,000	226,000
Depreciation	11,000	10,500
Total from operations	665,200	291,600
Cost of investments sold or redeemed	310,000	285,000
Increase in accounts payable, accrued expenses and group insurance premium payable	70,000	50,000
Total	1,045,200	626,600
Decrease in Cash Resulted From:		
Payment of group insurance premium based on participants' accumulated eligibility, death benefits, and benefits to retired participants	232,600	273,000
Purchases of investments	507,000	438,000
Equipment additions	14,700	17,400
Increase in receivable and other assets—net	37,500	10,000
Total	791,800	738,400
Increase (Decrease) in cash	$ 253,400	$ (111,800)

See Notes to Financial Statements.

PAM Employee Health and Welfare Benefit Fund
Notes to Financial Statements
(Year Ended April 30, 19X2)

General. The PAM Exployee Health and Welfare Benefit Fund was formed in 19XX under an agreement between the Contractors' Association and the Labor Union. The agreement provides, among other things, for employers of members of the Union to contribute X cents for each hours worked.

A plan of insurance provides for accident, hospital, medical, surgical, and disability benefits for eligible members as specified in the Plan.

Death benefits are provided for eligible members from contributions in excess of hours required for current coverage. The amount segregated for death benefits has been determined by application of the unit risk rates computed in accordance with actuarial principles.

Group Insurance. The group insurance contract with the insurance carrier provides that to the extent premiums paid exceed the sum of the claims paid and provided for and the insurance carrier's retention, a refund of premiums is to be made to the Fund. If the sum of the claims paid and provided for and the insurance carrier's retention exceed the premiums paid, such excess is carried forward to the succeeding policy years in the determination of the premium refunds, if any, to be paid to the Fund. As of April 30, 19X2, no significant adjustment of premium liability or refund is anticipated.

Group insurance premiums payable reflect the estimated cost of group insurance premiums to be paid subsequent to April 30, 19X2, based upon hours worked and contributions recorded prior to that date.

Depreciation. Depreciation is computed on the straight-line method over the estimated useful life of the equipment. Depreciation charged to administrative expenses was $11,000 in 19X2 and $10,500 in 19X1.

Estimated Liability for Future Benefits. The Fund provides benefits to certain active and retired members if such members have accumulated in the current or prior years credit amounts (expressed in hours) in excess of the hours required for current insurance coverage.

Under the Plan, accumulated credits equal to approximately one year's insurance coverage may be carried forward, and any credits in excess of approximately one year's insurance coverage are converted into specified amounts of paid-up death benefits.

Lease Commitments. The Fund operates in premises leased from the local labor union requiring annual rental payments of $10,000 through 19XX.

[b] Financial Statements of a Self-Insured Fund

Below is an example of financial statements of a self-insured fund from "Audits of Employee Health and Welfare Benefit Funds."

The SCS Employee Health and Welfare Benefit Fund is a self-insured plan providing primarily accident, hospital, medical, surgical, and disability benefits. This plan can be distinguished from the insured fund presented at ¶ 11.04[12][a] primarily because the plan has a direct liability for unpaid and unreported claims.

SCS Employee Health and Welfare Benefit Fund Balance Sheet

(April 30, 19X2 and 19X1)

Assets	April 30 19X2	19X1
Cash	$ 322,400	$ 69,000
Receivables:		
Estimated employers' contributions (less allowance for doubtful accounts of $8,000 in 19X2 and 19X1)	700,000	645,000
Accrued interest and dividends	3,000	4,500
Total	703,000	649,500
Investments—at Cost:		
United States Government bonds and noted (approximate quoted market value $921,000 in 19X2 and $570,000 in 19X1)	949,000	567,000
Corporate bonds and notes (approximate quoted market value $485,000 in 19X2 and $652,000 in 19X1)	487,000	653,000
Common stocks (approximate quoted market value $109,000 in 19X2 and $112,000 in 19X1)	83,000	102,000
Total	1,519,000	1,322,000
Equipment—at Cost (Less accumulated depreciation of $121,000 in 19X2 and $110,000 in 19X1)	328,300	324,600
Other Assets:		
Prepaid expenses	15,000	14,000
Miscellaneous	15,000	32,000
Total	30,000	46,000
Total Assets	$2,902,700	$2,411,100

Liabilities and Fund Balance	April 30 19X2	19X1
Liabilities:		
Accounts payable and accrued expenses	$ 38,000	$ 31,000
Claims payable	300,000	370,000
Estimated liability for claims incurred but not reported	563,000	430,000
Estimated liability for future payment of benefits based on participants' accumulated eligibility, arising from hours accumulated	430,000	275,000
Estimated liability for retired participants' benefits	385,000	300,000
Estimated liability for future death benefits	615,000	500,000
Total	2,331,000	1,906,000
Fund Balance	571,700	505,100
Total Liabilities and Fund Balance	$2,902,700	$2,411,100

See Notes to Financial Statements.

SCS Employee Health and Welfare Benefit Fund
Statement of Operation and Fund Balance

(For the Years Ended April 30, 19X2 and 19X1)

	Year Ended April 30	
	19X2	*19X1*
Revenues:		
Contributions:		
Employers	$ 9,700,000	$ 9,850,000
Employees	600,000	400,000
Interest and dividends	110,000	81,000
Gain on the sale of investments—		
met	42,600	1,000
Total Revenues	10,452,600	10,332,000
Expenses:		
Claims	9,932,800	9,974,000
Retired participants' benefits	162,200	53,000
Death benefits	190,000	136,000
Administrative expenses	101,000	113,900
Total Expenses	10,386,000	10,276,900
Excess of Revenues Over Expenses	66,600	55,100
Fund Balance:		
Beginning of year	505,100	450,000
End of year	$ 571,700	$ 505,100

See Notes to Financial Statements.

SCS Employee Health and Welfare Benefit Fund
Statement of Changes in Financial Position

(For the Years Ended April 30, 19X2 and 19X1)

	Year Ended April 30	
	19X2	*19X1*
Increases in Cash Resulted From:		
Excess of revenues over expenses	$ 66,600	$ 55,100
Add expenses not requiring outlay of operating funds:		
Provision for claims incurred but not reported, future benefits, retired participants' benefits, and death benefits	687,600	226,000
Depreciation	11,000	10,500
Total from operations	765,200	291,600
Cost of investments sold or redeemed	310,000	285,000
Total	1,075,200	576,600
Decreases in Cash Resulted From:		
Decrease (Incease) in accounts payable, accrued expenses, and claims payable	63,000	(50,000)
Payments of benefits based on participants' accumulated eligibility, death benefits, and benefits to retired participants	199,600	273,000
Purchases of investments	507,000	438,000
Equipment additions	14,700	17,400
Increase in receivables and other assets—net	37,500	10,000
Total	821,800	688,400
Increase (Decrease) in Cash	$ 253,400	$ (111,800)

See Notes to Financial Statements.

SCS Employee Health and Welfare Benefit Fund
Notes to Financial Statements
(Year Ended April 30, 19X2)

General. The SCS Employee Health and Welfare Benefit Fund was formed in 19XX under an agreement between the Contractors' Association and the Labor Union. The agreement provides, among other things, for employers of members of the Union to contribute X cents for each hour worked.

The Plan provides for accident, hospital, medical, surgical, and diability benefits for eligible members as specified in the Plan.

Death benefits are provided for eligible participants from contributions in excess of hours required for current coverage. The amount segregated for death benefits has been determined by application of the unit risk rates computed in accordance with actuarial principles.

Depreciation. Depreciation is computed on the straight-line method over the estimated useful life of the equipment. Depreciation charged to administrative expenses was $11,000 in 19X2 and $10,500 in 19X1.

Estimated Liability for Future Benefits. The Fund is required to provide benefits to certain active and retired members, if such members have accumulated in the current or prior years credit amounts (expressed in hours) in excess of the hours required for current coverage.

Under the Plan, accumulated credits equal to approximately one year's coverage may be carried forward, and any credits in excess of approximately one year's coverage are converted into specified amounts of paid-up death benefits.

Lease Commitments. The Fund operates in premises leased from the local labor union requiring annual rental payments of $10,000 through 19XX.

[c] Financial Statements of a Vacation Trust Fund

Below is an example of financial statements of a vacation trust fund from "Audits of Employee Health and Welfare Benefit Funds." The TCMT Vacation Trust Fund was set up in accordance with a union contract. The financial statements reflect the operating characteristics of a typical vacation plan described in the audit guide as follows:

> "Amounts received from employers by a vacation fund are generally allocated directly to the participants for whom the contributions were made. Therefore, they are not generally regarded as revenue of the fund but as liabilities to the participants.

> "Contributions received will be accumulated in, and benefits paid will be charged to, a separate account for each year.

> "Expenses of administration are generally provided for by investment income. Accounts should be established for investment income and administrative expenses. Any excess of investment income over administrative expenses may be carried forward to subsequent years, or distributed on some pro rata basis to participants, depending on action of the board of trustees.

> "Balances may remain in vacation fund accounts from prior years because of participants' failure to claim vacation benefits. Disposition of such balances will be governed by state laws and by action of the board of trustees based upon the advice of the fund's legal counsel."

TCMT Vacation Trust Fund
Balance Sheet

(April 30, 19X2 and 19X1)

| | April 30 | |
	19X2	19X1
Assets		
Cash	$ 17,000	$ 5,500
Certificate of Deposit	1,500,000	943,000
Contributions Receivable	152,000	146,000
Interest Receivable	9,000	8,200
Prepaid Expenses	9,000	7,300
Total Assets	$1,687,000	$1,110,000

See Notes to Financial Statements.

	April 30	
	19X2	*19X1*
Liabilities and Fund Balance		
Liabilities:		
Accounts payable	$ 17,000	$ 13,500
Vacation benefits payable:		
19X0 and prior Plan Years	25,000	47,000
19X1 Plan Year	31,000	1,013,000
19X2 Plan Year	1,600,000	
Total vacation benefits payable	1,656,000	1,060,000
Total Liabilities	1,673,000	1,073,500
Fund Balance	14,000	36,500
Total Liabilities and Fund Balance	$1,687,000	$1,110,000

TCMT Vacation Trust Fund
Statement of Operations and Fund Balance

(For the Years Ended April 30, 19X2 and 19X1)

	Year Ended April 30	
	19X2	*19X1*
Revenues:		
Interest	$ 70,000	$ 48,500
Other	500	500
Total Revenues	70,500	49,000
Expenses:		
Administrative fees	76,000	70,000
Professional fees	9,000	8,500
Insurance	2,000	2,000
Trustees' expenses	1,000	1,000
Corporate trustee fees	5,000	5,000
Total Expenses	93,000	86,500
Excess of Expenses Over Revenues	22,500	37,500
Fund Balance:		
Beginning of year	36,500	74,000
End of year	$ 14,000	$ 36,500

TCMT Vacation Trust Fund
Statement of Changes in Financial Position
(For the Years Ended April 30, 19X2 and 19X1)

	Year Ended April 30	
	19X2	*19X1*
Increases in Cash and Certificates of Deposit Resulted From:		
Increase in accounts payable	$ 3,500	$ 1,000
Increase in vacation benefits payable represented by employers' contributions:		
Plan Year 19X0 and prior years		20,000
Plan Year 19X1	10,000	1,018,000
Plan Year 19X2	1,653,000	
Total	1,666,500	1,039,000
Decreases in Cash and Certificates of Deposit Resulted From:		
Excess of expenses over revenues	22,500	37,500
Increase in receivables and prepaid expenses	8,500	1,000
Decrease in vacation benefits payable represented by vacation benefits paid to participants:		
Plan Year 19X0 and prior years	22,000	850,000
Plan Year 19X1	992,000	5,000
Plan Year 19X2	53,000	
Total	1,098,000	893,500
Increase in Cash and Certificates of Deposit	$ 568,500	$ 145,500

See Notes to Financial Statements.

TCMT Vacation Trust Fund
Note to Financial Statements

(Year Ended April 30, 19X2)

The TCMT Vacation Trust Plan was formed in 19XX under an agreement between the Contractors' Association and the Labor Union. The agreement provides, among other things, for employers of the labor union members to deduct from each member's wages X cents for each hour worked.

Contributions received are added to vacation accounts of employees. The amounts accumulated in each vacation account as of April 30 of each year are paid on or after June 1 to the members unless the member elects to continue to hold such amounts in his vacation account.

Chapter 12

INTERIM ACCOUNTING GUIDELINES

¶ 12.01   INTRODUCTION

Chapter 11 summarized the current status of generally accepted accounting principles (GAAP) for employee benefit plans, and Chapter 10 discussed the reporting and accounting requirements for financial statements included in annual reports to the Department of Labor (DOL). The various, and sometimes conflicting, requirements of the DOL, the American Institute of Certified Public Accountants (AICPA), and the Securities and Exchange Commission (SEC), and the proposed requirements of the Financial Accounting Standards Board (FASB) result in a number of alternatives for financial reporting. The purpose of this chapter is to provide guidance to plan administrators and accountants in selecting accounting principles from the alternatives.

The discussions in this chapter are primarily related to retirement benefit plans because, with the exception of the question of investment valuation, the AICPA industry audit guide appears to provide adequate guidance for welfare benefit plans. The question of investment valuation arises because the audit guide prescribes cost while the DOL prescribes market (current value) as the primary valuation basis. As a practical matter, the investments of most welfare benefit plans are short term and there is little significant difference between cost and market. For this reason, and in light of the DOL requirements and the FASB Exposure Draft on pension plans, presentation of welfare benefit plan investments at market is generally acceptable.

¶ 12.02   FORM AND BASIS OF FINANCIAL STATEMENTS

DOL reporting regulations, the FASB Exposure Draft, and Article 6C of Regulation S-X all require statements of assets and liabilities and income and changes in net assets. A separate statement of changes in financial position is not required by any of the above authorities. Although there are differences in the detailed statement requirements and in the statement titles, the requirements of each agency are similar.

Both the FASB and the SEC would require accrual-basis financial statements; however, the DOL also allows cash-basis financial statements adjusted for unrealized appreciation or depreciation of securities. It appears clear that to be in conformity with generally accepted accounting principles, financial statements for pension plans should be prepared on the accrual basis unless the effect of nonaccrual accounting is not material.

The principal difference between the requirements of the DOL and the SEC and the proposed requirements of the FASB is in the area of presentation and disclosure of plan obligations. The FASB Exposure Draft would require extensive presentation of a plan's obligation for accumulated benefits in separate statements of accumulated benefits and changes in accumulated benefits. The DOL reporting regulations specifically exclude presentation of actuarially determined obligations from presentation in financial statements. The SEC is silent on the matter; however, it should be noted that Article 6C is generally applicable only to contributory individual account plans where obligations are limited to plan assets.

Until a final FASB Statement is issued, it is recommended that presentation of plan obligations be limited to footnote disclosure. Recommended disclosures are discussed at ¶ 12.07.

¶ 12.03   VALUATION BASIS OF INVESTMENTS

The regulations of the DOL and of the Employee Retirement Income Security Act of 1974 (ERISA) require current value accounting either in the primary financial statements or in a schedule. In addition, Article 6C of Regulation S-X allows either cost or market as the primary valuation, and FASB Exposure Draft prescribes current value as the appropriate valuation method.

In practice, most plans have adopted current value accounting for plan investments; however, other valuation methods should continue to be acceptable under GAAP until a final FASB Statement is issued. Valuation methods which may be encountered in practice include:

- Cost;
- Lower of cost or market applied on a specific identification basis;
- Lower of cost or market applied on an aggregate basis;
- Amortized cost (for debt securities);
- Depreciated cost (for real estate);
- Current (market) value at statement date.

In addition to situations in which one method is applied consistently to all investments, accountants may encounter situations in which different types of investments will be valued on different bases.

For example, equity securities might be valued at market and debt securities at amortized cost. Any of the above-noted valuation methods or a reasonable combination of methods are currently considered acceptable if applied within the following guidelines:

- If securities are carried at cost, provision should be made for any permanent impairment in value.

- Other investments, such as real estate or royalty agreements, should not be valued in excess of currently realizable value. Generally, a periodic provision should be made for the decline in realizable value of other investments. A valuation based on future income will usually accomplish this goal, as will providing for depreciation on real estate.

- Provision should be made for uncollectible mortgages, loans, or other receivables.

¶ 12.04   DETERMINING COST AND CURRENT VALUE

As defined by Section 3 of ERISA, "the term 'current value' means fair market value where available and otherwise the fair value as determined in good faith by a trustee or named fiduciary . . . pursuant to the terms of the plan and in accordance with regulations of the Secretary, assuming an orderly liquidation at the time of such determination."

The FASB Exposure Draft defines "current value" as "the amount that the plan could reasonably expect to receive for the investment in a current sale and shall be measured by market value if an active market exists. If no active market exists for an investment but exists for similar investments, selling prices in that market may be helpful in estimating current value. If those prices are not available, a forecast of expected cash flows may aid in estimating current value, provided the expected cash flows are discounted at a rate commensurate with the risk involved."

In addition, the AICPA industry audit guide, "Audits of Investment Companies," published in 1973, requires that securities portfolios of investment companies be reported at "value," which is defined as "(a) with respect to securities for which market quotations are readily available, the quoted market value of such securities and (b) with respect to other securities and assets, fair value as determined in good faith by the board of directors." Factors to be considered in determining the current value and the cost of various types of investments are discussed in the following paragraphs.

[1] Equity and Debt Securities

The cost of equity and debt securities includes brokerage commissions and other acquisition costs. For securities contributed directly to the plan, such as stock contributed to an employee stock ownership plan (ESOP), cost would generally be the same as the cost to the sponsoring company determined in accordance with Accounting Principles Board (APB) Opinion No. 25.

The cost of debt securities also frequently includes a premium over or discount from the face value of the securities and accrued interest purchased. Generally, interest purchased should be accounted for separately as a receivable. Where discounts and premiums are significant and the plan intends to hold bonds for an extended period, discounts and premiums should be systematically amortized to income.

Market or current value of securites traded on organized exchanges or in the over-the-counter markets can usually be determined by reference to the latest published sales prices or bid and asked prices. The investment company audit guide states that "normally it is not acceptable to use the asked price alone." For securities in which the market is thin or sales are infrequent, the investment company guide suggests that determination of fair value by the trustees may be appropriate.

Securities for which the current value must be determined by the trustee or named fiduciary include privately placed debt securities (private placements) and restricted equity securities. "Audits of Investment Companies" contains the following discussion of such valuations:

> "As Accounting Series Release No. 118 states, no single standard for determining fair value in good faith can be laid down, since fair value depends upon the circumstances of each individual case. As a general principle, the current 'fair value' of an issue of securities being valued by the board of directors would appear to be the amount which the owner might reasonably expect to receive from them upon their current sale, although there usually is no intention to make a current sale. Current sale should be interpreted to mean realization in an orderly disposition over a reasonable period of time. Methods which are in

accord with this principle may, for example, be based on a multiple of earnings, or a discount (or less frequently a premium) from market of a similar, freely traded security, or a yield to maturity with respect to debt issues, or a combination of these and other methods. Some of the general factors which the directors should consider in determining a valuation method for an individual issue of securities include (1) the fundamental analytical data relating to the investment; (2) the nature and duration of restrictions on disposition of the securities; and (3) the evaluation of the forces which influence the market in which these securities are purchased and sold. In the case of investments made in several securities of the same issuer, such as those made by many SBICs (Small Business Investment Companies) and venture capital companies, the valuation of the 'package' as a whole may be appropriate. Among the more specific factors which must be considered are the type of security (debt or equity), financial standing of the issuer, availability of current financial statements, cost at date of purchase, size and period of holding, discount from market value of unrestricted securities of the same class at the time of purchase, special reports prepared by analysts, information as to any transaction or offers with respect to the security, existence of merger proposals or tender offers affecting the securities, reported prices and the extent of public trading in similar securities of the issuer or comparable companies, maintenance of investee's business and financial plan, use of new funds to achieve planned results, changes in economic conditions including those in the company or industry, and other relevant matters. This guide does not purport to delineate all factors which may be considered. The directors should take into consideration all indications of value available to them in determining the 'fair value' assigned to a particular security. The information so considered and, insofar as practicable, the basis for the board's decision, should be documented in the minutes of the directors' meetings and the supporting data retained for the inspection of the Company's independent auditor."

In addition to providing guidance on valuing nonreadily marketable securities, Accounting Series Release (ASR) No. 118 discusses the valuation of securities traded on national exchanges and over-the-counter securities. Although ASR No. 118 is directed at investment companies, the guidance provided on securities valuation is equally applicable to pension plans. Pertinent portions of ASR No. 118 are reproduced below.

"Securities Listed or Traded on a National Securities Exchange

"Ordinarily, little difficulty should be experienced in valuing securities listed or traded on one or more national securities exchanges, since quotations of completed transactions are published daily. If a security was traded on the valuation date, the last quoted sale price generally is used. In the case of securities listed on more than one national securities exchange the last quoted sale, up to the time of valuation, on the exchange on which the security is principally traded should be used or, if there were no sales on that exchange on the valuation date, the last quoted sale, up to the time of valuation, on the other exchanges should be used.

"If there was no sale on the valuation date but published closing bid and asked prices are available, the valuation in such circumstances should be within the range of these quoted prices. Some companies as a matter of general policy use the bid price, others use the mean of the bid and asked prices, and still others use a valuation within the range considered best to represent value in the circumstances; each of these policies is consistently applied. Normally, it is not acceptable to use the asked price alone. Where, on the valuation date, only a bid price is quoted or the spread between bid and asked prices is substantial, quotations for several days should be reviewed. If sales have been infrequent or there is a thin market in the security, further consideration should be given to whether 'market quotations are readily available.'

"Over-the-Counter Securities

"Quotations are available from various sources for most unlisted securities traded regularly in the over-the-counter market. These sources include tabulations in the financial press, publications of the National Quotation Bureau and the 'Blue List' of municipal bond offerings, several financial reporting services, and individual broker-dealers. These quotations generally are in the form of inter-dealer bid and asked prices. Because of the availability of multiple sources, a company frequently has a greater number of options open to it in valuing securities traded in the over-the-counter market than it does in valuing listed securities. A company (pension plan) may adopt a policy of using a mean of the bid prices, or of the bid and asked prices, or of the prices of a representative selection of broker-dealers quoting on a particular security; or it may use a valuation within the range of bid and asked prices considered best to represent value in the circumstances. Any of these policies is acceptable if consistently applied. Normally, the use of asked price alone is not acceptable.

"Ordinarily, quotations for a security should be obtained from more than one broker-dealer, particulaly if quotations are available only from broker-dealers not known to be established market-makers for that security, and quotations for several days should be reviewed. If the validity of the quotations appears to be questionable, or if the number of quotations is such as to indicate that there is a thin market in the security, further consideration should be given to whether "market quotations are readily available." If it is decided that they are not readily available, the security should be considered one required to be valued at 'fair value as determined in good faith by the board of directors (trustees).' "

[2] Investments in Insurance Policies or Contracts

Chapter 1 of this manual describes the various types of insurance contracts and deposit arrangements. A basic distinction between types of insured plans is whether premiums or deposits are allocated to purchase benefits for specific individuals or are unallocated. The FASB Exposure Draft provides: "For a plan that is partly or entirely financed through one or more insurance company contracts, inclusion of those contracts as assets depends on their nature. If the contract requires the insurance company to provide certain specified benefit payments (such as a deferred group annuity contract), it shall not be included. If no benefits are required to be provided by the insurance company, such as in the case of deposit administration and immediate participation guarantee contracts, the contracts shall be included."

Benefits fully guaranteed by insurance companies include those provided under individual ordinary life insurance contracts, individual retirement income or annuity contracts, group permanent contracts, and group annuity contracts. In addition, benefits payable under most deposit administration contracts are provided by the purchase at retirement of an annuity fully guaranteed by the insurer.

Deposits to deposit administration accounts (DA) and immediate participation guarantee accounts (IPG) can be invested wholly in the general assets of the insurer or partly in the general assets and partly in separate accounts. Accounting for deposits invested in separate accounts is discussed at ¶ 12.04[3]. Assets invested in the general assets of the insurer are credited with earnings at the guaranteed or declared rate, and are reduced by the cost of purchased annuities in the case of a DA account and direct benefits for an IPG account, and by administrative expenses charged to the account. These amounts will be reported annually by the insurance company. In effect, earnings less expenses are automatically reinvested, and the amount reported by the insurance company represents the adjusted cost of the investment. Since there are no separately identifiable assets related to the investment and the insurance company is contractually liable for the amount, it also represents the current value of the deposit provided the investment remains with the insurer. However, discontinuance charges or penalties are normally imposed if the contract is terminated and the investment is transferred to another funding agency. These potential charges generally range up to 5 percent of the active life fund and are specified in the contract. In addition, the insurance company usually reserves the right to pay out accumulated deposits in installments, generally over a period of five years. In lieu of discontinuance charges, some insurance companies will make a lump-sum settlement based on actual liquidation value of securities or formulas relating historical yields to current yields. Unless a decision has been made to change the funding agency, no provision need be made to reduce cost or current value of the investment.

[3] Investments in Common Trust Funds and Insurance Company Separate Accounts

Some portion of the deposits under DA or IPG contracts may be invested in insurance company separate accounts. Trusteed plans may invest all of a portion of their assets in bank-sponsored common or collective trusts. The proper accounting for investments in separate accounts and common trusts is identical. Under both of these funding instruments, investment units are purchased at a cost based on the current value of the assets in the fund. Thereafter, income, realized securities gains and losses, and unrealized gains and losses are accounted for on a unit basis. Unit values, income, etc., are normally computed monthly or quarterly, and additional investments and withdrawals are restricted to these valuation dates. From a plan standpoint, current value would be represented by the initial investment plus reinvested income distributions from the trust or separate account, and applicable undistributed realized and unrealized gains (losses), and would be equivalent to the number of units owned times the current unit value.

In practice, the cost of investments in common trusts or separate accounts is determined in either of two ways as follows:

(1) Investment cost is adjusted for reinvested income distributions, but not for gains and losses realized by the trust or separate account but not distributed to member plans.

(2) Investment cost is adjusted for both income distributions and the plan's share of realized gains and losses on sales of investments.

The second method seems preferable. If a plan does not recognize its share of realized gains and losses, the auditor should satisfy himself that there is not a permanent impairment in the value of a plan's investment in a common trust or separate account. As an example, the existence of unrealized gains in excess of realized losses would indicate there is no permanent impairment in value.

[4] Other Investments

The most common investments of pension plans are equity and debt securities; however, many plans do have some portion of their funds invested in other types of assets. Other investments may include real estate (including lease arrangements), mortgage loans, production payments, and oil and coal royalties.

Determining the cost of these types of investments presents no special problems except when assets are transferred to the pension plan by the employer in lieu of cash contributions. Since such transactions are nonmonetary transactions, the principles of APB Opinion No. 29 would be applicable. Paragraph 18 of that opinion states:

> "The Board concludes that in general accounting for nonmonetary transactions should be based on the fair values of the assets (or services) involved which is the same basis as that used in monetary transactions. Thus, the cost of a nonmonetary asset

acquired in exchange for another nonmonetary asset is the fair value of the asset surrendered to obtain it. . . . The fair value of the asset received should be used to measure the cost if it is more clearly evident than the fair value of the asset surrendered."

Paragraph 25 discusses determining fair value as follows:

"Fair value of a nonmonetary asset transferred to or from an enterprise in a nonmonetary transaction should be determined by referring to estimated realizable values in cash transactions of the same or similar assets, quoted market prices, independent appraisals, estimated fair values of assets or services received in exchange, and other available evidence. If one of the parties in a nonmonetary transaction could have elected to receive cash instead of the nonmonetary asset, the amount of cash that could have been received may be evidence of the fair value of the nonmonetary assets exchanged."

It should also be noted that while transfers of nonmonetary assets in lieu of cash contributions were fairly common in the past, such transfers will probably be less prevalent in the future because of the prohibited transaction rules of ERISA.

Determining current values of investments other than securities presents more difficult problems. The FASB Exposure Draft suggests that selling prices for similar investments, discounted cash flows, or appraisals may be useful in estimating current value. Real estate appraisers use three techniques for estimating current value: (1) cost of replacing the property, (2) sales of comparable property, and (3) the future income value of the property. The concepts behind these techniques may be equally valid (or invalid) in determining current value of other types of investments of pension plans.

☐ *Replacement cost.* The SEC now requires that disclosure of replacement cost be made for certain assets of operating companies. The SEC defined "replacement cost" as "the lowest amount that would have to be paid in the normal course of business to obtain an asset of equivalent operating or productive capability." Based on this definition, which is similar to previous definitions of the phrase, the concept does not appear appropriate for valuing assets of a pension plan because a plan is not an operating or producing entity.

☐ *Sales of comparable property.* This appraisal technique estimates current value based upon the amount which could be realized in a current sale of the asset using recent sales of comparable property as the determinant. This technique may be useful in estimating current value of non-income-producing assets such as land, assets which produce income based on factors other than the passage of time such as royalties, or assets held for or in the process of disposal. But it is not generally appropriate in valuing income-producing investments, such as leased property, mortgages, or production payments, whose value to the plan is derived from their ability to produce a periodic investment return.

☐ *Future income value.* The other investment assets of plans are generally held for the production of income; accordingly, the present value of the future stream of income is an appropriate measure of current value for many of these investments. In measuring the present value of future income, current prevailing market interest rates should be used to discount the future income. For example, the current value or a building under a lease arrangement covering its entire estimated useful life is determined by discounting the future lease payments to their present value using an appropriate interest rate. The major difficulty in this approach is the determination of the appropriate interest rate. Some guidance for determining appropriate interest rates is contained in paragraphs 13 and 14 of APB Opinion No. 21.

Other difficulties in determining current values relate primarily to valuing residual property rights and renewal options.

¶ 12.05   INVESTMENT TRANSACTIONS

Investment transactions include purchases and sales of investments, distributions of securities to participants, receipt or accrual of income, and, if investments are carried at current value, recognition of unrealized appreciation and depreciation.

[1] Purchase and Sale Transactions

Determination of the cost of purchased investments has been discussed previously. Generally, securities transactions should be recorded at the trade date rather than at the settlement date. However, the FASB Exposure Draft would allow the use of settlement date accounting if its effect is not significant. The use of trade-date accounting will result in receivables and payables relating to transactions occurring immediately before year-end. Private placements and transactions in other investment assets should be recorded when an enforceable contract is executed. For real estate transactions, the AICPA industry accounting guide, "Accounting for Profit Recognition on Sales of Real Estate," requires actual consummation of the transaction and the exchange of consideration before recording the transaction.

The proceeds from securities sold should be reduced by brokerage commissions and other direct expenses in determining the amount of sale. Identification of the cost of investments sold can be accomplished using specific identification; first-in, first-out; last-in, first-out; or an average cost basis. The average method is preferable. The investment company audit guide states that "if the cost of securities sold is determined on other than the average cost basis the company should disclose (required for a registered company) in a note, if practicable, what gain or loss would have resulted if average cost had been used."

However, for plans which provide for allocation and distribution of securities to individual participants, such as in a savings plan where employee contributions are used to purchase employer stock, the cost of securities distributed should be accounted for on a specific identification basis.

Realized gains and losses from sale of investments are determined by reference to original cost. This is true for current value statements as well as for cost-basis statements.

[2] Investment Income

Interest income normally should be accrued on a daily basis and includes amortization of discounts and premiums. Dividends receivable should be accrued on the record date if investments are valued at current value since the market value of the stock theoretically includes the dividends until that date. If investments are valued at cost, dividends receivable should be accrued when they are declared. Dividends representing a return of capital, stock splits, and stock dividends should not be recorded as income. Dividends representing a return of capital should be credited to the investment account.

[3] Unrealized Appreciation/Depreciation

The difference between current value and cost of investments at the balance sheet date is the unrealized appreciation or depreciation. Typically, amounts reported for unrealized appreciation or depreciation during the year are adjusted for realized gains or losses incurred during the year and reported separately. The FASB Exposure Draft would require reporting of realized gains or losses only in a footnote and would segregate the change in unrealized appreciation or depreciation between that applicable to investments held at year-end, and that applicable to investments sold during the year to the date of sale. The amount of unrealized appreciation or depreciation included in plan equity at the beginning and end of the period should be disclosed.

¶ 12.06 OTHER ASSETS

Assets other than investments could include cash, receivables (e.g., investment income, proceeds from sale of investments, contributions, notes), prepaid expenses (e.g., prepaid insurance), and buildings, equipment, and furniture and fixtures used in the operations of the plan. There are no apparent accounting questions with respect to cash, prepaid expenses, or receivables in general. The questions of current value versus cost and related charges for depreciation arise concerning operating assets. The nature of the sponsor's obligation gives rise to questions concerning contributions receivable.

[1] Operating Assets

The FASB Exposure Draft provides that assets employed in the operations of a plan should be measured at historical cost, less accumulated depreciation or amortization. This is at variance with the DOL regulations which require that current value be used in measuring such assets in financial data filed with the Department. This difference in valuation should not present a problem for most plans since operating assets are normally not significant. However, presentation of significant amounts of operating assets at current value would be a variance from current GAAP.

[2] Contributions Receivable

The proposed FASB Statement calls for reporting as plan receivables only those amounts that are legally or contractually required to be paid by the employer to the plan. The terms "legally" and "contractually" are not defined; however, it can be assumed that "legally" refers to amounts required to be contributed in accordance with the minimum funding standards and "contractually" refers to amounts due under union contracts or other formal agreements. This would vary from current practice, which generally is to record as a receivable of the plan those amounts accrued as a liability by the sponsor.

¶ 12.07   OBLIGATION FOR PENSION BENEFITS

The most significant obligation of a pension plan is the obligation to pay future benefits. Presentation of this obligation in plan financial statements is a subject of considerable current controversy. The FASB Exposure Draft would require separate statements of accumulated benefits and changes in accumulated benfits. In current practice, obligations to pay pension benefits other than those currently payable (e.g., where a plan provides that monthly benefits are payable to retirees living on the last day of the month) are rarely recognized as a liability in the financial statements. We do not believe that current generally accepted accounting principles require accounting recognition of the obligation to pay future benefits. We do believe that a comparsion of the assets of a plan and some measure of benefits payable from those assets is appropriate. Vested benefits represent a currently available measure of plan obligations which also provides a valid comparison with assets on a current value basis. We recommend that presently available information regarding actuarially determined obligations be disclosed in a footnote as follows:

(1) The present value of vested benefits at the most recent valuation date. If available, a breakdown of vested benefits between those applicable to individuals currently receiving benefits and those whose benefits will commence in the future should be given (see ¶ 5.03 for a discussion of vested benefits).

(2) The primary actuarial assumptions used to determine the present value of vested benefits (see Chapter 7 for a discussion of actuarial assumptions).

(3) The cost method and assumptions actually used to determine the funding requirements of the plan and the period over which past and prior service costs are being amortized (see Chapter 8 for a discussion of actuarial methods).

(4) The date of the most recent actuarial valuation. If the most recent actuarial valuation date is not the same as the financial statements date, an estimate of the effect of any subsequent plan amendments on vested benefits should be disclosed.

¶ 12.08   OTHER LIABILITIES

Liabilities of pension plans, other than the obligation to pay bene-fits, usually are not significant. Generally, liabilities will be limited to amounts payable for securities purchased and administrative expenses —although some plans may have mortgage obligations on real estate or an employee stock ownership plan may have incurred debt to pur-chase stock. Generally, there are no unique aspects to accounting for other liabilities of pension plans except that Form 5500 requires pre-sentation of liabilities as well as assets at current value. Adjusting liabil-ities to current (present) value is not a generally accepted accounting principle except in the original valuation of a transaction (see APB Opinion No. 21). For purposes of compliance with Form 5500, the current value of amounts currently payable would be the face amount of the liability. This would also be true for long-term obligations bear-ing a rate of interest approximating the current market rate. The prin-ciples included in APB Opinion No. 21 should be applied to significant long-term liabilities bearing an unrealistically high or low interest rate.

Part IV

AUDITING
AND REPORTING

Chapter 13

GENERAL AUDITING CONSIDERATIONS

¶ 13.01   INTRODUCTION

The Department of Labor (DOL) annual audit requirements are discussed in Chapter 10. As noted at ¶ 10.02[2], regulations issued by the DOL provide that plans may elect to exclude assets held by banks or insurance companies and transactions involving those assets from the scope of the independent auditor's examination. An examination of plan financial statements when this exclusion has been elected is commonly known as an ERISA limited-scope examination. The American Institute of Certified Public Accountants (AICPA) Auditing Standards Executive Committee (AudSEC) has provided guidance for conducting and reporting on such an examination in an Interpretation issued in November 1976.

As a result of the DOL regulations, one of the principal decisions that plans and plan sponsors will have to make with regard to the audit is whether they want a complete examination in accordance with generally accepted auditing standards (GAAS) or whether they want to limit compliance to the minimum audit requirements provided for by the regulations. In making that decision, plans should consider the audit procedures employed in a complete examination which would not be performed in a limited-scope examination. These procedures may be beneficial in helping plan administrators and sponsors meet their general fiduciary, administrative, and reporting responsibilities. The procedures would include the following:

- Review of internal accounting controls over transactions and the safeguarding of trusteed assets;
- Tests of purchases and sales of trusteed assets;

- Tests of income from trusteed assets;
- Tests of the detail records relating to trusteed assets;
- Tests or confirmation of the existence and ownership of trusteed assets;
- Tests of valuations.

In any event, the decision as to the type of examination has to be made by the plan, not the auditor. The auditor should be prepared to conduct either a full-scope examination or a limited-scope examination.

This chapter discusses general auditing requirements for limited-scope ERISA examinations and for full-scope examinations. It also discusses planning the audit, which is extremely important, considering the varied ways in which plans operate. Separate chapters discuss reviewing internal accounting controls and conducting the audit.

¶ 13.02   ERISA LIMITED-SCOPE EXAMINATION

DOL Regulations Section 2520.103-8 provides that "the examination and report of an independent accountant need not extend to any statement or information prepared and certified by a bank or similar institution or insurance carrier." The information can be excluded from the independent accountant's examination if the bank or similar institution or insurance carrier is regulated and supervised and subject to periodic examination by a state or federal agency, and if the information is "certified" by the institution.

[1]   Procedures in Limited-Scope Examinations

The information covered by the exemption from audit is limited to information regarding assets held by the "certifying" institution and transactions in those assets. Accordingly, an auditor *should perform the same procedures he would perform in full-scope examination in areas not related to information certified by a bank or an insurance company*. The auditor does not have to verify the existence of the assets held or transactions therein, either through confirmation or otherwise, nor does he have to verify the propriety of asset valuations or the amounts at which transactions are reported.

In addition, however, the AudSEC Interpretation specifies certain procedures an auditor should perform with respect to the information certified to by the bank or insurance company as follows:

- Compare the information to the amounts included in the financial statements and schedules, and ascertain that it is presented in compliance with the DOL rules and regulations.
- Test amounts reported by the trustee as received from and disbursed at the direction of the plan administrator (e.g., contributions, benefits, and expenses) for proper determination in accordance with the terms of the plan.

The auditor should also inquire as to the basis on which the information as to plan assets is prepared for purposes of footnote disclosure of accounting principles and practices, and review the reported information for possible violation of restrictions or limitations imposed by plan documents or ERISA.

[2] Reporting on Limited-Scope Examinations

The November 1976 AudSEC Interpretation prescribes a form of report to be used when the auditor's scope is limited and the excluded assets are material irrespective of whether the financial statements are prepared in conformity with the statutory requirements, the alternative method, GAAP, or non-GAAP. The AudSEC Interpretation notes that DOL regulations require footnote disclosure of departures from GAAP, and says that if the auditor is satisfied that the financial statements include adequate disclosure of departures from GAAP, the prescribed form of report may be issued without modification. The form of report prescribed by AudSEC is discussed at ¶ 16.02.

[3] Reporting When Required Procedures Are Not Performed

Because of the confusion generated by DOL regulations, some plans may resist having auditors perform any procedures, such as those described at ¶ 13.02[1] with respect to information certified by a bank or insurance company. The Interpretation states, "If the auditor is precluded from performing these procedures, he should issue a disclaimer of opinion in accordance with SAS No. 1, Section 516." The DOL has indicated that a standard disclaimer would not be acceptable, and that it would reject a filing containing such a disclaimer.

[4] Sample Footnote Summarizing Unaudited Information

The explanatory paragraph of the report included in the AudSEC Interpretation refers to a footnote summarizing the information certified by a bank or an insurance company. Following is an example of such a footnote.

The *ABC* Bank, corporate trustee of the Plan, holds the Plan's investment assets and executes transactions therein. Financial information relating to those assets is included in the accompanying financial statements based on information provided by the trustee. That information, which has not been examined by independent accountants is summarized below:

| | *December 31* | |
	19XX	*19XX*
Net Assets:		
Cash	$ 5,000	$ 4,000
United States Government securities	750,000	718,000
Corporate bonds and notes	1,461,000	1,998,000
Common stocks	5,068,000	4,318,000
	$7,284,000	$7,038,000

| | *Year Ended December 31* | |
	19XX	*19XX*
Changes in Net Assets:		
Additions:		
Contribution from Employer Company	$ 828,000	$1,063,000
Interest and dividend income	364,000	351,000
	1,192,000	1,414,000
Deductions:		
Benefit payments	562,000	885,000
Loss on sale of securities—net	362,000	415,000
Administrative expenses	74,000	70,000
	998,000	1,370,000
	194,000	44,000
Unrealized appreciation in aggregate current value of securities	52,000	116,000
NET ADDITIONS	$ 246,000	$ 160,000

Alternatively, where assets held by a bank or an insurance company comprise all, or substantially all, of a plan's assets, a statement to that effect along with an indication of the total amounts covered may be substituted for the tabular presentation of assets and transactions.

¶ 13.03   FULL-SCOPE EXAMINATIONS

As previously noted at ¶ 13.01, some plans will want the auditor to perform a full-scope examination of plan financial statements in accordance with GAAS in spite of the DOL regulations allowing limited-scope examinations.

Generally accepted auditing standards are comprised of general standards, standards of fieldwork, and standards of reporting. These standards are applicable to examinations of financial statements of employee benefit plans as well as to examinations of financial statements of other entities. By way of emphasis, the general standards and standards of fieldwork contained in Statement on Auditing Standards (SAS) No. 1, Section 150.02, are as follows:

General Standards

(1) The examination is to be performed by a person or persons having adequate technical training and proficiency as an auditor.

(2) In all matters relating to the assignment, an independence in mental attitude is to be maintained by the auditor or auditors.

(3) Due professional care is to be exercised in the performance of the examination and the preparation of the report.

Standards of Fieldwork

(1) The work is to be adequately planned and assistants, if any, are to be properly supervised.

(2) There is to be a proper study and evaluation of the existing internal control as a basis for reliance thereon and for the determination of the resultant extent of the tests to which auditing procedures are to be restricted.

(3) Sufficient competent evidential matter is to be obtained through inspection, observation, inquiries, and confirmation to afford a reasonable basis for an opinion regarding the financial statements under examination.

[1] Applying Generally Accepted Auditing Standards to Trusteed Plans

The second and third standards of fieldwork are particularly troublesome with respect to many employee benefit plan audits. This is true because of the unique relationship of many plans to bank trust departments whereby many of the accounting records are maintained by the bank trust departments. These relationships are discussed in more detail in Chapter 1.

The assets of many employee benefit plans currently are held in trust by banks. A bank's function with respect to a particular plan may range from custodial responsibility for the investments and related transactions to almost complete discretionary control over the assets, transactions, and accounting records of the plan. In effect, in many cases, internal controls relating to plan operations are exercised by the trust department rather than the plan. Similarly, necessary competent evidential matter is also maintained by the bank.

The procedures for auditing trusteed assets include review of internal accounting controls over investments, testing of investment transactions by examination of competent evidential matter such as investment authorizations and broker's advices, testing of recorded gains and losses on investment transactions and investment income, and verification of the existence and valuation of assets.

When a bank is performing more than custodial functions for a plan, confirmation of transactions will normally not constitute adequate audit procedures and some independent testing of the records and documentation of plan transactions and assets maintained by a bank will be necessary. The extent of the required testing of plan records maintained by a bank will vary depending upon the extent of functions performed by the bank and the adequacy of internal accounting control. The varying types of trust arrangements and the services provided by bank trust departments are described at ¶ 1.04[1].

The procedures for auditing trusteed assets as described in the preceding paragraph are applicable whether the trustee relationship is solely custodial, fully discretionary, or somewhere in between. The necessity to visit a bank trust department to audit a discretionary trust account depends on the amount of discretion vested in a trustee and the existence of independent records and documentation maintained by a plan or other sources external to the trustee. These factors differ from plan to plan. The auditor should use his judgment to determine where and how these audit procedures should be applied. This requires an understanding of how the plan operates and its relationship to the trust department. Where the trustee has complete discretionary authority and maintains the primary accounting records of the plan, the tests of internal accounting controls and transactions will probably have to be performed at the bank trust department. However, certain or even all of these tests could be performed outside of the bank if the plan administrator or other external sources maintain sufficient controls and accounting records. In either instance, the auditor should be satisfied through substantive audit procedures that there is a basis for relying on the completeness and accuracy of the investment records.

[2] Single-Auditor Approach to Auditing Trusteed Assets

Banks are understandably opposed to having numerous plan auditors visit their trust department to review their internal accounting controls and make tests of records they maintain for employee benefit plans. As an alternative to having individual plan auditors perform these procedures, a number of banks, particularly the larger ones, have engaged their own auditors to review and test the trust department's internal accounting control as it relates to the employee benefit plans serviced by the bank, and issue a report on this review.

A single-audit review of a bank's trust department would normally include: (1) a review and evaluation of the system of internal accounting control over legal compliance, physical existence of assets, and trust activity; (2) tests of trust department procedures; and (3) tests of trust account activity. The objectives of such a review are to ascertain that the controls and procedures are adequate and in use and operating as planned, and that assets exist and are properly safeguarded.

An example of a typical report on a signal-auditor review is as follows:

Date ....

Board of Directors and Stockholders
ABC Bank

We made a study for the year ended December 31, 19XX of the system of internal accounting control in the Employee Benefit Trust Department of *ABC* Bank controlling assets held for others in trust, investment advisory, and custody accounts for the purpose of reporting on our evaluation of the system. In making our study, we reviewed and tested the system (including the procedures employed as they affect internal control, the extent of the segregation of duties within and among the various departments, and the scope of the internal audit program) to the extent we considered necessary to evaluate the system as required by generally accepted auditing standards. Our study included inspection and confirmation, on a test basis, of assets held for others in trust, investment advisory, and custody accounts as of November 19, 19XX, examination of administration of selected accounts, and observation and review of the procedures followed by the internal auditing department.

The objective of internal accounting control is to provide reasonable, but not absolute, assurance as to the safeguarding of assets against loss from unauthorized use or disposition, and the reliability of financial records for preparing financial statements and maintaining accountability for assets. The concept of reasonable assurance recognizes that the cost of a system of internal accounting control should not exceed the benefits derived and also recognizes that the evaluation of these factors necessarily requires estimates and judgments by management.

There are inherent limitations that should be recognized in considering the potential effectiveness of any system of internal accounting control. In the performance of most control procedures, errors can result from misunderstanding of instructions, mistakes of judgment, carelessness, or other personal factors. Control procedures whose effectiveness depends upon segregation of duties can be circumvented by collusion. Similarly, control procedures can be circumvented intentionally by management with respect either to the execution and recording of transactions or with respect to the estimates and judgments required in the preparation of financial statements. Further, projection of any evaluation of internal accounting control to future periods is subject to the risk that the procedures may become inadequate because of changes in conditions and that the degree of compliance with the procedures may deteriorate.

Our study and evaluation of the aforementioned system of internal accounting control in the Employee Benefit Trust department controlling assets held for others in trust, investment advisory, and custody accounts, which was made for the purpose of reporting on our evaluation of such system of internal accounting control, would not necessarily disclose all weaknesses in the system. However, such study and evaluation disclosed no conditions that we believe to be material weaknesses.

Bank Auditor

[a] Professional Recognition of the Single-Auditor Approach

The AICPA Employee Benefits Plan Committee is in the process of preparing an industry audit guide for audits of pension plans. As a part of this project, an issues paper on auditing trusteed assets was released for comment in April 1977. The principal thrust of the paper was to determine the circumstances, if any, under which audit procedures need to be performed at a bank trustee's offices. Those believing that audit procedures need to be performed at the bank were asked to comment on the following two methods:

(1) One method is to visit the trustee and perform the audit procedures considered necessary in the circumstances at the offices of the trustee. These procedures might include evaluation of the system of internal accounting controls, including vault control procedures, inspection of securities, and examination underlying documentation, including authorization in support of transactions.

(2) Another method would involve the engagement by a bank trust department of an independent auditor to perform a review and evaluation of the trust department's internal accounting controls, and the issuance of a report to the bank setting forth the scope of the review and results of the evaluation. This report would then be available to the auditors of employee benefit plans to enable them to satisfy themselves as to the requirement for the study and evaluation of internal accounting control. Those who hold this view believe that it greatly reduces the duplication of effort in the review of internal accounting controls, the test of block trades, and to some extent, the inspection of securities that would otherwise be necessary if each plan auditor were to conduct his own examination at the bank trust department.

The second standard of fieldwork does not contemplate that the auditor will place complete reliance on internal control to the exclusion of other auditing procedures with respect to material amounts in the financial statements (see SAS No. 1, Section 320.71). Some plan auditors, after establishing the scope of examination by reference to the internal accounting control report, believe that such a report supplemented by other audit procedures not involving bank records are sufficient for an examination made in accordance with generally accepted auditing standards. Some plan auditors recognize that it may be necessary to review and discuss with the bank auditor the scope of his examination, his working papers, and the results of his examination. They may request the bank auditor to perform specific tests of trust department records to provide the plan auditor with evidential matter with respect to plan transactions.

Although the single-auditor approach to auditing trusteed assets as described in (2) above has not been officially sanctioned by the AICPA, it is used in practice; and many plan auditors are accepting and using the reports of other auditors on a bank trustee's internal accounting controls.

[b] Other Considerations in Using the Single-Auditor Approach

In discussing the single-auditor approach, the AICPA issues paper points out the concern of many auditors that a review of internal accounting control and a report thereon may not be sufficient for a plan auditor to express an opinion unless he is satisfied with the results of specific tests of transactions of the plan under examination.

The single-auditor approach contemplates that specific tests of transactions will be made to verify the system of internal accounting control. While these tests may not encompass tests of transactions of a specific plan under examination, they do provide a basis for reliance by the plan auditor on the integrity of the bank's system and its ability to provide reliable information, which can then be tested without reference to the bank's records.

Alternatively, many banks have engaged the firm conducting the review of internal control to be available to test specific transactions or perform other procedures as requested by the plan auditor.

A footnote to the discussions of the single-auditor approach contained in the AICPA issues paper reads as follows:

> "The approach discussed above has caused some to express concern about the question of whether the plan auditor may have to express reliance on the auditor engaged by the bank or whether he may be the principal auditor of the plan. Others maintain that there is guidance in existing literature, for example, sections 640.04 and 543 of SAS No. 1, to establish precedent for using the reports of other auditors on internal control without express-

ing reliance on those auditors or affecting the principal auditor role of the plan auditor."

Using the reports of other auditors on internal accounting control would not seem to affect the plan auditor's role as principal auditor, nor would it seem to result in expressing reliance on other auditors. This is true primarily because the plan auditor only uses the report on internal control in setting the scope of his examination, not as a substitute for his own audit procedures.

Similarly, use of other auditors to examine source documents should not have an effect on the plan auditor's report. In effect, the plan auditor determines the procedures to be performed and the items to be tested, and accepts responsibility for the work of the other auditor.

¶ 13.04 PLANNING THE AUDIT

Obviously, the first step in planning an audit of an employee benefit plan is to determine whether the plan elects to have a limited-scope examination or a full-scope examination. However, regardless of the type of examination, planning is an integral part of the examination. Only the depth of the planning will be affected by the type of audit. As an example, the amount of coordination required with a bank trust department (see ¶ 13.04[2]) may be less when the audit scope is limited.

The requirement for planning is covered by the first standard of fieldwork, which states: "The work is to be adequately planned. . . ." Effective and timely planning is essential to the performance of efficient audits. It provides for considered development of the overall audit plan and effective utilization of available resources. Various forms of planning are required as an audit progresses: however, initial planning for the engagement should take place prior to or in conjunction with the review and evaluation of internal accounting control and the preparation of the audit program.

The various aspects of initial planning for an audit of an employee benefit plan should include the following:

- Determining how the plan operates;
- Coordinating with outside parties;
- Coordinating with audit of sponsoring employer;

- Identifying current developments affecting the plan's operations;
- Developing the overall scope of examination, including identification of areas of audit emphasis;
- Establishing the timing of significant phases of the audit and determining the extent of client assistance;
- Developing the general staffing plan.

[1] Determining How the Plan Operates

Chapter 1 discusses the various types of employee benefit plans and the different ways in which they can be administered and funded. The most logical first step in the audit of a plan is to understand its specific operating characteristics. This can usually be accomplished through discussions with personnel of the plan or plan sponsor and review of plan documents. Documents of value in reviewing and understanding the provisions and operations of a plan would include the following:

- Written plan agreement;
- Plan description filed with the DOL (Form EBS-1);
- Summary plan description;
- IRS determination letter or request for determination;
- Trust agreement;
- Annual report of trustee;
- Minutes of meetings of board of trustees and/or administrative committee;
- Actuarial reports;
- Internal audit reports;
- Insurance contracts;
- Insurance company reports;
- Annual return/report to the IRS and the DOL.

[2] Coordinating With Outside Parties

In most cases, some record-keeping functions will be performed for the plan by outside organizations (e.g., a bank trust department). This will necessitate coordination with corporate trustees, insurance companies, and actuaries to determine when and where data necessary to audit the plan will be available.

[3] Coordinating With Audit of Sponsoring Employer

One of the auditor's principal responsibilities in auditing a plan is to ascertain compliance with both plan and ERISA provisions. Many of the audit procedures in these areas involve participant data, much of which is generated and/or maintained by the employer's payroll or accounting department. For this reason, testing of this data in most instances should be performed in conjunction with the employer audit. Coordination of these audit efforts is particularly important where the plan records are decentralized.

[4] Identifying Current Developments Affecting the Plan's Operations

The identification of current developments affecting a plan's operations generally is achieved through early discussions with key members of a plan's management and staff and by reference to various available sources of information. Of concern are those developments which may give rise to potential auditing, accounting, or reporting problems, such as:

- Changes in plan provisions;
- Changes in accounting principles or estimates;
- Changes in actuarial methods or assumptions;
- Changes in key plan personnel, actuaries, trustees, outside investment advisers, or others rendering services to the plan;
- Changes in internal accounting controls, procedures and systems, or location of accounting records;
- Changes in applicable government regulations;
- New contracts, agreements, litigation, or contingencies.

[5] Developing the Overall Scope of Examination

The overall audit scope should provide adequate audit coverage of significant financial statement items. In establishing the audit scope, the auditor should identify the areas of audit emphasis—i.e., those areas or issues involving risks and exposure that could result in significant audit adjustments or require financial statement or schedule disclosures.

The principal audit areas for most employee benefit plans are investments; plan transactions such as contributions, benefit payments, and investment purchases and sales; participant data including withdrawals, terminations, and forefeitures; and, possibly, actuarial determinations. An overriding audit responsibility is to determine that the plan is operating in accordance with its provisions and that the plan and its operations are in compliance with ERISA.

The overall audit plan should not be regarded as inflexible. Appropriate changes to the audit scope should be made when changing circumstances warrant them. For example, the procedures performed at the bank trust department should be challenged if the trust agreement is changed from a discretionary account to a custodial account.

[6] Establishing the Timing of Significant Phases of the Audit and Determining the Extent of Client Assistance

The timing of significant phases of the audit and tentative deadlines for their completion should be determined at an early date and a timetable prepared. Significant audit dates might include dates for benefit payment confirmation, commencement and completion of interim work, year-end work, trustee meetings, meetings with actuaries, closing conference, and the issuance of the audit report and management letter.

To the extent the plan or the sponsoring employer has internal auditors, it would generally be appropriate to discuss the scope and findings of their work during the current year and the planned scope of their work for the remainder of the current year, and to tentatively determine the availability of internal audit personnel for direct assistance. At a later date, the effect of the internal audit function on the scope of the audit should be determined by reviewing and evaluating the competence and objectivity of the internal audit staff in accordance with SAS No. 9.

The extent of client assistance to be provided during the audit engagement should be determined as early as possible. Prior to beginning the fieldwork, a listing of schedules and analyses to be provided by the client, with identification of the dates they are to be completed, and by whom, should be prepared and reviewed with the client. So that the specific information required (e.g., schedule of account activity for the year or analysis of year-end balance) is obtained, it may be desirable to provide the client with the formats of schedules and analyses, as well as written instructions for preparation.

[7] Devloping the General Staffing Plan

A general staffing plan should be developed based upon the tentative timetables and overall time estimates. Consideration should be given to assigning personnel with adequate experience and specialized knowledge. For example, if the plan's records are highly automated, assignment of an electronic data processing specialist would be appropriate. In most plan audits, tax personnel would be extremely helpful in determining the plan's compliance with ERISA.

Chapter 14

REVIEW OF INTERNAL ACCOUNTING CONTROL

¶ 14.01   INTRODUCTION

The second standard of fieldwork requires that

"There is to be a proper study and evaluation of the existing internal control as a basis for reliance thereon and for the determination of the resultant extent of the tests to which auditing procedures are to be restricted."

The basic concepts governing the review and evaluation of internal accounting control are discussed extensively in Section 320 of Statement on Auditing Standards No. 1. Section 320.50 states:

> "The study to be made as the basis for the evaluation of internal control includes two phases: (a) knowledge and understanding of the procedures and methods prescribed and (b) a reasonable degree of assurance that they are in use and are operating as planned. These two phases of study are referred to as the review of the system and tests of compliance, respectively."

Following is an internal control questionnaire which has been developed to assist the auditor in the first phase of his review, that is, obtaining knowledge and understanding of the procedures and methods prescribed. It has been developed to cover the significant assets, liabilites, and operations of most types of plans.

The questionnaire does not contain sections on cash receipts and disbursements as these functions are usually performed by others on behalf of the plan, nor does it contain sections on certain other functions which may be performed by the plan. Where applicable, this questionnaire should be supplemented by appropriate additional questions, flow charts, and narrative procedural descriptions.

Although the internal accounting controls of others (e.g., corporate trustees) performing functions such as cash receipts and disbursements for plans is important to plans, they are not within the scope of this questionnaire. Where applicable, the internal accounting controls of such institutions should receive the full and adequate consideration of the auditor. See ¶ 13.03[1] for a discussion of this area.

The sponsoring employer's internal controls over personnel records and payroll are also important to the operations of many plans and should be considered in the overall evaluation of internal control of the plan.

The questions have been so devised that a "yes" answer would indicate a satisfactory degree of internal control. "No" answers should influence the auditor to consider whether, in order to make the questionnaire as informative as possible, such negative answers should be amplified or the related questions covered by a supplemental statement. For example, it may be that a "no" answer should be coupled with a statement to the effect that some alternative procedure followed by the client provides the same degree of control in the circumstances.

Questions that are not applicable to a particular plan should be answered by inserting "N/A" in the "answer" section.

Answering the questions does not complete the investigation of the system of internal controls; the accountant in charge must be satisfied, by observations and/or test-check, that the procedures indicated by the answers are being carried out in practice.

Space is also provided at the end of each section of the questionnaire for notations as to the adequacy or inadequacy of the system as it relates to the particular section. In addition, space is also provided for cross-referencing the questionnaire to the final audit program to relate audit procedures implemented to test specific areas of control weakness. (Use insert pages if necessary.)

¶ 14.02   GENERAL INFORMATION

Client personnel (name and title) from whom answers were obtained:

....

....

(1) Describe the type of plan under examination giving consideration to the following attributes:
   (a) Is the plan a welfare benefit or pension benefit plan?
   (b) Is the plan a defined benefit or defined contribution pension plan?
   (c) If the plan is a defined contribution pension plan, is it a profit-sharing, money-purchase, stock bonus, target benefit, or savings plan?
   (d) If the plan is a welfare benefit plan, what type of welfare benefits are provided (e.g., health, vacation, etc.)?
   (e) Is the plan contributory or noncontributory?
   (f) Is the plan a single-employer or multiemployer plan?
   (g) Is the plan established through collective bargaining?

....
....
....
....
....
....
....

(2) Is the plan a trusteed plan, an insured plan, or a combination plan? (Describe.)

....

....

....

(3) If the plan is a trusted plan or a combination plan, list the trustee(s) and, if individuals, their affiliation with the employer/union.

Name   *Affiliation*

....

....

....

....

....

....

(4) If the plan is an insured plan or a combination plan, indicate the name of the insurance company(ies) and the type of contract (e.g., deposit administration, immediate participation guarantee, individual policy, group annuity, etc.)

Company   *Type of Contract*

....

....

....

(5) (a) List the name and title or capacity of any person who under ERISA is a fiduciary to the extent he or she: (i) exercises discretionary authority or control over the plan or the disposition of its assets; (ii) renders investment advice to the plan for a fee; (iii) has any discretionary authority or responsibility in administration of the plan.

....

....

....

....

....

....

(b) Indicate which of the above are named fiduciaries as defined by Section 403(a) of ERISA.

....

....

(6) Who is responsible for plan administration? An administrative committee, a retirement committee, the board of trustees, an individual?

....

(7) If applicable, list the names and affiliations of the administrative or retirement committee.

Name	*Affiliation*
....	....
....	....
....	....
....	....
....	....
....	....

(8) Designate principal executives, department heads, etc., involved in day-to-day administration of the plan.

Name	*Position*	*Principal Duties*
....	....	....
....	....	....
....	....	....
....	....	....
....	....	....
....	....	....
....	....	....

(9) List the names of the custodian(s) of plan assets. (Note: This will normally be either a bank trust department or an insurance company.)

....

....

....

....

(10) List the names of any independent investment managers employed by the plan other than corporate trustees.

....

....

....

....

(11) List the name, address, professional qualification, and enrollment status of the plan's actuary, if applicable (i.e., for a defined benefit pension plan).

....

....

....

....

(12) Designate which accounting and participant records are maintained by or for the plan and by whom (e.g., administrator, sponsor, bank, insurance company, actuary).

Type of Record	*By Whom*
....	....
....	....
....	....
....	....
....	....
....	....
....	....
....	....

	Answer		*Answer Substantiated During Audit*	
	Yes	*No*	*Observation*	*Test*
(a) Are the plan accounting records kept separate from plan sponsor records?	☐	☐	☐	☐

| | | Answer | | Answer Substantiated During Audit | |
		Yes	No	Obser-vation	Test
(b) Are the plan accounting records kept separate from the plan sponsor's other benefit plan records?		☐	☐	☐	☐
(13) If records are maintained for the plan by bank, insurance company or other outside party:					
(a) Are formal reports of plan activity furnished?		☐	☐	☐	☐
(b) Are such reports reconciled to internally generated information?		☐	☐	☐	☐
(c) Is the institution rendering the report audited by independent accountants?		☐	☐	☐	☐
(14) Is the responsibility of maintaining accounting records of the plan completely separated from:					
(a) The plan's cash receipts and disbursements?		☐	☐	☐	☐
(b) The investment department?		☐	☐	☐	☐
(c) The participants' eligibility records?		☐	☐	☐	☐
(d) Custodianship of the assets?		☐	☐	☐	☐
(15) Is a general ledger maintained?		☐	☐	☐	☐
(a) How often is it posted?					
(b) Is it posted in sufficient detail?		☐	☐	☐	☐

	Answer Yes	No	Answer Substantiated During Audit Observation	Test

(16) In a contributory plan, is a subsidiary ledger of participants' balances maintained? □ □ □ □

    (a) How often is it updated and reconciled to the general ledger?

    ....

    (b) How often are valuation adjustments posted to participants' accounts?

    ....

(17) In a multiemployer plan, is a subsidiary ledger of employer and employee balances maintained? □ □ □ □

    (a) If such ledgers are maintained, how often are they updated and reconciled to the general ledger?

    ....

(18) Are journal entries approved by:

    (a) The plan administrator? □ □ □ □

    (b) Other designated employee? □ □ □ □

(19) Are standard journal entries used for the regularly recurring monthly closing entries? □ □ □ □

(20) Are journal entries explained or supported by substantiating data? □ □ □ □

			Answer Substantiated During Audit	
	Answer		*Obser-*	
	Yes	*No*	*vation*	*Test*

(21) Is electronic data processing (EDP) equipment or service used? If so, by whom (plan, plan sponsor, service bureau, etc.)? If EDP equipment is used, consideration should be given to reviewing the controls and procedures of the EDP Department.

....

(22) Are periodic financial statements prepared for the plan?   ☐ ☐ ☐ ☐

   (a) Is so, by whom?

   ....

   (b) How often? ....

   (c) Are they sufficiently informative to bring to light abnormal fluctuations in income, contributions, benefits paid, expenses, etc.?   ☐ ☐ ☐ ☐

(23) Is a written record retention program in effect, including participant eligibility, payroll and personnel records, in accordance with ERISA?   ☐ ☐ ☐ ☐

(24) Does the plan or plan sponsor have an internal auditor or audit staff?   ☐ ☐ ☐ ☐

(25) If internal auditors are employed:

   (a) To whom are they responsible (employer, Board of Trustees / Administrative Committee, etc.)?

   ....

			Answer Substantiated During Audit	
	Answer		*Obser-*	
	Yes	*No*	*vation*	*Test*
(b) Briefly describe below extent of testing and nature of reports, if any.				
....				
....				
....				
....				
....				
(c) Have their reports been reviewed?	☐	☐	☐	☐
(26) Does the plan's actuary make periodic actuarial valuations of the plan and issue formal reports?	☐	☐	☐	☐
If yes, how often?				
....				
....				
(27) Does the plan maintain a list of parties-in-interest?	☐	☐	☐	☐

Describe the plan's procedures for identifying transactions with parties-in-interest.

....
....
....
....

(28) Describe the plan's procedures for identifying transactions in excess of 3 percent of plan assets.

....
....
....
....
....
....

(29) Obtain copies of the following, where applicable:

(a) Written plan agreement, including amendments

(b) Internal Revenue Service determination letter

(c) Trust agreement

(d) Insurance contracts

(e) Minutes of Trustee/Committee meetings

(f) Organization chart

(g) Chart of accounts

(h) Accounting manual

(i) Trustee's reports

(j) Actuary's reports

(k) Filings with Internal Revenue Service and Department of Labor

Comment on the adequacy of internal control and indicate how audit procedures were expanded/reduced to compensate for noted weaknesses/strengths in the plan's system of internal control.

....
....
....

In subsequent examinations, indicate areas where scope of examination was expanded/reduced because of changes in plan's internal control.

....
....
....
....

	Name	*Date*
Originally prepared by:	....	....
Reviewed and substantiated in subsequent examination by:	....	....
	....	....
	....	....
	....	....

¶ 14.03   CONTRIBUTIONS

Plan personnel (name and title) from whom answers were obtained:

....

....

	Answer Yes	No	Answer Substantiated During Audit Observation	Test
(1) Is the method of determining employer contributions prescribed by the plan agreement?	☐	☐	☐	☐

(2) Describe how contributions are determined (e.g., by actuarial calculation, based on hours worked, as a percentage of pay, as determined by the Board of Directors of the sponsor, as a percentage of employee contributions).

....

....

....

....

(3) Describe the frequency with which employer contributions are made (e.g., monthly, annually).

....

....

| (4) Are contributions reported as received by a trustee or insurance company compared to contributions as determined above? | ☐ | ☐ | ☐ | ☐ |

	Answer Yes	Answer No	Answer Substantiated During Audit Obser- vation	Answer Substantiated During Audit Test
(5) If the plan is contributory, are predetermined control totals established for employee contributions withheld?	☐	☐	☐	☐
(6) Are employee contributions remitted to trustees or insurance companies compared to control totals?	☐	☐	☐	☐
(7) Are employee contributions posted to individual participant accounts?	☐	☐	☐	☐

The following questions are applicable to most multiemployer plans and should be completed for such plans. In addition, such plans normally have a cash receipts function which should be reviewed.

	Yes	No	Obser- vation	Test
(8) Is initial accountability over contribution forms established when they are received?	☐	☐	☐	☐
(9) Are contribution forms checked as to:				
(a) Rate?	☐	☐	☐	☐
(b) Hours?	☐	☐	☐	☐
(c) Extensions?	☐	☐	☐	☐
(d) Footings?	☐	☐	☐	☐
(e) Social Security account number?	☐	☐	☐	☐
(f) New participants and/or terminations?	☐	☐	☐	☐
(g) Agreement to cash receipts?	☐	☐	☐	☐

| | *Answer* | | *Answer Substantiated During Audit* | |
	Yes	*No*	*Obser-* *vation*	*Test*
(10) Does the plan have adequate control procedures to insure proper accounting for new participants/terminations noted on the contribution form?	☐	☐	☐	☐
(11) Are the contribution forms adequately controlled throughout the processing operation from the time of receipt of funds to the final postings in employer and participant subsidiary records?	☐	☐	☐	☐
(12) Do such records provide detail sufficient to differentiate between employer and participant contributions?	☐	☐	☐	☐
(13) Are participants' self-payments adequately controlled from the time of receipt to posting to participant records?	☐	☐	☐	☐
(14) Does someone reconcile total contributions per contribution forms and postings to employer/ participant subsidiary records to cash receipts? (Designate.)	☐	☐	☐	☐
(15) (a) Has the plan or contract administrator adopted procedures which are adequate for disclosing:				
(i) Delinquent contribution reports?	☐	☐	☐	☐

			Answer Substantiated During Audit	
	Answer		Obser-	
	Yes	No	vation	Test
(ii) Employer/participant over/under payments?	☐	☐	☐	☐
(b) If so, are such differences recorded in the general ledger?	☐	☐	☐	☐
(16) (a) Are receipts for contributions furnished to participants?	☐	☐	☐	☐
(b) If so, are they sent on a timely basis?	☐	☐	☐	☐
(17) If union dues are included in contribution remittances, are they promptly turned over to the union?	☐	☐	☐	☐
(18) Are payroll audits performed by the plan?	☐	☐	☐	☐
(a) If yes:				
(i) Is the collective bargaining agreement reviewed to determine that the employer/plan sponsor has complied with the applicable provisions?	☐	☐	☐	☐
(ii) Are the total gross earnings shown by the employer's/plan sponsor's earnings records reconciled with total wages shown by the general ledger and the payroll tax report?	☐	☐	☐	☐

| | *Answer* | | *Answer Substantiated During Audit* | |
| | *Yes* | *No* | *Obser-vation* | *Test* |

(b) Is information shown on the contribution reports compared with the data shown on the participant's earning record on a test basis?   ☐ ☐ ☐ ☐

(c) Is information shown on the participant's earning record compared with data shown on the contribution report on a test basis?   ☐ ☐ ☐ ☐

(d) Are the employer's/plan sponsor's cash disbursement records reviewed to ascertain whether any payments not recorded as compensation have been made to the participant?   ☐ ☐ ☐ ☐

(e) For a selected group of participants, is the data shown in the payroll journal:

(i) Compared to the participant's earnings?   ☐ ☐ ☐ ☐

(ii) Compared to the participant's time records?   ☐ ☐ ☐ ☐

(iii) Are the related payroll checks examined?   ☐ ☐ ☐ ☐

Comment on the adequacy of internal control and indicate how audit procedures were expanded/reduced to compensate for noted weaknesses/strengths in the plan's system of internal control.

....

....

....

In subsequent examinations, indicate areas where scope of examination was expanded/reduced because of changes in plan's internal control.

....

....

....

	Name	*Date*
Originally prepared by:	....	....
Reviewed and substantiated in subsequent examination by:	....	....
	....	....
	....	....
	....	....

¶ 14.04   INVESTMENTS

Plan personnel (name and title) from whom answers were obtained:

....

....

	Answer Yes	Answer No	Answer Substantiated During Audit Observation	Answer Substantiated During Audit Test
A. *Marketable Securities*				
(1) Who maintains physical control over securities owned by the plan?				
(a) Plan administrator?	☐	☐	☐	☐

	Answer Yes	Answer No	Answer Substantiated During Audit Observation	Answer Substantiated During Audit Test
(b) Corporate trustee?	☐	☐	☐	☐
(c) Other? (Designate.)	☐	☐	☐	☐

....

(2) (a) If the plan administrator maintains physical control over securities owned by the plan, are they kept in a safe-deposit vault?   ☐   ☐   ☐   ☐

    (b) Does access thereto require signatures of two or more persons? (Designate.)   ☐   ☐   ☐   ☐

....
....

    (c) Are visits to the vault recorded?   ☐   ☐   ☐   ☐

(3) If physical control over securities owned by the plan is maintained by a corporate trustee:

    (a) How are securities registered?

        Nominee name: ....
....

        Plan name: ....
....

    (b) How are securities filed?

        By issue: ....
        By plan: ....

| | Answer | | Answer Substantiated During Audit | |
	Yes	No	Obser- vation	Test
(c) Are periodic securities counts made by independent CPAs?	☐	☐	☐	☐
(d) Do the independent CPAs issue a letter as to internal accounting control over securities?	☐	☐	☐	☐
(4) Are securities periodically inspected or confirmed with independent custodians and reconciled to subsidiary records by internal auditors or others?	☐	☐	☐	☐
(5) Have the plan's investment policies and responsibility for custody of securities been determined by:				
(a) Board of Trustees/Administrative Committee?	☐	☐	☐	☐
(b) Others? (Designate.)	☐	☐	☐	☐
(6) Are purchases and sales of securities authorized by:				
(a) The Board of Trustees/ Administrative Committee/ Investment Committee?	☐	☐	☐	☐
(b) A corporate trustee?	☐	☐	☐	☐
(c) An outside investment manager?	☐	☐	☐	☐
(d) Others? (Designate.)	☐	☐	☐	☐

	Answer		*Answer Substantiated During Audit*	
	Yes	*No*	*Obser-vation*	*Test*
(7) If investment transactions are authorized by the plan trustees or a plan committee, are investment decisions recorded in minutes?	☐	☐	☐	☐
(8) If investment transactions are authorized by a corporate trustee or outside investment manager, is the plan notified of investment decisions prior to execution?	☐	☐	☐	☐
(9) Is the plan notified of investment transactions after they are executed?	☐	☐	☐	☐
(10) Are securities and securities transactions recorded in a subsidiary ledger?	☐	☐	☐	☐
(11) If a subsidiary securities ledger is not maintained, do reports of the corporate trustee include details as to holdings and transactions?	☐	☐	☐	☐
(12) Are reports of corporate trustees reconciled to plan records and/or compared to investment transaction notification or minutes?	☐	☐	☐	☐
(13) Are all write-downs or write-offs of securities approved by the Board of Trustees/Administrative Committee?	☐	☐	☐	☐

		Answer		Answer Substantiated During Audit	
		Yes	No	Obser- vation	Test
(14) Are security investments which have been written off followed up as to possible realization?		☐	☐	☐	☐
(15) Who retains broker advices and other documentation of securities transactions?					
(a) Plan administrator?		☐	☐	☐	☐
(b) Corporate trustee?		☐	☐	☐	☐
(c) Other? (Designate.)		☐	☐	☐	☐
(16) Who receives investment income?					
(a) Plan administrator?		☐	☐	☐	☐
(b) Corporate trustee?		☐	☐	☐	☐
(c) Other? (Designate.)		☐	☐	☐	☐
(17) Are records and procedures adequate to determine that investment income due has been received? (Describe.)		☐	☐	☐	☐
(18) Does the plan utilize an investment service to "audit" investment performance, transactions, receipt of income, etc.?		☐	☐	☐	☐

	Answer Yes	Answer No	Answer Substantiated During Audit Observation	Test

(19) If assets are invested in bank-sponsored common trust funds, is the common trust audited by independent CPAs? If so, obtain a copy of their report.   ☐ ☐ ☐ ☐

B.   *Deposits With Insurance Company*

(1) Are deposits under insurance contracts invested in:

   (a) The general assets of the insurance company?   ☐ ☐ ☐ ☐

   (b) Separate accounts?   ☐ ☐ ☐ ☐

(2) Does the insurance contract contain a penalty clause for termination of the contract? (Describe.)   ☐ ☐ ☐ ☐

....

....

....

....

(3) If the insurance deposit is split between separate accounts or between the general assets of the insurance company and separate accounts, who determines the percent or amount invested in each?

   (a) The plan administrator?   ☐ ☐ ☐ ☐

   (b) The insurance company?   ☐ ☐ ☐ ☐

   (c) Other? (Describe.)   ☐ ☐ ☐ ☐

....

	Answer		*Answer Substantiated During Audit*	
	Yes	*No*	*Obser-vation*	*Test*

(4) Does the insurance contract contain provisions requiring a specified amount be invested in the general assets of the insurance company? (Describe.)   ☐ ☐ ☐ ☐

....
....
....
....

(5) If deposits are invested in separate accounts, are the separate accounts audited by independent CPAs? (If so, obtain a copy of their report.)   ☐ ☐ ☐ ☐

C. *Other Investments*

(1) List other investments, such as loans, real estate, leases, etc., held by the plan.

....
....
....
....

(2) Are purchases, sales, and other transactions relating to such investments authorized by:

   (a) The Board of Trustees/ Administrative Committee?   ☐ ☐ ☐ ☐

   (b) An investment committee?   ☐ ☐ ☐ ☐

   (c) Other? (Describe.)   ☐ ☐ ☐ ☐

....

	Answer		*Answer Substantiated During Audit*	
	Yes	*No*	*Obser-vation*	*Test*
(3) Are investment decisions documented in Board/Committee minutes?	☐	☐	☐	☐
(4) Are legal documents relating to other investments:				
(a) In the name of the plan?	☐	☐	☐	☐
(b) Kept in a secure place?	☐	☐	☐	☐
(5) Are subsidiary records maintained for other investments? (Describe.)	☐	☐	☐	☐

....

....

....

(6) Describe in a separate memo the accounting system relating to and control over other investments to the extent not previously covered. Example of items which should be covered are accounting for and control over investment income and control over securities held as collateral for loans.

Comment on the adequacy of internal control and indicate how audit procedures were expanded/reduced to compensate for noted weaknesses/strengths in the plan's system of internal control.

....

....

....

In subsequent examinations, indicate areas where scope of examination was expanded/reduced because of change in plan's internal control.

....

....

....

....

	Name	*Date*
Originally prepared by:	....	....
Reviewed and substantiated in subsequent examination by:	....	....
	....	....
	....	....
	....	....

¶ 14.05   BENEFITS

This section is applicable to all pension and welfare plans. The questions assume that benefit disbursements are made by a corporate trustee or insurance company. For plans where benefits are disbursed directly, internal controls over cash disbursements should be considered.

Plan personnel (name and title) from whom answers were obtained:

....

....

	Answer		*Answer Substantiated During Audit*	
	Yes	*No*	*Obser- vation*	*Test*
(1) Are signed applications obtained for all payments?	☐	☐	☐	☐
(2) Is initial accountability over applications established when they are received?	☐	☐	☐	☐
(3) Are procedures in effect to promptly notify the administrator of all payment requests?	☐	☐	☐	☐
(4) Are payment applications received and approved by a responsible official not involved in the original processing procedures?	☐	☐	☐	☐

	Answer		*Answer Substantiated During Audit*	
	Yes	*No*	*Obser-vation*	*Test*
(5) Does the individual in item (4) above check for:				
(a) Eligibility of beneficiary?	☐	☐	☐	☐
(b) Amount of benefit and compliance with benefit schedule provided in plan?	☐	☐	☐	☐
(c) Appropriate supporting documentation, such as medical bills, employment and payroll records, birth certificates, etc.?	☐	☐	☐	☐
(d) If appropriate, is a determination made that the benefits are not covered for reimbursements under state, federal, and other insurance programs?	☐	☐	☐	☐
(6) Are payments checked for clerical accuracy?	☐	☐	☐	☐
(7) Are predetermined control totals maintained for monthly pension benefit payments and compared to trustee or insurance company reports?	☐	☐	☐	☐
(8) Are approved orders for payment mailed without returning them to the person processing the benefit claim?	☐	☐	☐	☐

	Answer Yes	Answer No	Answer Substantiated During Audit Obser-vation	Answer Substantiated During Audit Test
(9) Does the plan sponsor or administrator periodically correspond with retired beneficiaries for the purpose of determining that they are receiving correct benefits and/or are still alive?	☐	☐	☐	☐
(10) Does the plan sponsor or administrator maintain adequate participant records to support eligibility (e.g., enrollment date, credited service, salary history)?	☐	☐	☐	☐
If not, who does? (Designate.)				
(11) Are adequate procedures employed to determine that deceased beneficiaries are promptly deleted from the pension and benefits file? (Describe.)	☐	☐	☐	☐
....				
(12) Does the Board of Trustees/ Administrative Committee of the plan or its designee approve all benefit/claim applications, and is a record maintained in the minutes?	☐	☐	☐	☐
If not, who does? (Designate.)				

Comment on the adequacy of internal control and indicate how audit procedures were expanded/reduced to compensate for noted weaknesses/strengths in the plan's system of internal control.

....
....
....

In subsequent examinations, indicate areas where scope of examination was expanded/reduced because of changes in plan's internal control.

....
....
....

	Name	*Date*
Originally prepared by:	....	....
Reviewed and substantiated in subsequent examination by:	....	....
	....	....
	....	....
	....	....

¶ 14.06 WITHDRAWALS AND FORFEITURES

Plan personnel (name and title) from whom answers were obtained:

....
....

	Answer Yes	Answer No	Answer Substantiated During Audit Observation	Answer Substantiated During Audit Test
(1) Are signed withdrawal requests obtained for all withdrawals?	☐	☐	☐	☐
(2) Is initial accountability over withdrawal requests established when they are received?	☐	☐	☐	☐

	Answer		Answer Substantiated During Audit	
	Yes	*No*	*Obser-vation*	*Test*

(3) Are procedures in effect to promptly notify the administrator of all withdrawal requests? ☐ ☐ ☐ ☐

    (a) Are all withdrawal requests approved by:

        (i)   The Administrator? ☐ ☐ ☐ ☐

        (ii) The Board of Trustees/Administrative Committee? ☐ ☐ ☐ ☐

        (iii) Other? (Designate.) ☐ ☐ ☐ ☐

        ....

(4) Does someone recompute the participant's equity and the percent vested? ☐ ☐ ☐ ☐

(5) Is an unpaid withdrawal file maintained to insure all withdrawals are processed and paid on a timely basis? ☐ ☐ ☐ ☐

(6) Is a file of paid withdrawals maintained? ☐ ☐ ☐ ☐

(7) Are the withdrawal forms adequately controlled throughout the processing operation from the time of receipt of the request to the final payment and posting in the participant subsidiary record? ☐ ☐ ☐ ☐

(8) Are the number of participants withdrawn from the participants' subsidiary ledger reconciled to

| | *Answer* | | *Answer Substantiated During Audit* | |
	Yes	*No*	*Obser-vation*	*Test*
the number of withdrawal requests received?	☐	☐	☐	☐

(9) Are forfeited nonvested employer contributions:

    (a) Used to reduce employer's contribution?

    (b) Allocated to other participants?

(a)	☐	☐	☐	☐
(b)	☐	☐	☐	☐

Describe how forfeitures are computed and allocated.

....
....
....

Comment on the adequacy of internal control and indicate how audit procedures were expanded/reduced to compensate for noted weaknesses/strengths in the plan's system of internal control.

....
....
....

In subsequent examination, indicate areas where scope of examination were expanded/reduced because of changes in plan's internal control.

....
....
....

	Name	*Date*
Originally prepared by:	....	....
Reviewed and substantiated in subsequent examination by:	....	....
	....	....
	....	....
	....	....

¶ 14.07   PARTICIPANT DATA

Plan personnel (name and title) from whom answers were obtained:

....

....

	Answer Yes	Answer No	Answer Substantiated During Audit Observation	Answer Substantiated During Audit Test
(1) Are applications for new enrollments reviewed by a responsible employee with regard to eligibility requirements, etc., before processing?	☐	☐	☐	☐
(2) Are enrollment applications for all participants maintained for future reference in the Plan Administration Department?	☐	☐	☐	☐
(3) Are the number of new participants entered into the participants' subsidiary ledger reconciled to the number of new enrollment applications received?	☐	☐	☐	☐
(4) In a multiemployer plan, are employer contribution reports reviewed for new participants?	☐	☐	☐	☐
(5) Are procedures in effect to insure such new participants are promptly included in the participants' subsidiary ledger? (Describe.)	☐	☐	☐	☐

....

....

	Answer Yes	No	Answer Substantiated During Audit Observation	Test
(6) Are procedures in effect to promptly notify an employee when he becomes eligible to participate in the plan?	☐	☐	☐	☐
(7) If an employee declines enrollment, is the refusal retained in the employee's personnel folder?	☐	☐	☐	☐
(8) Are new enrollment applications kept under numerical control?	☐	☐	☐	☐
(9) Are hours of service accumulated for purposes of determining eligibility for benefit accrual, vesting, breaks in service?	☐	☐	☐	☐
(10) Are adequate records maintained for terminated participants with deferred vested benefits?	☐	☐	☐	☐
(11) Are separate records maintained for different participant classifications (e.g., active, retired, terminated with deferred vested benefits)?	☐	☐	☐	☐
(12) Are participant classification records reconciled periodically with participant activity (e.g., new enrollment, death, withdrawal, retirement) records?	☐	☐	☐	☐
(13) For defined benefit plans, how often is participant data furnished the actuary? (Designate.)	☐	☐	☐	☐

		Answer		Answer Substantiated During Audit	
		Yes	*No*	*Obser-vation*	*Test*

(14) Is participant data furnished the actuary reconciled to plan sponsor payroll and personnel records? (Designate by whom.) □ □ □ □

....

....

(15) For a contributory plan, is a record maintained of:

    (a) Cumulative participant contributions? □ □ □ □

    (b) Cumulative employer contributions? □ □ □ □

    (c) Cumulative interest on participant's contributions? □ □ □ □

    (d) Pro rata participant's share of investment gains/losses? □ □ □ □

    (e) Other? (Describe.) □ □ □ □

    ....

    ....

    ....

(16) (a) Is a statement of account furnished each participant? □ □ □ □

    (b) If so, how often?

    ....

(17) Indicate what data is maintained on participants and by whom (e.g., plan personnel, personnel department of plan sponsor, account-

ing or payroll department of plan sponsor, corporate trustee, insurance company, actuary, other).

Data	*Maintained By*
Name	....
Sex	....
Social Security number	....
Birthdate and related verification data	....
Current address	....
Marital status	....
Benefit option selected	....
Beneficiary designation form	....
Social Security number and birthdate of joint annuitant	....
Years of service including hours worked	....
Salary history	....
Contribution authorization	....
....	....
....	....
....	....
....	....
....	....

Comment on the adequacy of internal control and indicate how audit procedures were expanded/reduced to compensate for noted weaknesses/strengths in the plan's system of internal control.

....

....

....

In subsequent examination, indicate areas where scope of examination was expanded/reduced because of changes in plan's internal control.

....
....
....
....

	Name	*Date*
Originally prepared by:	....	....
Reviewed and substantiated in subsequent examination by:	....	....
	....	....
	....	....
	....	....

¶ 14.08 ADMINISTRATIVE EXPENSES

Plan personnel (name and title) from whom answers were obtained:

....
....

(1) Who is charged for administrative expenses?

　　(a) Plan: ....

　　(b) Plan sponsor: ....

(2) Who makes disbursements?

　　(a) Plan?

　　(b) Corporate trustee?

　　(c) Plan sponsor?

　　(d) Other or combination? (Describe.)

　　　　...
　　　　...
　　　　...
　　　　...

| | | *Answer* | | *Answer Substantiated During Audit* | |
| | | *Yes* | *No* | *Obser-vation* | *Test* |

(3) If expenses are paid from plan assets, are charges:

    (a) Approved by a responsible official? □ □ □ □

    (b) Compared to contractual fee schedules (e.g., for trustee fees)? □ □ □ □

    (c) Compared to amounts disbursed by trustee? □ □ □ □

Chapter 15

CONDUCTING
THE AUDIT

¶ 15.01 GENERAL

Once the auditor has completed his review of internal accounting control, he is in a position to develop his audit program. The examination of an employee benefit plan's financial statements and the related reporting requirements imposed on independent accountants by the Employee Retirement Income Security Act of 1974 (ERISA) present the auditor with many unique auditing problems. This chapter discusses many of these problems in the areas which are normally significant to employee benefit plans. These discussions are general in nature; however, ¶ 15.07 contains a guide to specific procedures the auditor may want to consider in developing audit programs for plan examinations.

It should be emphasized that there is much current controversy over appropriate audit procedures in examinations of employee benefit plans—particularly in the areas of investment held by bank trustees and actuarial determinations. The AICPA Employee Benefit Plans and ERISA Committee is studying these and other areas with the objective of issuing an industry audit guide. The approaches and procedures described in this chapter represent the authors' recommendations until an audit guide is completed.

In general, the audit of an employee benefit plan will consist of:

(1) Auditing plan transactions and financial position;
(2) Auditing compliance with the provisions of ERISA, the Internal Revenue Code, and the specific plan provisions;
(3) Auditing information required in separate schedules (e.g., transactions in excess of 3 percent of plan sssets).

¶ 15.02 INVESTMENTS

The single most significant audit area in most employee benefit plan examinations is plan investments. The relationship of many plans to bank trustees and the audit problems encountered have been previously discussed (see ¶ 13.03). By way of emphasis, the audit objectives and procedures discussed in the following paragraphs are appropriate whether they are performed by the plan auditor or by a "single auditor." The objective of an audit of plan investments is to obtain reasonable assurance that

(1) The assets exist and are owned by the plan.

(2) Income from the assets has been received and is properly reflected in the financial statements.

(3) Purchase and sale transactions have been properly reflected in the financial statements and receipts and disbursements from such transactions have been accounted for.

(4) The assets are properly valued and presented in the financial statements.

[1] Existence and Ownership of Trusteed Assets

The existence and ownership of investments can be difficult to audit. Securities held in trust by a bank or trust companies are normally held in a nominee name. In addition, many trust departments file certificates by issuer rather than by trust account. These two factors make physical inspection of certificates impossible for any individual trust. In the past, confirmation of securities held by banks or trust companies has become a generally accepted auditing practice. This practice is acceptable in auditing employee benefit plans, provided the following guidelines are followed.

A confirmation is a third-party corroboration of information of which the auditor already has knowledge. Where securities are held by a bank or trust company and parties other than the bank or trust department exercise discretion and control over securities transactions, the auditor should have information as to assets the bank is supposed to have, and a confirmation from the bank would be acceptable audit evidence.

Where the bank or trust company exercises discretion and control over securities transactions, the auditor needs to satisfy himself as to investment transactions and securities, which should be held by the bank or trust company before a confirmation is acceptable. Normally, this would involve a review of internal accounting controls of the bank and tests of transactions or the receipt of a satisfactory single-auditor report. In either case, the auditor should be satisfied as to the reputation and financial responsibility of the institution.

[2] Investment Income

The objective in auditing investment income is to ascertain that all income due is received and properly recorded. When a bank or trust department controls the investments and receives income directly, the auditor obtains details of investment income if such detail is not included in the trustee's report. Once the auditor is satisfied that investment transactions, and therefore holdings at any point in time, are properly stated, investment income can be audited by testing to ascertain that income recorded is accurate based on the plan's holdings and all income due the plan has been received and credited. For example, the auditor could compare recorded dividend income to published dividend reports.

In addition, several brokerage and investment firms offer services which provide transaction analysis, schedules of dividends and interest, discrepancy reports, and other reports intended to "audit" the performance of the trustee. Utilization of such a service by the plan may enable the auditor to reduce his or her scope in testing investment income.

[3] Investment Transactions

Verification of transaction authorizations, prices for purchases and sales of investments, and the proper receipt and disbursement of funds are audit procedures normally accorded to investments. In this connection, much if not all of the supporting documentation may be maintained by the bank or trust department. In addition, supporting broker advices may be in a nominee name and include block (more than one trust) securities transactions. As with physical examination of securities, bank or trust company operations make it difficult for an individual trust auditor to perform necessary procedures at the institution. Again, the "single auditor approach" can be utilized to verify those transactions for which no support exists outside the bank or trust company.

[4] Investments in Commingled or Common Trust Funds

Commingled or common trusts are investment vehicles similar to mutual funds. A participating plan acquires investment units (units of participation), the unit price of which is determined periodically based on the current or market value of the assets held by the fund. Although many commingled trusts are audited by independent accountants, generally accepted auditing standards presently do not require such audits to support unit values for purposes of expressing an opinion on financial statements containing an investment in such trusts or accounts. However, the auditor should confirm the number of units held by the plan, the unit value, and the income distributions credited to the plan during the period, and he should test the plan's transactions in units of the fund by comparing the amounts confirmed by the bank to the plan's records.

[5] Investment Deposits Under Insurance Contracts

Deposits under insurance contracts are either invested in the general assets of the insurance company or in the pooled separate accounts sponsored by the insurance company. Confirmation of the deposits, credited earnings, transfers, etc., is sufficient evidence in auditing the existence and value of assets invested in the insurance company general account, provided the auditor is satisfied as to the reputation and financial responsibility of the insurance company. Pooled separate accounts of insurance companies are much like commingled or common trusts. Market risks are borne by the investor and unit values based on current market are reported periodically. Audit procedures for pooled separate account investments should be the same as for commingled trust funds.

[6] Auditing Current Value

Determination of current value has been previously discussed in Chapter 12. By way of emphasis, current value determination should be audited, not made, by accountants. In discussing audit requirements for securities held by investment companies carried at current value, the Securities and Exchange Commission (SEC) Accounting Series Release (ASR) No. 118 states:

> "In the case of securities for which market quotations are readily available, the independent accountant should independently verify all the quotations used by the company at the balance sheet date and satisfy himself that such quotations may properly be used under the standards stated above.

> "In the case of securities carried at 'fair value' as determined by the Board of Directors in 'good faith,' *the accountant does not function as an appraiser and is not expected to substitute his judgment for that of the company's directors*; rather, he should review all information considered by the board or by analysts reporting to it, read relevant minutes of directors' meetings, and

ascertain the procedures followed by the directors. If the accountant is unable to express an unqualified opinion because of the uncertainty inherent in the valuations of the securities based on the directors' subjective judgment, he should nevertheless make appropriate mention in his certificate whether in the circumstances the procedures appear to be reasonable and the underlying documentation appropriate.*

"When considering values assigned to securities by the company, the independent accountant should consider any investment limitations or conditions on the acquisition or holding of such securities which may be imposed on the company by the (Investment Company) Act, by its certificate or bylaws, by contract, or by its filings with the (Securities and Exchange) Commission. If such restrictions are met by a narrow margin, the independent accountant may need to exercise extra care in satisfying himself that the evidence indicates that the security valuation determinations were not biased to meet those restrictions."

Again, although the above-quoted ASR specifically applies to investment companies, its contents can also apply to employee benefit plans. For example, restrictions on investments contained in plan documents, such as percentage of equity investments, are similar to restrictions imposed on investment companies, and the auditor should exercise extra care as recommended by the ASR in reviewing valuations of restricted securities.

Audit procedures related to current value determinations should include a review to ascertain that the methods used have been reviewed and approved by the board of trustees (administrative committee, investment committee). In addition, these audit procedures should include inspection and testing of the documentation underlying the valuations.

The auditor may find it necessary under some circumstances to qualify his or her opinion if the plan owns material investments for which no readily ascertainable "current value" exists, or if the auditor is unable to form an opinion as to the fairness of the values so determined. An appropriate form of an accountant's report is included at ¶ 16.04.

---

* See ¶ 16.04 for an example of such a report.

¶ 15.03   PLAN TRANSACTIONS

Typical transactions of an employee benefit plan include receipt of employer and employee contributions, payment of benefits and other expenses, and previously discussed transactions involving investment income, sales, and purchases.

[1] Employer and Employee Contributions

In a single-employer plan, employer contributions should present few audit problems. Auditing employer contributions to multiemployer plans does present some problems which are discussed separately in connection with unique aspects of auditing multiemployer plans.

Auditing of employee contributions, while not difficult, can present some logistics problems if payroll records, deduction authorization, etc., are maintained on a decentralized basis.

Documentation to support the propriety of the amount and recording of both employer and employee contributions should be available from either the plan administrator or the employer. Such documentation could include the actuary's report, minutes of the sponsor's pension committee or board meeting, computations in accordance with the terms of the plan, and employee withholding authorizations.

[2] Benefit Payments

Broadly defined, benefit payments include not only normal (e.g., retirement or medical, etc.) benefits, but also withdrawal of employee contributions, and distributions and forfeitures upon employee termination. The primary objective in the audit of such transactions is to ascertain that the form and amount of distributions are properly authorized and in accordance with the plan provisions, and that the payment is received by the person entitled to it. For many plans, these disbursements are made by the bank or insurance company with which the funds are invested, while initiation of and support for the disbursements are handled by the plan or the employer.

To test the benefit disbursements, it is necessary to obtain the details of individual disbursements as well as the total of benefit disbursements. The details may be included in the trustee or insurance company report, or they may have to be requested separately from the institution. Audit procedures should be designed to verify that individual benefit disbursements made by the institution are properly supported, computed, and authorized by the plan. For example, these tests could include comparison of the amount disbursed to the amount authorized, and recomputation of the amount based on the terms of the plan. The auditor should also test from the plan records to the disbursement records to determine that authorized benefit payments are being made.

The above-described tests of plan benefit authorization and institution disbursements, however, do not provide evidence that (1) benefit payments are not being made to deceased beneficiaries, or (2) benefit payments are not being made to persons other than beneficiaries. Audit procedures to test for these possibilities include confirmations with beneficiaries of benefits received, and examination of canceled checks. Canceled checks are normally retained by the institution making the disbursements and, in the case of a bank, might not be readily available for examination. If the bank utilizes a "single auditor," that firm could be asked to examine checks (copies of beneficiary signatures should be supplied for comparative purposes). If no "single auditor" is available, arrangements should be made to examine canceled checks unless other controls coupled with benefit confirmations are considered adequate in the circumstances.

Other controls that are designed to prevent benefit payments to deceased or unauthorized persons include the following:

(1) Many plans will provide a death benefit to encourage timely notice of deaths.

(2) Some plans periodically check on the continued existence of older beneficiaries or all beneficiaries through phone calls or written communications.

(3) As an overall control against misappropriation of authorized benefits, the complete dependence of many beneficiaries on their pensions normally causes prompt correspondence if benefits are not received.

¶ 15.04   COMPLIANCE WITH PLAN PROVISIONS, ERISA, AND THE INTERNAL REVENUE CODE

Plan documents, including trust agreements and insurance contracts, generally contain very specific provisions as to how the plan must operate. These provisions are generally aimed at clearly defining the responsibilities of those administering the plan and the rights of the participants and beneficiaries.

The provisions of ERISA relating to participation, vesting, funding, fiduciary responsibility, and plan termination have been discussed in Chapter 2. Plan qualification and specific provisions of the Code have been discussed in Chapter 3. The importance of compliance with both the Department of Labor (DOL) provisions of ERISA and the Code cannot be overemphasized. The auditor should satisfy himself that the plan provisions are in accordance with applicable laws and regulations. Most plans should have an Internal Revenue Service (IRS) determination letter which indicates that the provisions of the plan meet the IRS qualification requirements. Normally, this should constitute sufficient evidence that the plan qualifies in its form.

However, the auditor may encounter situations where a plan has not applied for or received a determination letter. In these situations, the auditor should discuss plan qualification with the plan's legal counsel and management and, to the extent possible, obtain written representations that the plan meets the qualification requirements. In addition, the auditor may wish to review the plan provisions for compliance. The following checklist has been provided for this purpose.

[1] Checklist for Review of Pension Benefit Plans

This checklist has been designed to aid in the review of existing retirement plans that are affected by ERISA and have not received a current determination letter covering all plan amendments to date. It is intended to serve as a guide for a review as to the probable qualification of the plan. The checklist is not intended to be all inclusive, but should serve to highlight certain existing plan provisions that may require change or to point out provisions that may have to be added for the plan to meet the qualification requirements enumerated in Section 401(a) of the Code.

The questions are structured such that a "no" answer indicates a potential problem. In many instances, the Act provides exceptions, limitations, or transitional rules which may apply so that a "no" answer to a question does not necessarily mean that the plan must be changed immediately.

Following most of the questions, there is a reference to a specific section of the Code, a section of the DOL regulations, or a section of ERISA. This should provide the reviewer with a better understanding of the purpose of a particular question. It should also serve as a starting point for determining if there are exceptions, limitations, or regulations which indicate that a change in the existing plan is not required even though a question is answered in the negative.

[a] Participation and Coverage

	Yes	No	N/A

(1) If the plan does not provide for full and immediate vesting, does it provide for participation no later than the later of: (a) the date the employee attains age 25; or (b) the date the employee completes one year of service? [I.R.C. § 410(a)(1)(A)]   ☐   ☐   ☐

(2) If the plan does provide for full and immediate vesting, does it provide for participation no later than the later of: (a) The date the employee attains age 25; or (b) the date the employee completes three years of service? [I.R.C. § 410(a)(1)(B)]   ☐   ☐   ☐

(3) Does the plan provide that any employee who works at least 1,000 hours in a twelve-month period (measured from the time employment begins) will have one year of service in order to participate in the plan? [I.R.C. § 410(a)(3)(A) and DOL Reg. § 2530.202-2(a)]   ☐   ☐   ☐

(4) Is an employee required to complete no more than 1,000 hours of service during the computation period to be credited with a year of service? [I.R.C. § 410(a)(3)(A) and DOL Reg. § 2530.200b-1(a)]   ☐   ☐   ☐

(5) If the plan uses an "equivalency test," does it credit all employees with at least 1,000 hours of service? [DOL Reg. § 2530.200b-3(b)]   ☐   ☐   ☐

(6) If the plan uses the plan year as the computation period to measure years of service for purposes of eligibility after the first computation period, does the first such plan-year computation period include the first anniversary of the date of hire? [DOL Reg. § 2530.202-2(b)]   ☐   ☐   ☐

(7) Where the employee meets the eligibility requirements of the plan, does the plan use a
vesting computation period to measure years
of service for purposes of eligibility which
includes the last day of the eligibility computation period in which the employee first
completed the service requirement for participation in the plan? [DOL Reg. § 2530.202]   ☐   ☐   ☐

(8) Where the employer maintains the plan of a
predecessor employer, does the plan provide
that service with a predecessor employer is
counted as service with the employer? [I.R.C.
§ 414(a)(1)]   ☐   ☐   ☐

(9) Is a "break in service" defined as a computation period during which the employee
fails to complete more than 500 hours of service? [DOL Reg. § 2530.200b-4]   ☐   ☐   ☐

(10) Is the computation period for determining a
break in service the same as is used to compute a year of service for eligibility? [DOL
Reg. § 2530.202-2(c)(3)]   ☐   ☐   ☐

(11) In the case of an employee who has a vested
benefit, does such employee participate immediately on his return to the employ of the
employer after a break in service? [I.R.C. §
410(a)(5)(C)]   ☐   ☐   ☐

(12) In the case of an employee with no vested
benefit, who sustains a break in service, where
the number of years in which he incurred a
break in service are less than the number of
years in which he attained a year of service, does he participate immediately upon
his return to the employ of the employer?
[I.R.C. § 410(a)(5)(D) and Temp. Reg.
§ 11.410(a)-4]   ☐   ☐   ☐

	Yes	No	N/A

(13) After an employee satisfies the age and years of service requirements for participation, does the plan provide for commencement of participation no later than the earlier of: (a) the first day of the first plan year beginning after the employee satisfies the requirements; or (b) six months from the day the employee satisfies the requirements? [I.R.C. § 410(a)(4)]   ☐ ☐ ☐

(14) Are employees eligible for participation if their employment commences more than five years before the normal retirement age described under the plan? [I.R.C. § 410(a)(2)]   ☐ ☐ ☐

For defined contribution plans, are employees eligible to participate without regard to any maximum age conditions? [I.R.C. § 410(a)(2)]   ☐ ☐ ☐

(15) Does the plan limit eligibility conditions for participation to only those relating to length of service or age? [I.R.C. § 410(b)(1)(B)]   ☐ ☐ ☐

(16) Does the plan benefit 70 percent or more of all employees, excluding those who have not satisfied the minimum age and service requirements prescribed by the plan and those who are covered under a collective-bargaining agreement? [I.R.C. § 410(b)(1)(A)]   ☐ ☐ ☐

(17) If the answer to question 16 is "no," are 70 percent or more of all employees eligible to benefit under the plan and are 80 percent or more of those eligible actually benefited, excluding those who have not satisfied the minimum age and service requirements and those who are covered under a collective-bargaining agreement? [I.R.C. § 410(b)(1)(A)]   ☐ ☐ ☐

NOTE: If neither question 16 nor 17 is satisfied, the nondiscriminatory coverage requirements of Section 410(b)(1)(B) of the Code must be satisfied. (In this connection, see Rev. Rul. 66-12, 1966-1 C.B. 158; Rev. Rul. 70-200, 1970-1 C.B. 101; and the instruction to Form 5300.)

(18) Are the coverage requirements satisfied by considering this plan alone? If the answer is "no," identify the other plans which are considered as a "single plan" for purposes of qualification.   ☐   ☐   ☐

(19) If the answer to question 18 is "no," are benefits comparable between the plans?   ☐   ☐   ☐

(20) If the employer maintaining the plan is a member of a controlled group of corporation (within the meaning of Section 1563(a) of the Code), are the coverage requirements satisfied by the plan since all employees of corporations in the controlled group are considered as being employed by this employer? [I.R.C. § 414(b)]   ☐   ☐   ☐

(21) Are the coverage requirements satisfied when all employees of other trades or businesses (whether or not incorporated) under common control are considered as being employed by this employer? [I.R.C. § 414(c)]   ☐   ☐   ☐

[b] Vesting

(1) Does the plan provide that an employee's rights in the accrued benefit derived from his own contributions are nonforfeitable? [I.R.C. § 414(a)(1)]   ☐   ☐   ☐

(2) Does the plan provide that an employee's right to his retirement benefits derived from employer contributions are nonforfeitable

	Yes	No	N/A

upon reaching normal retirement age? [I.R.C. § 141(a)]   ☐ ☐ ☐

(3) Does the plan provide for vesting of employees' accrued benefits derived from employer contributions at least as fast as under one of the following minimum vesting standards?   ☐ ☐ ☐

(a) Ten-year vesting? [I.R.C. § 411(a)(2) (A)]

(b) Five-to-fifteen-year vesting? [I.R.C. § 411(a)(2)(B)]

(c) "Rule of 45"? [I.R.C. § 411(a)(2)(C)]

(4) If the "Rule of 45" minimum vesting standard is used by the plan, does it provide for at least 50 percent vesting after ten years of service and an additional 10 percent for each year of service thereafter without regard to age? [I.R.C. § 411(a)(2)(C)(ii)]   ☐ ☐ ☐

(5) Does the plan require separate accounting for the portion of each participant's accrued benefit derived from any voluntary employee contributions permitted under the plan? [I.R.C. § 411(b)(2)(A)]   ☐ ☐ ☐

For defined contribution plans, does the plan provide separate accounting for each participant? [I.R.C. § 411(b)(2)(B)]   ☐ ☐ ☐

(6) For defined benefit plans, does the plan provide for the accrual of benefits derived from employer contributions in accordance with one of the following alternative rules?   ☐ ☐ ☐

(a) 3 percent method? [I.R.C. § 411(b)(1) (A)]

(b) 133⅓ percent rule? [I.R.C. § 411(b) (1)(B)]

(c) Pro rata rule? [I.R.C. § 411(b)(1)(C)]

Yes   No   N/A

(7) For defined benefit plans, if the plan was in existence on January 1, 1974, does it provide that benefits which accrue, or accrued, during plan years prior to the first plan year beginning after December 31, 1975 are not less than the greater of: (a) the accrued benefit determined under the plan in effect prior to September 2, 1974; or (b) an accrued benefit that would have resulted if one of the alternative benefit accrual rules had applied with respect to such years? [I.R.C. § 411(b)(1)(D)]   ☐   ☐   ☐

(8) Does the plan define "year of participation" for vesting and benefit accrual purposes as a twelve-month period during which the employee has worked at least 1,000 hours? [I.R.C. §§ 411(a)(5), 411(b)(3)]   ☐   ☐   ☐

(9) For defined benefit plans, does the plan provide for at least ratable benefit accrual for less than full-time service if it exceeds 1,000 hours during the applicable twelve-month period? [I.R.C. § 411(b)(3)(B)]   ☐   ☐   ☐

(10) Does the plan provide for treatment of "breaks in service" in accordance with Section 411(a)(6) of the Code? [I.R.C. § 411(a)(4)(D)]   ☐   ☐   ☐

(11) Does the plan provide for full vesting upon its termination or partial termination?   ☐   ☐   ☐

For defined contribution plans, does the plan also provide for full vesting where a complete discontinuance of contributions occurs? [I.R.C. § 411(d)(3)]   ☐   ☐   ☐

(12) Does the plan provide that in the event it is merged or consolidated with, or the assets or liabilities of the plan are transferred to anoth-

Yes   No   N/A

er qualified plan after September 2, 1974, that every participant in the plan is entitled to receive a benefit immediately after the merger, consolidation, or transfer which is not less than the value of the benefit he would have been entitled to receive immediately before the event (if the plan had been terminated)? [I.R.C. §§ 401(a)(12), 414(1)]   ☐   ☐   ☐

(13) Does the plan *not* contain provisions for forfeitures of accrued benefits derived from employer contributions for any reason other than death? [I.R.C. § 411(a)(3)]   ☐   ☐   ☐

(14) If the answer to question 13 is "no," and the plan provides for forfeiture of accrued benefits derived from employer contributions because of the withdrawal of mandatory employee contributions by a participant who is not at least 50 percent vested, does it also provide for restoration of the forfeited accrued benefit upon repayment of the full withdrawal plus interest? [I.R.C. § 410(a)(3)(D)]   ☐   ☐   ☐

NOTE: See Section 401(a)(19) of the Code for prohibition against forfeiture of any accrued benefits derived from employer contributions due to withdrawal of mandatory employee contributions if the participant is at least 50 percent vested.

[c] Minimum Funding Standards

(1) Has the client considered the impact of the new funding standards?   ☐   ☐   ☐

(2) Do our files contain a copy of the last actuarial report?   ☐   ☐   ☐

Yes   *No*   *N/A*

(3) Has provision been made for valuation of the plan's liabilities and determination of experience gains and losses at least once every three years? [I.R.C. §§ 412(b), 412(c)(9)]   □   □   □

(4) If the minimum funding standard applies, have arrangements been made for the filing of an actuarial report? [I.R.C. § 6059]   □   □   □

(5) For money-purchase and "target benefit" pension plans, if the employer has ever missed a contribution under the plan, or if a lesser amount than required was contributed, has it been treated as a past service liability?   □   □   □

[d] Limitation on Benefits

(1) For defined benefit plans, does the plan limit the annual benefit payable to the lesser of: (a) $75,000 adjusted for allowable cost-of-living changes; or (b) 100 percent of the participant's average compensation for his high three years? [I.R.C. § 415(b)(1)]   □   □   □

(2) For defined contribution plans, does the plan limit the annual addition to a participating employee's account to the lesser of: (a) $25,000 adjusted for allowable cost-of-living changes; or (b) 25 percent of the participant's compensation? [I.R.C. § 415(c)(1)]   □   □   □

(3) For defined benefit plans, does the plan provide for a proportionate reduction in the above limitations for each year of service less than ten? [I.R.C. § 415(b)(5)]   □   □   □

(4) For defined benefit plans, does the plan provide for an adjustment of the $75,000 limita-

	Yes	No	N/A

tion if the benefit under the plan begins before age fifty-five? [I.R.C. § 415(b)(2)(C)] ☐ ☐ ☐

(5) If the employer maintains both a defined benefit plan and a defined contribution plan, are the limitations on benefits from the defined benefit plan and the limitation on annual additions to the defined contribution plan such that an employee participating in both plans could not obtain a combined defined benefit plan fraction and a defined contribution plan fraction in excess of 1.4 for any year? [I.R.C. § 415(e)] ☐ ☐ ☐

(6) If the employer maintaining the plan is a member of a controlled group of corporations (using "more than 50 percent" instead of "at least 80 percent" for measuring control), are the applicable limitations satisfied when benefits payable (or annual additions to employees' accounts) to participating employees from plans maintained by other members of the controlled group are taken in account? [I.R.C. § 415(h)] ☐ ☐ ☐

(7) If the plan provides for the payment of benefits upon retirement in the form of an annuity, does it provide for a joint and survivor annuity unless the employee elects otherwise? [I.R.C. § 401(a)(11)] ☐ ☐ ☐

[e] Fiduciary Responsibility and Prohibited Transactions

(1) Does the plan provide for one or more named fiduciaries? [ERISA § 402(a)(1)] ☐ ☐ ☐

(2) Does the plan provide a procedure for establishing and carrying out a funding policy? [ERISA § 402(b)(1)] ☐ ☐ ☐

	Yes	No	N/A

(3) Does the plan describe any procedure for the allocation of responsibility for the operation and administration of the plan? [ERISA §§ 402(b)(2), 405(b)(1), 405(c)]   ☐ ☐ ☐

(4) Does the plan provide a procedure for amending the plan and for identifying the persons who have authority to amend the plan? [ERISA § 402(b)(4)]   ☐ ☐ ☐

(5) Does the plan specify the basis on which payments are to be made from the plan? [ERISA § 402(b)(4)]   ☐ ☐ ☐

(6) Does the plan provide that any person or group of persons may serve in more than one fiduciary capacity with respect to the plan? [ERISA § 402(c)(1)]   ☐ ☐ ☐

(7) Does the plan provide that a fiduciary may employ one or more persons to render advice with regard to any responsibility such fiduciary has under the plan? [ERISA § 402(c)(2)]   ☐ ☐ ☐

(8) Does the plan provide that the named fiduciary with respect to control or management of the assets of the plan may appoint an investment manager or managers to manage (including the power to acquire and dispose of) any assets of a plan? [ERISA § 402(c)(3)]   ☐ ☐ ☐

(9) Do our files contain a listing of the persons or organizations qualifying as "parties in interest" ("disqualified persons" for purpose of the tax provisions)? [ERISA § 3(14), and I.R.C. § 4975(e)(2)]   ☐ ☐ ☐

	Yes	*No*	*N/A*
(10) Have steps been taken to insure that fiduciaries with respect to the plan are aware of the transactions that may constitute "prohibited transactions"? [ERISA §§ 406, 408, 409, and I.R.C. §§ 4975(c), 4975(d)]	☐	☐	☐
(11) Have we reviewed post-July 1, 1974 transactions to be sure there are no such transactions which carry over beyond December 31, 1974 and constitute prohibited transactions? [ERISA § 2003(c)(2)]	☐	☐	☐
(12) Are we sure that the plan does not hold any employer securities or employer real property acquired *after July 1, 1974* which are not qualifying employer securities or qualifying employer real property? [ERISA §§ 407(a)(1), 414(c)]	☐	☐	☐
(13) If the plan *is* an eligible individual account plan, does it specifically provide for the acquisition and holding of qualifying employer securities and/or qualifying employer real property in excess of the 10 percent limitation on investments in such employer assets? [ERISA §§ 407(d)(3)(A), 407(d)(3)(B)]	☐	☐	☐
(14) For defined benefit plans, are we sure that the plan has not acquired qualifying employer real property or qualifying employer securities in excess of 10 percent of the fair market value of plan assets immediately after any such acquisition? [ERISA §§ 407, 414(c)]	☐	☐	☐
(15) For defined benefit plans, has the plan made an election permitting it to disregard appreciation in the value of employer securities after December 31, 1974 for purposes of the 10 percent limitation? [ERISA § 407(c)(3)]	☐	☐	☐

                                                          Yes   *No*   *N/A*

(16) Where any of the plan's assets are invested
     in employer securities, has a Form 4575 been
     filed with the Internal Revenue Service?   ☐   ☐   ☐

[f] Joint and Survivor Annuity

(1) Does the plan provide payment of benefits in
    the form of a life annuity? (If the answer to
    question 1 is "no," then do not complete the
    remaining questions in this section.) [DOL
    Reg. § 11.401(a)-11(a)]   ☐   ☐   ☐

(2) If the plan provides forms of benefit in addi-
    tion to a joint and survivor annuity, are joint
    and survivor annuity payments automatically
    provided at retirement unless a participant
    elects otherwise? [DOL Reg. §§ 11.401(a)-
    11(a), 11.401(a)-11(d)]   ☐   ☐   ☐

(3) If the plan provides benefits prior to normal
    retirement age, is a joint and survivor annuity
    automatically provided on the later of early
    retirement or ten years prior to normal retire-
    ment age, unless the participant elects other-
    wise? [DOL Reg. §§ 11.401(a)-11(d)(2)(i),
    11.401(a)-11(d)(2)(ii)]   ☐   ☐   ☐

(4) If the plan provides benefits during the period
    specified in question 3, does it provide for the
    election of a survivor annuity in the event of
    the death of the participant prior to retire-
    ment if the participant so elects? [DOL Reg. §
    11.401(a)-11(d)(3)]   ☐   ☐   ☐

(5) If the plan provides the election provided in
    question 4, does it also require that payments
    to the survivor not be less than specified in
    Section 11.401(a)-11(d)(3)(iv) of the DOL
    Regulations?   ☐   ☐   ☐

Yes   No   N/A

(6) Is the joint and survivor annuity payable under the plan "qualified"? [DOL Reg. § 11.401(a)-11(b)(1)]   ☐   ☐   ☐

(7) Is any marriage requirement for eligibility to a joint and survivor annuity limited to not more than one year? [DOL Reg. § 11.401(a)-11(e)]   ☐   ☐   ☐

(8) Will an election (or revocation of an election) *not* to take a joint and survivor annuity *not* be given effect (except as provided in the regulations) if a participant dies within two years of making such election (or revocation)? [DOL Reg. § 11.401(a)-11(f)]   ☐   ☐   ☐

[g] Miscellaneous Provisions

(1) Does the plan contain a provision that a participating employee's benefits may not be assigned or alienated? [I.R.C. § 401(a)(13)]   ☐   ☐   ☐

(2) Does the plan provide that payment of benefits will begin to the participating employee, unless he otherwise elects, within sixty days after the close of the plan year in which (a) the participant reaches age 65, or any other normal retirement age specified in the plan; (b) the tenth anniversary of the time the participant commenced participation in the plan; or (c) the time the participant terminates his service with the employer, whichever is later? [I.R.C. § 401(a)(14)]   ☐   ☐   ☐

(3) Do plan distributions which meet the requirements of question 2 provide no more than incidental death benefits?   ☐   ☐   ☐

(4) If benefits payable under the plan are integrated with Social Security, does the plan

Yes   No   N/A

prohibit the reduction of benefits being paid
to retired employees, or to be paid to terminated employees who have nonforfeitable
rights to benefits because of an increase in
Social Security benefits? [I.R.C. § 401(a)(15)]   ☐   ☐   ☐

(5) Does the employer maintain sufficient records
to provide the necessary information for the
annual registration statement (Form 5500,
Schedule SSA) required to be filed with the
IRS and to provide active participants (upon
their request) with a yearly statement of their
vesting and accrued benefit status? [ERISA
§§ 105, and 209, and I.R.C. § 6057]   ☐   ☐   ☐

(6) Does the plan specifically designate a plan
administrator? [I.R.C. § 414(g)]   ☐   ☐   ☐

(7) Have arrangements been made for filing a
plan description with the Secretary of Labor
and furnishing summary plan description to
plan participants by September 30, 1977?
[ERISA §§ 102, 104(b)]   ☐   ☐   ☐

(8) If the plan is subject to the plan termination
insurance provisions of the Act, has Form
PBGC-1 been filed and the applicable premium paid? [ERISA § 4007]   ☐   ☐   ☐

(9) Have steps been taken to insure that the plan
administrator is aware of what constitutes a
"reportable event" for purposes of reporting
to the Pension Benefit Guaranty Corporation?
[ERISA § 4043]   ☐   ☐   ☐

[2] Compliance in Operations

In addition to a responsibility to ascertain that the plan provisions
are in accordance with applicable laws and regulations, the auditor
should satisfy himself that the plan is operating in accordance with the
specific plan provisions and regulatory requirements. Various aspects
of this responsibility are discussed in the following paragraphs.

[a] Participation, Vesting, Benefit Accrual, and Related Participant Data

All pension benefit plans will contain provisions as to participation and vesting. Defined benefit pension plans will also contain provisions governing the accrual of benefits, while defined contribution plans will contain provisions as to how contributions are to be allocated to individual participants' accounts. Both defined benefit and defined contribution plans may contain provisions concerning participants' mandatory or voluntary contributions. Audit tests of benefit payments and participants' individual accounts should include testing the proper application of the provisions. For example, if employee contributions are limited to a percentage of compensation, the auditor should consider comparing individual contributions to the computed amount on a test basis.

In addition to affecting benefit payments and participants' individual accounts, participant data has a significant impact on the actuarial computations for defined benefit plans. The extent of the auditor's responsibility for auditing actuarial determinations has not been determined. However, ERISA does permit the actuary to rely on accountants with respect to accounting data used in the actuarial computations. For this and other reasons, it is necessary that the auditor satisfy himself that the plan is operating in accordance with plan provisions as to participation, vesting, and benefit accrual, and that data submitted to actuaries reflect proper service credit, salary, age, and other pertinent items. The extent of the auditor's responsibility for auditing actuarial determinations is discussed later in this chapter.

[b] Fiduciary Responsibility

The fiduciary responsibility provisions of ERISA have a far greater effect on plan operations than on specific plan provisions. In general, the primary thrust of the fiduciary responsibility provisions is to define responsibility for the management of the assets of a plan. The provisions generally require prudence in the management of investments and diversification of the investments. In addition, certain types of transactions are specified as prohibited transactions.

What constitutes prudence and diversification is a matter of judgment not susceptible to setting rigid guidelines. However, some specific rules, such as limitations on holding of employer securities and real property, are included in ERISA. In general, the auditor's responsibility with respect to compliance with fiduciary responsibility provisions should be limited to ascertaining that the plan has instituted controls to monitor compliance, and that the controls are reasonably effective. Generally, this involves no more than an awareness of who are parties-in-interest and the types of prohibited transactions.

Prohibited transactions as defined in ERISA are discussed in Chapter 2. An audit objective should be to identify transactions with parties-in-interest and whether they are prohibited. Prohibited transactions, however, have a greater impact on the other party to the transaction than they do on the plan. ERISA penalty provisions for an excise tax on the amount of the prohibited transaction are levied on the other party to the transaction. Disclosure of the transaction in the plan financial statements, including how the transaction will be undone, normally will be necessary; however, a qualification in the accountant's report generally will not be necessary. Any plan asset acquired in the transaction, such as a loan receivable or real estate, must be evaluated in terms of collectibility or realizable value.

[c] Tax Qualification

As noted previously, plans should have obtained an IRS determination letter as to tax qualification of the plan. The plan, however, must continue to qualify in its operation as well as in its original form. Particularly troublesome in this respect are the combined limitations on contributions and benefits and the application of discrimination provisions. Certain items of Form 5500 are designed to point out problems in specific areas of qualification, and the contents of this form should be reviewed for indications of qualification problems. In addition, the auditor should be aware of possible qualification problems in all phases of the audit.

The penalty for nonqualification is that the trust would be liable for income taxes. Generally, an auditor's reporting responsibilities are similar to those with respect to income tax liabilities of commercial organizations. In most cases, recording a tax liability should not be necessary unless one has been agreed to with the IRS. If disqualification has been proposed, but a liability has not been agreed to, disclosure and possible qualification of the auditor's report probably would be necessary.

[d] Funding

Funding is the responsibility of the sponsoring employer, and penalties for underfunding in the form of excise taxes are assessed against the sponsor. Most plans, however, will contain provisions as to how contributions are determined, and the auditor should ascertain that the plan is funded in accordance with these provisions. For example, in a profit-sharing plan, the auditor should consider recomputing the contributions based on the sponsor's profit and the provisions of the plan. In defined benefit plans and certain money-purchase pension plans, a funding standard account must also be maintained (see ¶ 2.05[3]). Again, the extent of the accountant's responsibility for auditing this account is unclear due to the involvement of the actuary in determining and "certifying" to the amounts reflected in the account. At a minimum, the auditor should review the entries to the account and determine that the actuary has certified to the balance.

[e] Reporting and Disclosure

ERISA contains numerous reporting and disclosure requirements to the DOL, IRS, PBGC, and plan participants and beneficiaries. These requirements are described in Chapter 11. A general audit procedure should be to ascertain that the required reports have been filed and disclosures made.

Specific audit considerations arising from the reporting and disclosure requirements include the financial statements and schedule requirements of the annual report and the financial statements in the summary annual report. In particular, the schedules require accumulation and testing of detailed information not ordinarily necessary to express an opinion on the financial statements.

¶ 15.05   ACTUARIAL DETERMINATIONS

Actuarial determinations affect several aspects of a plan's financial statements. Depending on the type of plan (i.e., defined benefit or defined contribution), these areas may include contributions received during the year, contributions receivable at year-end, benefit payments and other distributions, and benefit obligations. As previously discussed in Chapter 11, the Financial Accounting Standards Board (FASB) has proposed a requirement that accumulated benefits and changes in accumulated benefits be reported in separate financial statements, while the current practice is generally to disclose the value of vested benefits in a footnote to the plan financial statements. Regardless of the measure of benefit obligation presented or the way it is presented, actuaries will usually be involved in the determination.

[1] Using the Work of an Actuary

The auditor is responsible for obtaining sufficient competent evidential matter as a basis for forming an opinion on plan financial statements. The actuary is responsible for the actuarial valuation and determination of plan obligations. Actuarial information required to be filed as a part of the annual return/report is included on Schedule A of the series 5500 forms. That schedule requires a statement signed by the actuary: "To the best of my knowledge, the information supplied in this schedule and on the accompanying statement, if any, is complete and accurate, and in my opinion the assumptions used in the aggregate (a) are reasonably related to the experience of the plan and to reasonable expectations, and (b) represent my best estimate of anticipated experience under the plan."

Although the auditor needs to have a general awareness and understanding of actuarial concepts and practices as described in Part II of this manual, he or she does not have to have professional qualifications in actuarial science. Accordingly, to the extent actuarial determinations affect the plan financial statements, the auditor needs to use the work of an actuary. Statement on Auditing Standards (SAS) No. 11, "Using the Work of a Specialist" provides guidance for using the work of specialists, including actuaries, in performing an examination of financial statements in accordance with generally accepted auditing standards.

[2] Applying SAS No. 11 to Plan Audits

The importance of auditing participant data has been discussed at ¶ 15.04[2][a]. A specific provision of SAS No. 11 calls for the auditor to "make appropriate tests of the accounting data provided by the client to the specialist." In the case of an actuarial valuation of a pension plan, the accounting data is the participant data. Other provisions of SAS No. 11 are as follows:

(1) *Selecting a specialist.* SAS No. 11 provides that the auditor should satisfy himself as to the professional qualifications and reputation of the specialist. There is no single organization of actuaries to establish their professional credentials. Membership in the American Academy of Actuaries or the Society of Actuaries would generally be acceptable evidence of professional qualification; however, it should be noted that some actuaries confine their practice to life or casualty insurance matters. These qualifications do not necessarily prepare the actuary to practice in the pension area. In addition, membership in

other organizations, such as the Conference of Actuaries in Public Practice, and the actuarial enrollment procedures and examinations prescribed for practice with the IRS and DOL may provide evidence of professional qualification.

The SAS also provides that the specialist does not have to be independent with respect to the plan; however, "work of a specialist unrelated to the client usually provides the auditor with greater assurance of reliability because of the absence of a relationship that might impair objectivity."

(2) *Reference to the specialist in the auditor's report.* The SAS proscribes making reference in an unqualified opinion to the work or findings of a specialist.

(3) *Using the findings of the specialist.* The responsibility for the appropriateness of methods or assumptions used is that of the specialist.

The auditor's responsibility is to obtain an understanding of the methods and assumptions sufficient to determine "whether the findings are suitable for corroborating the representations in the financial statements." The auditor should also ascertain that the methods or assumptions are consistently applied.

In using the findings of the specialist, "the auditor should consider whether the specialist's findings support the related representations in the financial statements." This section also requires the accountant to test the accounting data used by the specialist.

Although the SAS does not require the specialist to be independent of the plan, it does indicate that the auditor "should consider employing additional procedures when the specialist is related to the client."

Additional procedures (to those prescribed by the SAS) could be performed by the auditor, or he could employ an independent specialist to perform such procedures. Normally, additional procedures should not be necessary when the actuarial valuation has been performed by a qualified independent actuary.

¶ 15.06   WELFARE   BENEFIT   AND   MULTIEMPLOYER PLANS

As discussed in Chapter 11, an AICPA audit guide, "Audits of Employee Health and Welfare Benefit Funds," was issued in 1972. The guide discusses accounting, auditing, and reporting for welfare benefit plans. Prior to ERISA, most benefit plans which were audited were multiemployer plans, so particular emphasis was given to such plans. In addition, some of the unique features and auditing problems related to multiemployer welfare plans are equally applicable to multiemployer pension plans. Primary among these areas are contributions and administrative expenses. The guide also discusses accounting for and auditing of fully insured plans (i.e., plans where all risks are borne by the insurance company in return for payment of a premium). Accounting for and auditing of fully insured employee benefit plans is not discussed at any length in this manual because most such plans are small and will not be required to be audited.

The audit guide should be read before commencing the audit of any welfare benefit plan, multiemployer pension plan, or fully insured plan. Certain areas covered by the guide are discussed briefly in the following paragraphs.

[1] Contributions

The involvement of more than one employer in making contributions to the plan is one feature of a multiemployer plan which presents unique auditing requirements. Contributions to multiemployer plans normally are stated as a flat amount per hour worked, and are received from employers on a self-assessed basis. Procedures employed by multiemployer plans to establish control over contributions include the use of lock boxes, mailing of periodic statements to employee participants, confirming hours worked as submitted by the employers, and periodic payroll audits of contributing employers. The auditor should review the results of these procedures performed by the administrator, as well as employer over- and underpayments, and delinquent employer contributions.

[2] Administrative Expenses

Another feature somewhat unique to multiemployer plans is allocated administrative expenses, normally in the form of an administrator's fee. This fee may be determined by various criteria, such as the number of plan participants, number of checks issued, or employers' reports processed. The reasonableness of such fees should be reviewed.

[3] Claims

Multiemployer plans are also unique in that they comprise the majority of funded, self-insured welfare benefit plans. Auditing of claims and claim liabilities is of primary importance in this type of plan. The auditor's primary responsibility is to satisfy himself as to the validity of claims paid and as to the adequacy of established claim liabilities.

¶ 15.07 GUIDE TO AUDIT PROCEDURES

Following is a guide to audit procedures which has been developed as an aid to help the auditor in developing an audit program. The guide is not intended to set forth any minimum procedures which should be followed in all cases, or to suggest procedures that would meet all unusual situations. Further, the guide does not contain procedures for auditing areas such as cash, property, and accounts payable, which are not unique or normally significant to employee benefit plans.

The auditor should select procedures that apply to the particular engagement after considering such plan characteristics as type, benefits paid, administration, funding and accounting methods, and size. The guide should not be regarded as a substitute for individual judgment and initiative.

[1] General

(1) Obtain (or update) copies of the following documents for the permanent file; review and extract significant provisions. Copies obtained should be of signed originals or should be compared thereto.

(a) Plan agreement;

(b) Plan description (Form EBS-1) filed with the DOL;

(c) Trust agreement;

(d) Annual report of trustee;

(e) Agreement with investment adviser;

(f) Actuarial reports;

(g) Information filed with the IRS and the DOL;

(h) IRS determination letter;

(i) Minutes of the board of trustees or administrative committee.

(2) If an IRS determination letter has not been received, consideration should be given to completing a tax qualification checklist.

(3) Make inquiries of appropriate plan representatives regarding contingencies and commitments of the plan.

(4) Request an attorney's letter from the plan's counsel (see SAS No. 12).

(5) Obtain letter of representation (see SAS No. 19).

[2] Investments

The auditor's objectives in the examination of investments are to satisfy himself that (1) the plan has ownership of, and accounting control over, its investment portfolio; (2) income and gains and losses from investment transactions are properly accounted for; (3) any restrictions imposed by the plan and ERISA as to the selection of investments have been complied with; and (4) the basis on which securities or other investments are carried in the accounts conforms with generally accepted accounting principles.

ERISA provides that the separate schedules required to be included with the annual report reflect the "current value" of all assets held for investment purposes. Current value as defined by the Act means fair market value where available and otherwise the fair value as determined in good faith by the trustees or a named fiduciary. In the case of securities and other investments for which market quotations cannot be obtained, determinations of current value can be a difficult and troublesome area to audit. The independent accountant, however, does not function as an appraiser and is not expected to substitute his judgment for that of management; rather, he is to review all information considered by management and ascertain that the procedures followed appear to be reasonable and adequate in the circumstances.

In addition to separate schedules reflecting current value, ERISA prohibits certain transactions involving parties-in-interest and investments of plan assets in employer securities and real estate. Further, disclosure is required of all party-in-interest transactions and certain other specified investment transactions. Suggested auditing procedures applicable to various types of investments made by employee benefit plans are outlined below.

[a] Securities

(1) Obtain listings of securities owned at date of the statement of assets and liabilities setting forth details substantially as follows:

(a) Description of securities.

(b) Securities on hand at beginning of year including number of shares owned and the cost thereof.

(c) Purchases during the year including date purchased, number of shares or principal amount, and cost and current value.

(d) Sales or redemptions during the year including proceeds, cost of securities sold, date of sale, and realized gains and losses.

(e) Securities on hand at end of year including:

  (i)   Number of shares or total principal amount;

  (ii)   Cost and current value;

  (iii)   Unrealized appreciation/depreciation;

  (iv)   Market price per unit;

  (v)   Location of investment, and if hypothecated, with whom and for what purpose;

  (vi)   Maturity date—if applicable;

  (vii) Interest rate—if applicable.

(2) Test the footings of the listing and trace totals to the general ledger.

(3) Reconcile investment activity per the plan's record to the trustee's report and the statement of cash receipts and disbursements.

(4) Determine that cash remitted to the trustee has been invested on a timely basis by comparing the date it was received by the trustee to the date it was invested.

(5) Inspect securities on hand in presence of plan's representative (preferably at date of the statement of assets and liabilities) and obtain signed receipts for return of securities to custodian. If the date of inspection is other than the date of the statement of assets and liabilities, account for transactions in the intervening period. If the securities are in a safe-deposit box, a letter from the safe-deposit company attesting to nonentry to the box during the interim period will eliminate the need to account for intervening transactions.

(6) While inspecting securities, see that stock certificates and registered bonds are made out in the name of the plan, are endorsed so as to be transferable to the plan, or are accompanied by powers of attorney. Watch for past-due bond interest coupons and for coupons clipped in advance of maturity date.

(7) Request confirmation of securities held by trustees or others as of the date of inspection of securities on hand.

(8) Obtain confirmation of the number of common trust fund units held by the plan, and a copy of the financial statements of the common trust fund.

(9) If the date of the financial statements of the common trust fund does not coincide with the plan-year end, additional procedures should be considered as follows:

(a) Confirm the total units outstanding as well as the units held by the plan.

(b) Obtain a confirmation of the details of investments held by the common trust as of the plan-year end.

    (i) Compare investment portfolio and valuations to investments at common trust audit date. Investigate significant differences through inquiry of common trust personnel.

    (ii) Test securities valuations as of plan-year end.

(10) On a test basis, examine broker's advices or other evidence in support of purchases and sales during the year. Ascertain that investment transactions have been approved by a responsible person or committee. Check the computation of gain or loss on sales, noting whether cost is determined by first-in, first-out, specific certificate, or average-cost method. Determine that method used is consistently applied. See step 12 below if trustee is investment manager for plan.

(11) Obtain a schedule of investment income received or receivable for the period under review.

(a) Foot and trace to general ledger income accounts.

(b) Reconcile income per the general ledger to income as shown on the trustee's report.

(c) Test the computation of accrued income.

(d) Test interest and dividend income by reference to financial publications (e.g., Moody's Dividend Record).

(12) When security investments are held in a nominee name by a trustee and/or investments are managed by a trustee and the auditor is not able to perform the above steps:

(a) Ascertain what reports are issued by or can be obtained from the trustee's independent auditors and what use the auditor can make of such reports in rendering his or her opinion on the plan's financial statements

(i)   Obtain copy of trustee's auditor's report on internal accounting control, if available.

(ii) Consider obtaining trustee's auditor's report on trust account cash receipts and disbursements, if available.

(iii) Consider having trustee's auditor support selected transactions applicable to the plan's investments.

(b) Arrangements should be made to perform the work discussed in (i) and (ii) above if the trustee's auditors are not available to perform such work, or if a determination is made that the auditor cannot rely upon their work.

[b] Insurance Contracts

(1) Obtain copy of agreement with insurance company.

(2) Request confirmation from the insurance company of beginning balance, deposits, credited earnings, transfers and benefit payments, as applicable, and information as to the existence of contingencies relative to discontinuance charges and penalties.

(3) Consider reputation and financial responsibility of insurance company and obtain copy of recent audited financial statements, if available.

(4) Obtain copy of financial statements for investments in separate accounts maintained by the insurance company.

(5) If the date of the financial statements of the separate account does not coincide with the plan-year end, additional procedures should be considered as follows:

(A) Confirm the total units outstanding as well as the units held by the plan.

(B) Obtain a confirmation of the details of investments held by the separate account as of the plan-year end.

(1) Confirm the total units outstanding as well as the units held by the plan.

(2) Obtain a confirmation of the details of investments held by the separate account as of the plan-year end.

(a) Compare investment portfolio and valuations to investments at separate account audit date. Investigate significant differences through inquiry of separate account personnel.

(b) Test securities valuations as of plan-year end.

[c] Other Investments

(1) Obtain schedules of other plan investments setting forth details substantially as follows:

(a) Description of investment;

(b) Cost at beginning of year;

(c) Current year additions;

(d) Current year disposals;

(e) Cost at end of year;

(f) Realized gains and losses;

(g) Current value at beginning and end of year;

(h) Collateral, if applicable.

(2) Examine support for significant additions to the investment accounts by reference to invoices, contracts, authorizations, and other documentation, as applicable.

(3) Examine deeds or other evidence of title and closing documents pertaining to acquisitions of land and buildings.

(4) Request confirmation of the balances and terms of loans and mortgages, including such items as interest paid, accrued and/or in arrears, and collateral.

(5) Examine documentation in support of sales of investments and tie in gain or loss on disposal of investments.

(6) Obtain copies or brief leases, royalty, and other agreements pertaining to plan investments. Recompute rental and other income by reference to the terms of the agreement and tie in to general ledger and trustee's report.

[d] Current Value Considerations

(1) For listed securities, check market prices and indicate source and basis, such as last sales price, bid price, etc.

(2) Determine that the current value assigned to investments for which market quotations cannot readily be obtained are reasonable by:

(a) Reviewing reports, appraisals, and other documentation in support of current value determinations;

(b) Noting that current values were determined or approved by the trustees or named fiduciary of the plan;

(c) Obtaining representations from qualified independent experts as to the reasonableness of values assigned, if applicable.

(3) Determine whether an allowance for loss on investments is required.

[e] Compliance With Plan Documents and ERISA

(1) Determine that the investments entered into by the plan have not violated any restrictions or limitations imposed by plan documents and that investment transactions were properly authorized.

(2) Review investments for any prohibited transactions, employer securities, or real estate. Consider transitional rules regarding investments in employer securities and employer real estate entered into prior to July 1, 1974.

(3) Review investments for party-in-interest transactions, transactions which either singularly or in the aggregate amounted to 3 percent of the current value of plan assets (as of the beginning of the plan year), loans or leases in default, and other matters requiring disclosure by ERISA.

[3] Contributions Receivable

The auditor's objective in the examination of contributions receivable is to determine their authenticity, collectibility, and the propriety of the amounts at which they are stated.

[a] Single-Employer Plans

(1) Request confirmation of contribution receivable from plan sponsor and tie into related liability account in plan sponsor's accounting records.

(2) Reconcile contribution receivable to total required contribution for period and payments made to the plan.

(a) Agree total of contribution to amount determined by actuary in defined benefit plans or applicable plan provisions in other types of plans.

(b) Tie in payments to plan records and/or trustee report.

(c) Reconcile payments and contribution receivable to contribution income accounts.

(3) Examine plan records and/or trustee reports subsequent to year-end to determine accrued contribution was paid.

(4) Request confirmation from plan sponsor of amounts withheld from participants in contributory plans and not transmitted to plan and/or trustee as of year-end. Note subsequent payment of amount due.

[b] Multiemployer Plans

(1) Obtain details of contributions receivable as of year-end.

(a) Test footing and trace balance to general ledger control account.

(b) Compare recorded receivable to collections in subsequent months and review on a test basis the related employer contribution reports to ascertain that such receipts apply to the period under examination.

(2) Request positive confirmations on a test basis from employers making contributions during the period. The request should include total contributions paid for the period as well as the amount payable at year-end.

(a) Send second requests to employers not responding to initial requests after a reasonable period of time.

(b) Perform alternative procedures for employers not responding to confirmation requests.

(c) Tie in contributions receivable and total contributions paid to plan subsidiary records.

(d) Obtain explanation from plan personnel for any exceptions received. Investigate propriety of explanations.

(3) Review controls and procedures designed to disclose delinquent or unreported contributions. Ascertain that arrangements for handling delinquent contributions are in accordance with ERISA requirements.

(4) Review adequacy of the allowance for doubtful accounts.

(5) Determine that write-offs of delinquent contributions are properly supported and approved.

[4] Liabilities

The auditor's primary objective in the examination of liability accounts is to determine, as far as possible, that all significant liabilities are included in the financial statements.

Auditing procedures for liabilities that are unique to employee benefit plans (primarily applicable to welfare benefit plans) are outlined below:

(1) Obtain a listing of withdrawal requests received but not paid as of year-end.

    (a) Test footings and trace balance to general ledger.

    (b) Compare amounts to individual account records on a test basis.

    (c) Review subsequent payments to withdrawn participants to determine that balances payable were properly recorded and none were omitted.

    (d) Examine withdrawal requests received subsequent to year-end to determine whether liability to withdrawn participants was properly recorded.

(2) Request direct confirmation from insurance company of the total amount of benefits and premiums paid during the year, premium payments due, and other liabilities and deposits at year-end.

(3) Trace pertinent data confirmed by insurance company to accounting records of the plan and to insurance contract.

(4) Review insurance contracts to determine if supplemental premium payments may be due under certain circumstances, such as an unfavorable experience loss ratio.

(5) Review computation of retrospective premiums. Determine that computation is in accordance with the insurance contract. Trace appropriate data to fund's records. Examine subsequent payments. In this regard, examine claims audit report.

(6) For plans in which benefits are not paid by an insurance company, obtain listing of claims filed but not paid as of year-end.

    (a) Test footings and trace balance to general ledger.

    (b) Select a sample of claims and examine participant file noting propriety of the amount of the claim.

(7) Review subsequent claim payments to determine:

    (a) The adequacy of the claim liability;

    (b) That all claims are recorded in the proper period.

(8) Review the analysis supporting the estimated amount of claims incurred but not yet reported to the plan. Such review should be

based on the number of eligible employees, eligibility period, and claim experience.

(9) Where a plan provides for accumulation of eligibility credits of participants for payment of benefits, such as vacation pay, obtain details of accrued liability.

(a) Foot listing and reconcile total with the general ledger control account.

(b) Compare eligibility credits on listing to participant eligibility records on a test basis.

(c) Check accuracy of amount recorded by reference to credited hours worked and the applicable plan rates or employer contribution reports. Determine that amounts recorded are in accordance with plan provisions.

[5] Benefit Payments

The auditor's primary objective in the examination of benefit payments is to determine that the forms and amount of the distributions are properly authorized and in accordance with the plan provisions and that the payment is received by the person entitled to it. Suggested auditing procedures applicable to the several classes of benefits commonly paid from employee benefit plans are outlined below.

(1) Obtain an analysis of the benefit accounts for the period under review.

(a) Test the footings and trace balance to the general ledger.

(b) Reconcile total benefits paid for the period to the amount shown in the cash disbursements book and/or trustee's report.

(2) Select a sample of participants receiving benefits during the period under audit and determine propriety of individual benefits paid.

(a) Examine participant's file noting nature of claim and propriety of approvals. Trace approval of benefit payment to board of trustees or administrative committee minutes, as applicable.

(b) Determine participant's eligibility for benefits received by reference to terms of the employee benefit plan, age, eligibility files, and credited service, as applicable.

(c) For pension benefits, examine evidence of age, benefit option forms, and employment history data. Compare employment dates, credited service, and earnings to payroll records. Recompute pension benefit based upon plan provisions and option selected, and balance in participant's individual account, if applicable.

(d) For supplemental pension plan benefits such as death and disability, examine copy of death certificate and beneficiary form, physician's statement, etc., as applicable. Recompute amount of benefit based upon participant data and plan provisions.

(e) For welfare benefits, examine supporting medical data and bills, cumulative hours register, or other supporting data, as applicable. Determine that the benefit paid to the participant or beneficiary was in accordance with the plan. Determine that cumulative benefits paid to participant or beneficiary did not exceed plan limitations.

(f) Compare amount of benefit payment to cash disbursement records or trustee reports.

(g) Examine canceled checks noting agreement to cash disbursement records of amount, payee, and date. Compare endorsement to participant's application.

(3) In many instances, benefit payments will be made on behalf of a plan by a bank or other trustee and paid checks will not be available for support of benefit payments. To determine that pension benefits are not being paid to deceased participants or persons other than eligible beneficiaries, benefit confirmation procedures should be considered as follows:

(a) Request positive confirmation of benefits paid during the period for a sample of participants.

(b) Send second requests to participants not responding to initial requests after a reasonable period of time.

(c) Compare signature on confirmation reply with signature on benefit application form.

(d) Obtain explanation from plan personnel on any exceptions received. Investigate propriety of explanations.

(e) Consider supplemental procedures such as phone calls, certified delivery, etc., for participants not responding to confirmation requests.

(4) Review monthly benefit payments for unusual fluctuations.

(5) Test insurance premium payments by comparing the number of eligible participants, as shown by the eligibility records, to premium computation, and by tracing the applicable premium rates to the insurance contract.

(6) Request confirmation of total amount of premiums paid during the period.

(7) Review insurance company's claim audit reports.

[6] Contributions

The auditor's primary objective in auditing contributions is to determine that amounts due to the plan have been received and properly recorded and participant records related to contributions are being properly maintained.

Employee benefit plan contributions and accounting records relative thereto vary according to the type of plan. The auditing procedures for the various types of contributions are outlined below.

[a] Single-Employer Plans

Auditing procedures with regard to contributions should be coordinated with related contributions receivable work. Confirmation procedures and procedures relating to reconcilement of amounts received and accrued are outlined in ¶ 15.07[3]. Procedures relative to the testing of the propriety of the amount of the contribution and other matters are outlined below.

(1) Test the amount of the employer's annual contribution by reference to applicable provisions of the plan agreement. Procedures include:

    (a) Comparison of amount recorded with actuary's report;

    (b) Examination of plan sponsor board of director's minutes for approval of amount paid;

    (c) Agreement of amount of contribution to tax return filed by plan sponsor;

    (d) Recomputation of amount based upon predetermined plan formula;

    (e) Comparison of amount with participant contributions, taking into consideration allocation of terminations and forfeitures, as applicable.

(2) Compare amounts received by trustee to amounts recorded in plan records. Note if any time lag exists between date of payment by plan sponsor and the date amount was credited to the plan's account.

(3) See ¶ 15.07[b][c] for procedures relative to participant contributions and allocation of employer contributions.

[b] Multiemployer Plans

Auditing procedures with regards to contributions should be coordinated with related contributions receivable work. Such procedures outlined in ¶ 15.07[3], include confirmation of contributions made by selected employers. Additional tests of contributions are outlined below:

(1) For a selected period(s), reconcile total cash receipts shown by the cash receipts books to the:

(a) Total amount credited to the general ledger contribution accounts;

(b) Total amount posted to the employer's record;

(c) Deposits shown by the bank statements.

(2) Select a sample of individual employer contributions per the cash receipts book and compare to the amount shown on the employer's contribution report and to the amount posted to the individual employer records.

(3) Select a sample of employer contributions per the individual employer records and compare to the amount shown on the employer's contribution report and to the cash receipts book.

(4) For the selected employer's contribution report:

(a) Determine that time reported has been properly credited to the participants' eligibility records.

(b) Test the clerical accuracy of the report, noting that the correct contribution rate has been used. On a test basis, foot the time and amounts reported by the employer and verify extensions.

(5) Select a sample of postings to participant eligibility records and trace to employer contribution report.

(6) Reconcile the total of participants' credits posted to the records for a selected period to the credits shown by employer's contribution report.

Where a central bank account is used to accumulate employer contributions to several related benefit funds, the amounts transferred to the appropriate fund's bank account should be tested.

(8) Review general ledger entries to contribution accounts for the period under examination. Investigate unusual entries and significant fluctuations.

(9) Review internal audit reports on employer payroll audits.

(10) If payroll audits of contributing employers are not performed by internal auditors for the plan, or the auditor is not satisfied with the results of such audits, consider performing the following procedures on selected employer payroll records (note: the plan administrator should make the necessary arrangements):

(a) Review the applicable collective-bargaining agreement to determine that the employer has complied with the provisions.

(b) Reconcile the total gross earnings shown by the employees' earnings records with total wages shown by the general ledger and the payroll tax reports.

(c) Review selected employees' personnel files to determine they are eligible for inclusion in the plan.

(d) Compare information shown on the employer's contribution report for a selected number of participants with the data shown on the employees' earnings records. In addition, compare a selected group of participants' earnings records with the employer's contribution report to ascertain that they have been properly included or excluded from the report.

(e) Review the employer's general cash disbursements to determine whether any payments not recorded as compensation have been made to employees.

(f) Compare the data shown in the payroll journal for a selected group of employees to the employee earnings records and time records, and examine the related canceled checks.

[c] Individual Account Plans

ERISA requires individual accounts for each participant to be maintained for voluntary participant contributions to employee benefit plans. In addition, individual accounts are normally maintained for all defined contribution plans. Balances in individual accounts consist of participant and/or employer contributions and the income, expenses, gains and losses attributable thereto. Auditing procedures to determine that participant individual account records are being properly maintained are outlined below.

(1) Select a sample of employees eligible to participate in the plan and examine personnel records.

(a) Examine signed enrollment applications, noting amount of payroll deduction authorized.

(b) For a selected period(s) recompute employees' payroll deductions on a test basis, noting that they are in accordance with plan provisions.

(c) Compare payroll deductions tested above to employer's contribution report to plan.

(d) Compare total of employer's contribution report to plan's cash receipt records.

(e) Trace posting of amount withheld to participant individual account record.

(f) Note that employer matching of participant contribution is in accordance with plan provisions, if applicable.

(2) Select a sample of participant contributions made directly to the plan from cash receipts records. Note that application to participants' accounts is in accordance with plan provisions.

(3) Select a sample of postings to participants' accounts and trace to cash receipts and employer contribution report.

(4) Reconcile the total of employer contributions to the total amount posted to participants' accounts for a selected period(s).

(5) Determine that participants' and/or employer contributions were properly applied to the investment funds selected, if applicable.

(6) Select a sample of participants eligible to share in the employer's annual contribution to the plan. Determine that employer's contribution was allocated to participants' accounts in accordance with plan provisions (see Single-Employer Plans, ¶ 15.07[6][a], for procedures used to test total amount of employer contributions).

(7) The participant samples selected to test participant and/or employer contributions should also be tested to determine that plan provisions have been complied with in regard to the following allocations:

(a) Plan income, expenses, gains, and losses.

(b) Plan terminations and forfeitures.

(8) Obtain trial balance of participant individual account balances as of year-end.

   (a) Foot trial balance and reconcile the total with the general ledger control account.

   (b) Test the accuracy of amounts by reference to the individual accounts.

(9) Where there are a large number of relatively small accounts, tests and samplings may be used in place of trial balances of all accounts. Make sure that the total of the subsidiary controls agrees with the general ledger control and that samples are representative of the whole.

(10) Attach negative confirmation requests to a selected number of annual statements mailed to participants.

(11) Investigate confirmation exceptions by reference to participant payroll records, withholding authorizations, etc., and plan provisions.

[7] Withdrawals, Terminations, and Forfeitures

The auditor's primary objective in the examination of withdrawals, terminations, and forfeitures is to determine that (1) withdrawn participants are promptly removed from eligibility records, (2) distributions and forfeitures are computed in accordance with the terms of the plan, and (3) deferred vested benefits for terminated employees are properly accounted for.

(1) Obtain analysis of the withdrawals paid and forfeiture accounts for the period under review.

   (a) Test footings and trace balance to general ledger.

   (b) Reconcile withdrawals paid during the period to the amount shown in the cash disbursements book and/or trustee's report.

   (c) Trace balance of forfeitures to amount distributed to active participants' accounts or to reduction of employer's contribution as applicable.

(2) Determine what procedures are in effect to notify the plan administrator of employee terminations and/or membership withdrawals. On a test basis, select terminated employees from plan sponsor payroll records and trace to plan withdrawal or termination lists.

(3) Select a representative sample (from participant listings, cash disbursements journal, or withdrawal lists) of members' withdrawals during the period under audit. For the selected members:

(a) Examine application for or notice of withdrawal.

(b) Examine waiver of claims and/or election of optional withdrawal provisions (if applicable) signed by withdrawing member.

(c) Examine subsidiary ledger of participant's equity. Recompute amount payable to participant, including vested and forfeited portions thereof in accordance with the terms of the plan.

(d) Determine that the basis for valuation of plan assets distributed to withdrawn participants is in accordance with the terms of the plan. Where applicable for securities distributed, check market value to publish sources. For cash distributions, examine canceled check and supporting documentation and trace to disbursements journal.

(e) Note approval by administrative committee or board of trustees.

(f) Consider confirmation of distributions to withdrawn participants.

(4) Determine whether terminated employees are entitled to deferred vested benefits. Check computation of such benefits and trace to inclusion in deferred vested benefit register and to report filed with IRS.

[8] Participant Data

The auditor's primary objective in the examination of participant data is to determine that adequate controls exist for the adjustment of plan records for new participants, terminations, and deceased retirees, and that information supplied to a plan's actuary for valuation purposes is substantially accurate.

Certain tests of the accuracy of participant data are performed in connection with tests of benefits payments, contributions and withdrawals, terminations and forfeitures. For example:

(a) Benefit payments are tested to determine that they are not being made to deceased participants or persons other than eligible beneficiaries.

(b) In multiemployer plans, employer contributions reports are compared to plan records to determine that participants have been included.

(c) Plan withdrawals and terminations are tested to determine that plan records reflect deferred vested benefits.

Additional procedures to test participant data and to determine that information supplied to a plan's actuary is substantially accurate are outlined below:

(1) Review plan controls and procedures designed to insure that all eligible participants have been included in plan records and that terminated and deceased participants are reported to the plan on a timely basis.

(2) Test procedures by selecting a sample of employees from the plan sponsor's records and tracing to their inclusion in plan records.

(3) Review control registers maintained for active, deferred vested, retired, and other participants. Select a sample from the registers of participants withdrawing during the period under review, and perform the following:

(a) Examine participant file and determine reason why participant was withdrawn from active, deferred vested benefit or retired register, and examine propriety of supporting documentation thereto.

(b) Determine that proper adjustment was made to plan records for terminated employee entitled to deferred vested benefits.

(c) Determine that participants withdrawn from active register for reason of retirement or disability were properly added to the retirement and disability registers.

(d) Determine that proper entries were made in plan records for deceased participants with survivor options.

(4) Obtain listing from plan sponsor of claims for benefits under the company's death benefit insurance program. On a test basis, determine that proper and timely adjustments were made to the plan's records by examination of participant's file and withdrawals and entries into applicable registers.

(5) Review procedures related to the accumulation of participant data for the plan's actuary. Note if there is any systematic exclusion of certain participants, such as those with less than a specific number of years of service.

(6) Reconcile control totals in participant data registers and/or plan sponsor personnel department with totals of participant data submitted to the actuary.

(7) Select a sample of participants from the lists submitted to the actuary.

    (a) Examine plan sponsor personnel records to determine that the participants' age, sex, employment data, and compensation are accurate.

    (b) Determine that the plan has properly considered breaks in service in reflecting credited service on the listing.

[9] Operations

To express an opinion on a statement of changes in net assets available for benefit payments or a statement of operations, the auditor must review the accounting methods and test income and expense accounts to a degree sufficient to determine whether the statement has been prepared in accordance with generally accepted accounting principles applied on a basis consistent with that of the preceding period. Furthermore, such tests are necessary to determine that appropriate disclosure is made of certain transactions as required by ERISA.

Much of this work has been accomplished through the review and evaluation of the plan's system of internal control and accounting procedures, tests of benefit payments, investment transactions, and analysis of asset and liability accounts. The following audit procedures are designed to supplement this work.

(1) Compare the individual accounts for the period under audit with those of the preceding period. Investigate changes in classification, unusual fluctuations between years, and all new or unusual accounts.

(2) Obtain a detailed analysis of all significant administrative expense accounts, including name of payee, description of expenditure and amount. Examine supporting documentation on a test basis, noting propriety of approval.

(3) Determine that trustee and investment adviser fees are in accordance with the respective agreements.

(4) Test reasonableness of Pension Benefit Guarantee Corporation insurance premium by reference to the number of plan participants and rates currently in effect.

(5) Review operating accounts to identify any transactions involv-

ing 3 percent of the current value of plan assets (as of the beginning of the plan year), or other reportable transactions under ERISA. Parties-in-interest should be determined by review of plan documents, employer company executive lists, plan internal control questionnaires, and through inquiry of the plan administrator. Obtain or prepare summaries of all reportable transactions.

(6) Where administrative and other expenses are paid directly by the plan sponsor, obtain details thereof and examine supporting documents on a test basis.

(7) Where several plans are maintained by one administrator, test allocation of common expenses (such as data processing, payroll, rent, etc.) to the plan. Determine that the allocation is in accordance with the administration agreement and is approved by the board of trustees or administrative committee.

[10] Actuarial Liabilities and Disclosures

The auditor's responsibility for determining the accuracy of participant data submitted to the plan's actuary is covered in Participant Data, ¶ 15.07[8]. The auditor's objective in the examination of the resultant actuarially computed liabilities and disclosures is to satisfy himself that the assumptions and methods used by the actuary are reasonable and compatible with actual experience and expectations of the plan and that the actuarial calculations are reasonably accurate. In addition, the auditor should satisfy himself as to the professional qualifications and reputation of the actuary.

(1) Ascertain whether the actuary is "enrolled" with the Joint Board established under ERISA.

(2) Ascertain whether the actuary is a fellow or associate of the Society of Actuaries or a member of another recognized actuarial organization.

(3) Make additional inquiries as to the reputation and competenace of the actuary, if considered necessary under the circumstances. For example, if the actuary is not a member of a recognized firm of consulting actuaries and is not a fellow or associate of the Society of Actuaries, such inquiries would be appropriate.

(4) Obtain information as to the methods and assumptions used by the actuary and the consistency of their application.

(5) Determine that the participant data examined was the same as that used by the actuary in making the actuarial computations.

(6) Review the actuarial assumptions and methods for reasonableness in light of plan provisions and experience.

(7) Review pension costs and actuarial liabilities for latest several valuations and obtain explanation of significant variations.

(8) If unusual situations exist, consider engaging a consulting actuary to assist in reviewing and testing actuarial data.

(9) Review the entries to the funding standard account and determine that the balance in the account has been certified to by the actuary.

Chapter 16

REPORTING ON PLAN FINANCIAL STATEMENTS

¶ 16.01   GENERAL REPORTING REQUIREMENTS

The end product of an auditor's examination of plan financial statements is his report containing his opinion on the financial statements. Section 150 of the Statement on Auditing Standards (SAS) No. 1 provides four standards of reporting as follows:

(1) The report shall state whether the financial statements are presented in accordance with generally accepted accounting principles (GAAP).

(2) The report shall state whether such principles have been consistently applied in the current period in relation to the preceding period.

(3) Informative disclosures in the financial statements are to be regarded as reasonably adequate unless otherwise stated in the report.

(4) The report shall either contain an expression of opinion regarding the financial statements, taken as a whole, or an assertion to the effect that an opinion cannot be expressed. When an overall opinion cannot be expressed, the reasons therefor should be stated. In all cases where an auditor's name is associated with financial statements, the report should contain a clear-cut indication of the character of the auditor's examination, if any, and the degree of responsibility he is taking.

Further elaboration of these standards is also contained in SAS No. 1; SAS No. 2, "Reports on Audited Financial Statements"; SAS No. 14, "Special Reports"; and SAS No. 15, "Reports on Comparative Financial Statements."

¶ 16.02   REPORTING ON LIMITED-SCOPE EXAMINATIONS

The Department of Labor (DOL) regulations covering limited-scope examinations and an Auditing Standard Executive Committee (AudSEC) Interpretation relating to the conduct of such an examination are discussed at ¶ 13.02. In its Interpretation, AudSEC prescribed a form of special report to be used in reporting on such an examination. The form of report is as follows:

We have examined the statement of assets and liabilities and the schedule of assets held for investment of XYZ Pension Plan as of December 31, 19XX, and the related statement of changes in net assets available for plan benefits and the schedules of transactions or series of transactions in excess of 3 percent of the current value of plan assets, and loans and fixed-income obligations in default or classified as uncollectible for the year then ended. Except as stated in the following paragraph, our examination was made in accordance with generally accepted auditing standards (GAAS) and, accordingly, included such tests of the accounting records and such other auditing procedures as we considered necessary in the circumstances.

The plan administrator has elected the method of compliance permitted by Section 2520.103-8 of the Department of Labor Rules and Regulations for Reporting and Disclosure under the Employee Retirement Income Security Act of 1974. Accordingly, as permitted under such election, the plan administrator instructed us not to perform, and we did not perform, any auditing procedures with respect to the information certified by the *ABC* Bank, the trustee of the Plan, except for comparing the information which is summarized in Note X, to the related information included in the financial statements and schedules. We have been informed by the plan administrator that the trustee holds the Plan's investment assets and executes transactions therein. The plan administrator has obtained a certification from the trustee that the information provided to the plan administrator by the trustee is complete and accurate.

Because of the significance of the information which we did not audit, we are unable to, and do not, express an opinion on the accompanying financial statements and schedules taken as a whole. The form and content of the information included in the financial statements and schedules, other than that derived from the information certified by the trustee, have been examined by us and, in our opinion, is presented in compliance with the Department of Labor Rules and Regulations for Reporting and Disclosure under the Employee Retirement Income Security Act of 1974.

The form of report prescribed by AudSEC covers only the current year and will need to be modified when comparative financial statements are presented. DOL regulations for the alternative method require a comparative statement of assets and liabilities, but only a single-year statement of changes in net assets available for plan benefits. When the financial statements of the preceding year have not been examined (e.g., in the initial reporting year or the year in which the plan attains 100 participants), the modification would involve the addition of a sentence such as the following to the end of the first paragraph:

> The financial statements (statement of assets and liabilities) for the preceding year were (was) not examined by independent accountants.

When the financial statements for both years have been subjected to a limited-scope examination, a modification to the scope paragraph will be necessary. A suggested modification follows:

> We have examined the statements of assets and liabilities of *XYZ* Pension Plan as of December 31, 19X2 and 19X1, the related statements of changes in net assets available for plan benefits for the years then ended, and the schedules of assets held for investment, transactions in excess of 3 percent of the current value of plan assets, and loans and fixed-income obligations in default or classified as uncollectible as of or for the year ended December 31, 19X2. Except as stated in the following paragraph, our examinations were made in accordance with generally accepted auditing standards and, accordingly, included such tests of the accounting records and such other auditing procedures as we considered necessary in the circumstances.

More difficult reporting problems arise when the financial statements for one year are subjected to a limited-scope examination and those for the other year to a full-scope examination.

[1] Full-Scope Examination—Current Year; Limited-Scope Examination—Prior Year

Because of the confusion over DOL requirements, or for other reasons, some plans may decide to have a full-scope examination when they have previously had a limited-scope examination. SAS No. 15, "Reports on Comparative Financial Statements," provides that "a continuing auditor should update his report on the individual financial statements of the one or more prior periods presented on a comparative basis with those of the current period." An example of a report on comparative financial statements under these circumstances follows:

> We have examined the statements of assets and liabilities of *XYZ* Pension Plan as of December 31, 19X2 and 19X1, the related statements of changes in net assets for the years then ended, and the schedules of assets held for investment, transactions in excess of 3 percent of the current value of plan assets, and loans and fixed-income obligations in default or classified as uncollectible as of and for the year ended December 31, 19X2. Except as explained in the following paragraph with respect to the 19X1 financial statements, our examinations were made in accordance with generally accepted auditing standards and, accordingly included such tests of the accounting records and such other auditing procedures as we considered necessary in the circumstances.

> As permitted by Section 2520.103-8 of the Department of Labor Rules and Regulations for Reporting and Disclosure under the Employee Retirement Income Security Act of 1974, investment assets held by *ABC* Bank, the trustee of the Plan, and transactions in those assets were excluded from the scope of our examination, for the year ended December 31, 19X1, except for comparing the information provided by the Trustee which is summarized in Note X, to the related information included in the financial statements. Because of the significance of the information which we did not audit, we are unable to, and do not, express an opinion on the financial statements for the year ended December 31, 19X1.

> In our opinion, the statement of assets and liabilities of *XYZ* Pension Plan as of December 31, 19X2, and the related statement of changes in net assets available for plan benefits for the year then ended present fairly the financial position of *XYZ* Pension Plan as of December 31, 19X2, and the changes in net assets available for plan benefits for the year then ended, in conformity with generally accepted accounting principles applied on a basis consistent with that of the preceding year. Further, it is our opinion that the schedules referred to above present fairly the information set forth therein in compliance with the Department of Labor Rules and Regulations for Reporting and Disclosure under the Employee Retirement Income Security Act of 1974.

Under certain circumstances it may be possible and desirable for the auditor to render an opinion on financial statements on which he or she previously disclaimed an opinion. Under these circumstances paragraph 7 of SAS No. 15 requires a separate explanatory paragraph disclosing the type of opinion previously expressed and the reason for the change in opinion.

[2] Limited-Scope Examination—Current Year; Full-Scope Examination—Prior Year

Auditors can also anticipate that some plans which had a full-scope examination of the prior year financial statements will elect to exclude assets held by banks or insurance companies in the current year. Again, to the extent they are presented, the auditor should report on prior year financial statements in accordance with SAS No. 15.

Although SAS No. 15 states that the accountant's report should ordinarily be dated as of the completion of the most recent examination, the procedures performed in a limited-scope examination generally are not sufficient to enable the auditor to update his or her report on the prior year financial statements. Accordingly, the auditor should consider double-dating his or her report. An example of such a report follows:

> We have examined the statements of assets and liabilities of *XYZ* Pension Plan as of December 31, 19X2 and 19X1, the related statements of changes in net assets for the years then ended, and the schedules of assets held for investment, transactions in excess of 3 percent of the current value of plan assets, and loans and fixed-income obligations in default or classified as uncollectible as of and for the year ended December 31, 19X2. Except as stated in the following paragraph with respect to the 19X2 financial statements and schedules, our examinations were made in accordance with generally accepted auditing standards and, accordingly, included such tests of the accounting records and such other auditing procedures as we considered necessary in the circumstances.
>
> The plan administrator has elected the method of compliance permitted by Section 2520.103-8 of the Department of Labor Rules and Regulations for Reporting and Disclosure under the Employee Retirement Income Security Act of 1974. Accordingly, as permitted under such election, the plan administrator instructed us not to perform, and we did not perform, any auditing procedures with respect to the information certified by the *ABC* Bank, the trustee of the Plan as of and for the year ended December 31, 19X2,

except for comparing the information which is summarized in Note X, to the related information included in the financial statements and schedules. We have been informed by the plan administrator that the trustee holds the Plan's investment assets and executes transactions therein. The plan administrator has obtained a certification from the trustee that the information provided to the plan administrator by the trusee is complete and accurate.

In our opinion, the statement of assets and liabilities of *XYZ* Pension Plan as of December 31, 19X1, and the related statement of changes in net assets available for plan benefits for the year then ended present fairly the financial position of *XYZ* Pension Plan as of December 31, 19X1, and the changes in net assets available for plan benefits for the year then ended, in conformity with generally accepted accounting principles applied on a basis consistent with that of the preceding year.

Because of the significance of the information which we did not audit in 19X2, we are unable to, and do not, express an opinion on the accompanying financial statements and schedules as of and for the year then ended taken as a whole. The form and content of the information included in the financial statements and schedules, other than that derived from the information certified by the trustee, has been examined by us and, in our opinion, is presented in compliance with the Department of Labor Rules and Regulations for Reporting and Disclosure under the Employee Retirement Income Security Act of 1974.

May ⸺ 19X2, except for the third paragraph, the date of which is Nov. ⸺ 19X1.

¶ 16.03   REPORTING ON EXAMINATIONS IN ACCORDANCE WITH GAAS

As discussed in Chapter 10, DOL regulations allow for financial statements that are not prepared in conformity with generally accepted accounting principles. Such financial statements may be examined in accordance with GAAS or subjected to the limited-scope examination provided in DOL regulations. Depending on the alternatives selected, the auditor may be reporting on a GAAS examination of GAAP financial statements or non-GAAP financial statements.

[1] Full-Scope Examination of GAAP Financial Statements

When the plan has *not* elected to exclude significant assets or transactions from the auditor's examination, and the financial statements are prepared in conformity with GAAP, a report similar to that shown below should be used. The example assumes that the financial statements for the preceding year are presented but were not examined by independent accountants.

> We have examined the statement of assets and liabilities and the schedule of assets held for investment of XYZ Pension Plan as of December 31, 19XX, and the related statement of changes in net assets available for plan benefits and the schedules of transactions or series of transactions in excess of 3 percent of the current value of plan assets, and loans and fixed-income obligations in default or classified as uncollectible for the year then ended. Our examination was made in accordance with generally accepted auditing standards and, accordingly, included such tests of the accounting records and such other auditing procedures as we considered necessary in the circumstances. The financial statements (statement of assets and liabilities) for the preceding year were (was) not examined by independent accountants.

> In our opinion, the financial statements referred to above present fairly the financial position of *XYZ* Pension Plan at December 31, 19XX, and the changes in net assets available for plan benefits for the year then ended, in conformity with generally accepted accounting principles applied on a basis consistent with that of the preceding year. Further, it is our opinion that the schedules referred to above present fairly the information set forth therein in compliance with the Department of Labor Rules and Regulations for Reporting and Disclosure under the Employee Retirement Income Security Act of 1974.

If the prior year financial statements were examined, or if no prior year statements are presented (e.g., under the statutory method), the accountant's report should be modified accordingly.

[2] Full-Scope Examination of Non-GAAP Financial Statements

When a plan elects to prepare its financial statements on a basis other than GAAP, and the auditor's examination has been performed in accordance with GAAS, a modified report should be used. The following example assumes that the auditor is reporting only on the current year.

(Scope Paragraph—same as previous example)

As described in Note X, the Plan's policy is to prepare its financial statements and schedules on the basis of accounting practices prescribed or permitted by the Department of Labor. These practices differ in some respects from generally accepted accounting principles. Accordingly, the accompanying financial statements and schedules are not intended to present financial position and results of operations in conformity with generally accepted accounting principles.

In our opinion, the financial statements referred to above present fairly the assets and liabilities of *XYZ* Pension Plan as of December 31, 19XX, and the changes in net assets available for plan benefits for the year then ended, on the basis of accounting described in Note X, which basis has been applied in a manner consistent with that of the preceding year. Further, it is our opinion that the schedules referred to above present fairly the information set forth therein in compliance with the Department of Labor Rules and Regulations for Reporting and Disclosure under the Employee Retirement Income Security Act of 1974.

¶ 16.04   REPORTING WHEN SIGNIFICANT INVESTMENTS NOT HAVING A READILY ASCERTAINABLE CURRENT VALUE EXIST

ERISA defines "current value" as "fair market value where available and otherwise the fair value as determined in good faith by a trustee or a named fiduciary." Investments for which fair market value is not readily ascertainable may include restricted securities, private debt placements, and real estate investments. When such investments are material to the plan under examination and a full-scope audit is conducted, the auditor should consider following the guidance in the AICPA industry audit guide, "Audits of Investment Companies." The following example assumes that the financial statements are in conformity with GAAP.

(Standard Scope Paragraph)

As we discussed more fully in Note X to the financial statements, securities amounting to $____ (____% of the net assets) have been valued at fair value as determined by the trustees. We have reviewed the procedures applied by the trustees in valuing such securities and have inspected underlying documentation; while in the circumstances the procedures appear to be reasonable and the documentation appropriate, determination of fair values involves subjective judgment which is not susceptible to substantiation by auditing procedures.

In our opinion, subject to the possible effect on the financial statements of the valuation of securities determined by the trustees as described in the preceding paragraph, the financial statements referred to above present fairly the financial position of *XYZ* Pension Plan as of December 31, 19XX, and the changes in net assets available for plan benefits for the year then ended, in conformity with generally accepted accounting principles applied on a basis consistent with that of the preceding year. Further, it is our opinion, which is qualified as explained above, that the schedules referred to above present fairly the information set forth therein in compliance with the Department of Labor Rules and Regulations for Reporting and Disclosure under the Employee Retirement Income Security Act of 1974.

It should be noted, however, that on October 31, 1977, AudSEC issued an exposure draft of an SAS, "Auditor's Report When There are Contingencies," which would prohibit the use of the "subject to" opinion. Presumably, this SAS, if adopted in its present form, would cover the above example.

¶ 16.05 REPORTING WHEN THE FINANCIAL STATEMENTS OMIT DISCLOSURE OF ACTUARIAL LIABILITIES

GAAP currently does not require accounting recognition of an actuarially determined liability to pay future benefits. However, as discussed at ¶ 12.07, disclosure of vested benefits and the related actuarial methods and assumptions is strongly recommended. If actuarial disclosures are not made, the auditor should consider an appropriate qualification. An example of such a qualification follows:

Explanatory paragraph
The accompanying financial statements do not include disclosure

of the actuarially computed value of vested benefits, or a description of the actuarial assumptions and methods used in their determination. Such disclosures are necessary for a fair presentation of the financial position of the plan in conformity with generally accepted accounting principles.

Opinion paragraph

In our opinion, except for the omission of the disclosures as described in the preceding paragraph, the final statements. . . .

INDEX

[References are to paragraphs (¶).]

A

Accountant
actuarial terminology, 4.04
actuary's reliance on, 4.02[1]
role in determining funding requirements, 2.05[1]

Accounting control
administrative expenses, 14.08
  charged for whom, 14.08
  disbursements made by whom, 14.08
administrative responsibility, 14.02
benefits, 14.05
  applications, 14.05
  checking of payments, 14.05
  control totals, 14.05
  deceased beneficiaries, 14.05
  notification of administrator, 14.05
  records adequate, 14.05
contributions, 14.03
  checking of forms, 14.03
  determined how, 14.03
  frequency, 14.03
  payroll audits, 14.03
custodians and actuaries, 14.02
ERISA fiduciaries, 14.02
internal auditors, 14.02
investments, 14.04
  audit by independent CPA, 14.04
  authorized transactions, 14.04
  decisions documented, 14.04
  filing, 14.04
  income received, 14.04
  insurance company deposits, 14.04
  investment service used, 14.04
  legal documents, 14.04
  personnel interviewed, 14.04
  physical control over securities, 14.04
  registering, 14.04
  separate accounts or general assets, 14.04
  subsidiary records, 14.04
journal entries and financial statements, 14.02
participant data, 14.07
  classification records, 14.07
  new participants, 14.07
  notification of eligibility, 14.07
parties-in-interest, 14.02
past examinations, 14.02
personnel answering, 14.02
questionnaire, 14.01-14.08
record retention program, 14.02
review and evaluation, basic concepts, 14.01
transactions in excess of 3 percent of assets, 14.02
type of plan described, 14.02
withdrawals and forfeitures, 14.06
  accountability over, 14.06
  computing and allocating, 14.06

Accounting guidelines
cost and current value determination, 12.04
  equity and debt securities, 12.04[1]
  future income value, 12.04[4]

I-1

[References are to paragraphs (¶).]

[References are to paragraphs (¶).]

[References are to paragraphs (¶).]

[References are to paragraphs (¶).]

[References are to paragraphs (¶).]

[References are to paragraphs (¶).]

[References are to paragraphs (¶).]

[References are to paragraphs (¶).]

[References are to paragraphs (¶).]

[References are to paragraphs (¶).]

[References are to paragraphs (¶).]

[References are to paragraphs (¶).]

[References are to paragraphs (¶).]

[References are to paragraphs (¶).]

[References are to paragraphs (¶).]